The Band

Pioneers of Americana Music

Craig Harris

ROWMAN & LITTLEFIELD
Lanham • Boulder • New York • Toronto • Plymouth, UK
2014

Published by Rowman & Littlefield
 Forbes Boulevard, Suite 200, Lanham, Maryland 20706
http://www.rowman.com

 Road, Plymouth PL6 7PY, United Kingdom

Copyright © 2014 by Craig Harris

 reserved. No part of this book may be reproduced in any form or by any electronic or mechanical means, including information storage and retrieval systems, written permission from the publisher, except by a reviewer who may quote in a review.

 Library Cataloguing in Publication Information Available

 of Congress Cataloging-in-Publication Data

 Craig, 1953 December 20-, author.
 : pioneers of Americana music / Craig Harris.
  bibliographical references and index.
  978-0-8108-8904-0 (cloth : alk. paper) -- ISBN 978-0-8108-8905-7 (ebook) 1. Band (Musical Rock musicians--United States--Biography. I. Title.
ML421.B32H37 2014
782.42166092'2--dc23
2013044054
 978-0-8108-9501-0 (pbc : alk. paper)

 The paper used in this publication meets the minimum requirements of American Standard for Information Sciences Permanence of Paper for Printed Library Materials, ANSI/NISO Z39.48-1992.

Dedicated to my uncle, Albert Cornell, who introduced me to the music of Bob Dylan and The Band; my much-missed father, Stanley Watsky, who encouraged me; and Vicki Ruth Sterling, who helps to keep me inspired.

Contents

Acknowledgments		vii
1	Bob Dylan and the Band: At the Top of the World	1
2	Ronnie Hawkins and the Hawks	39
3	Voices from the Mountain	65
4	The Band	79
5	Rise and Descent	119
6	Resurrection	157
7	Extending Community	173
8	Coda	193
Bibliography		195
Index		197
About the Author		215

Acknowledgments

The members of The Band, and those whose paths intersected with theirs, have been extremely open about their experiences. Some quotes from this book came from interviews that I conducted with Rick Danko, Robbie Robertson, Ronnie Gilbert, Pete Seeger, Eric Andersen, John Hammond, and Happy Traum. Others came from Levon Helm's autobiography, *This Wheel's on Fire: Levon Helm and the Story of The Band*, cowritten with Stephen Davis (Chicago Review Press, 1993), and Ronnie Hawkins's *Last of the Good Ol' Boys* (Stoddardt Publishing, Toronto, 1989). Others come from more than four decades of interviews, reviews, and essays by Peter Aaron, Greg Alexander, Joshua Baer, Michael Bailey, Ron Balley, Michael Berick, Rob Bowman, Peter Stone Brown, Paul Burch, John Burke, Klas Burling, Robert Christgau, Jay Cocks, Michael Corcoran, Elvis Costello, Peter Crowley, Mark Deming, Nick De Rosa, Stephen Deusner, Bob Doerschuk, Susan Edmiston, Stephen Thomas Erlewine, John Feins, Robyn Flans, Larry Getlin, Andy Gill, Mikal Gilmore, Milton Glaser, Ralph J. Gleason, Susan Gordon, Andy Greene, Joseph Haas, Jill Henderson, Nat Hentoff, Clifton Heylin, Robert Hilburn, Barney Hoskyns, Dan Hyman, Mark Jacobson, Paul James, Scott Jordan, Hank Kalet, Greg Kot, Harvey Kupernik, Jon Landau, Martin Levy, Michael March, Justin Martell, Olivia Mather, Melinda McCracken, Larry McMahon, John Metzger, Ross W. Muir, Rory O'Connor, Clive Owen, Chris Parker, John Poppy, Mike Ragogna, Seth Rogovoy, Paul J. Robbins, Kevin Ronsom, William Ruhlman, Jason Schneider, Karen Schoemer, David Schultz, Robert Shelton, Sam Shepard, Irwin Silber, John Sinclair, Ronald Sklar, Paul Smart, Ruth Alpert Spencer, Scott Spencer, Margaret Steen, Bonnie Stiernberg, Jane Stevenson, Adam Thomas, Walter Tunis, Brian Turk, Twinker Twina, Peter Viney, Richard C. Walls, Robert Wilonsky, and Peter Yarrow, appearing in (or broadcast by) *Adirondack Daily Enterprise, All about Jazz, All Music Guide, American Songwriter, Austin American Statesman,* BBC, *Berkshire Eagle, Billboard,* Bluesmobile.com, CBS Radio, *Chicago Daily News, Chicago Tribune,* CNN, *Colorado Springs Independent, Crawdaddy, Daily Beacon, Dirty Linen, Echo, Esquire, Fusion, Goldmine, Gritz, Guitar Player, In Beat,* Jamband.com, *Keyboard, Lexington Herald-Leader, Look, Los Angeles Free Press, Los Angeles Times, Melody Maker, Midland Free Press, Modern Drummer, Mojo, Music Box, Musician,* National Academy of Songwriters, National Public Radio (NPR), *New York, New Yorker, New York Post, New York Times, No Depression, Offbeat, Paste, Playboy,* PopEntertainment.com, PopMatters.com, *Relix, Rolling Stone, San Francisco Chronicle, Sheffield University Press, Show Me, Sing Out, Something Else Reviews, Sputnik Music, Sun Media, Time, Times Herald Record, Toronto Globe and Mail, Toronto Life, Toronto Star Weekly, Tucson Weekly, USA Weekly, Village Voice, Woodstock Journal*, and the *Woodstock Times*. Additional quotes come from the liner notes of the New World Singers' eponymous debut album (Atlantic, 1963), Bob Dylan's *Biograph* (Columbia, 1985), The Band's *Music from Big Pink* (Capitol, 1969), and John Herald's self-produced, posthumously released *Just Another Bluegrass Boy* (2006). Authorized video, *The Band Reunion: The Band Is Back with Its Greatest Hits Live* (1983), Martin Scorsese's Dylan documentary *No Direction Home* (2005), Bob Smeaton's *Festival Express* (2003), Jacob Hatley's Levon Helm biopic *Ain't in It for My Health* (2012), and *Rolling Stone*'s interviews with Robbie Robertson (2011), were additional sources. I am extremely indebted to the Band website, www.thebandhiof.com, run by Jan Hoiberg of Norway's Ostofold University College.

As a musician, writer, educator, and photographer, I have been able to experience music from a variety of angles. Photographs in this book's centerfold represent more than three decades of my camera work. Although I had opportunity to photograph Levon Helm, Garth Hudson, and the late Rick Danko and Richard Manuel after The Band's reunion, Robbie Robertson has so far eluded me, though he graciously consented to a telephone interview, for which I am greatly appreciative.

ONE

Bob Dylan and the Band

At the Top of the World

I

Triumph! As the packed-to-capacity arena erupted in approval, thirty-three-year-old Bob Dylan, alongside The Band's Levon Helm, from Arkansas's side of the Mississippi Delta, and Robbie Robertson, Rick Danko, Richard Manuel, and Garth Hudson, from Ontario, Canada, soaked it in. It had been less than a decade since the Hibbing, Minnesota–born singer-songwriter's shift to electric music had caused one of the great schisms in America's musical history, but the crowd was now on its feet, holding lighters aloft, pleading for "just one more." "We did the exact same thing as when everybody was booing us," Robertson told the *Los Angeles Times*. "We didn't change a thing, the world changed. [People] had evolved and accepted what we were doing. We felt like we had won the battle—like we had come out the other end."

Despite the tour's financial and critical success, Dylan claimed to have hated every minute of the six weeks between January 3 and February 14, 1974. "We were cleaning up," he recalled in the liner notes of 1985's *Biograph*, "but it was an emotionless trip." The Band's guitarist and chief composer, Robbie Robertson, offered a different perspective. "With all the time [that I've] spent on the road," he told *Rolling Stone*, "there [were] maybe three times I've actually enjoyed it. The '74 tour was one of those times."

Demand for tickets (available by mail order only) had been phenomenal. According to tour promoter Bill Graham, whose FM Productions netted half a million dollars, there were twenty-four times as many requests as available seats (at a top price of $9.50). Nearly 4 percent of the

American population sent more than ninety-two million dollars, in checks and money orders, hoping to see one of the shows (those unable to score tickets had their money returned). "We grossed between forty and fifty million dollars in two months," Rick Danko told me during an interview for *Dirty Linen* in 1991. "We had a private plane with bedrooms. It was first class all the way; I got turned-on to fine wines. I'd never done anything so extravagant in my life."

"We lived and traveled like kings amid the excesses of all that seventies rock and roll money," remembered Helm in *This Wheel's on Fire*, "the fastest jet, the longest limos, and the biggest suites, tons of white powder."

Rehearsals for the tour balanced with sessions for *Planet Waves*—surprisingly, Dylan and The Band's first official collaborative album. "[It was] like cutting a blues album," Robertson told Band biographer Barney Hoskyns. "We were rehearsing songs, figuring out how we were going to do the tour, and we were making the album in our spare time."

A lot had changed in the eight years since The Band first played with the former Robert Zimmerman. They had apprenticed as Arkansas-born Ronnie Hawkins's Canada-based rockabilly band, The Hawks, in the early 1960s and accompanied Dylan on his 1966 world tour, but Robbie Robertson, Levon Helm, Richard Manuel, Rick Danko, and Garth Hudson were no longer mere backup musicians. As The Band, their first two albums—*Music from Big Pink*, in 1968, and its top-ten eponymous follow-up a year later—had reenergized America's musical roots with precise ensemble playing, distinctive lead vocals, earthy harmonies, and extremely literate lyrics, and set the foundation of what has become known as "Americana."

Success had come at a price, though. Drugs, alcohol, greed, and a fear of being in the public spotlight haunted the group. The darker palette of their third album, *Stage Fright*, in 1970, intensified on *Cahoots* a year later. "Clearly, they spent less time developing the material," said music journalist Don Ignacio, "and their inspired creative juices had almost entirely been drained."

In late December 1971, The Band performed five nights at New York's Academy of Music, culminated by a New Year''s Eve guest appearance by Bob Dylan. A two-disc live album, *Rock of Ages* (expanded in 2013 as a four-CD collection, *Live at the Academy of Music 1971*) temporarily revived their early momentum, but it would be the last time The Band would play together for a year and a half.

II

Bob Dylan had been gesturing toward electric music for most of his career. He had arrived in New York's Greenwich Village on January 24,

1961, looking and sounding like a ragamuffin version of Woody Guthrie, but he had cut his musical teeth on rock and roll. A longtime fan of Buddy Holly and Little Richard, he had even done a gig (as Elston Gunnn) in 1959 with Bobby Vee and his band, The Shadows. Dylan had gotten the gig by convincing the Holly-esque pop singer's brother that he had toured with country singer Conway Twitty. Speaking to Ronald Sklar of PopEntertainment.com in 1999, Vee recalled, "[Dylan] played [piano] pretty good in the key of C."

"I always wanted to be Little Richard," Dylan told *Fusion* magazine's Michael March. "If ya don't believe me, look in my old high-school yearbook. I used to stand there with the piano and scream."

Dylan told Joseph Haas of the *Chicago Daily News* that he had been playing rock and roll from the age of thirteen, "but I couldn't make it that way. The image of the day was Frankie Avalon or Fabian, or this athletic super-cleanness bit. . . . You could not carry around an amplifier and electric guitar and expect to survive; it was just too much of a hang-up. It cost bread to buy an electric guitar, and then you had to make more money to have enough people to play the music—you need two or three [other musicians] to create some conglomeration of sound."

Inspired by Woody Guthrie, Ramblin' Jack Elliott, Spider John Koerner, and Odetta, Dylan had turned to folk music as the 1950s gave way to the '60s. As he told Nora Ephron and Susan Edmiston in August 1965, he had ulterior motives. "I became interested in folk music," he confessed, "because I had to make it somehow. Obviously, I am not a hard-working cat—I played the guitar—that was all I did."

Dylan further discussed folk music in a May 1965 interview with Nat Hentoff of *Playboy* magazine. "Folk music is a bunch of fat people," he said. "It comes about from legends, Bibles, plagues, and it revolves around vegetables and death . . . all these songs about roses growing out of people's brains and lovers who are really geese and swans that turn into angels—they're not going to die. It's all those paranoid people who think that someone's going to come and take away their toilet paper—they're going to die."

Originating with the songs of cowboys, sailors, miners, and African American slaves, along with spiritual hymns and English, Irish, and Scottish ballads, American folk music had become synonymous with political struggle. The Industrial Workers of the World (IWW), or "the Wobblies," had used music as an effective tool since the early twentieth century. When Volunteers of America and Salvation Army bands attempted to drown out the IWW's call for "one big union" during a Free Speech protest in Spokane, Washington, in 1908, James H. Walsh formed a union band, and choir, to overpower the cacophonous brass. A lumberjack who played bass drum in Walsh's band, Harry "Haywire Mac" McClintock, would go on to write "Hallelujah! I'm a Bum," based on the Salvation Army's "Revive Us Again," and "The Big Rock Candy Mountain," possibly based on a late-seventeenth century Scottish ballad. "The IWW band often hid in a doorway," said Linda Allen in the liner notes of *Washington Notebook*, "while one [union] member, dressed in a bowler hat and carrying a briefcase and umbrella, yelled to the crowd, 'Help! I've been robbed!' The crowd rushed over only to hear, 'I've been robbed by the capitalist system!' He then launched into a short speech, and the makeshift band stepped out of the doorway and played their songs."

A committee of IWW members collected pro-union songs and parodies and published, in 1909, a four-page song card that sold for ten cents. Originally titled *Songs of the Workers, On the Road, In the Jungle, and In the Sky: Songs to Fan the Flames of Discontent*, the book continued to be expanded and published, as the *Little Red Songbook*, until 1995 (and periodically afterward). The son of a railroad conductor, Joel Emmanuel "Joe Hill" Hagglund (1879–1915) became the greatest of the IWW songwriters. Nearly a century after his premature death, his songs remain a cornerstone of labor union organizing and protest.

Immigrating to the United States, in 1902, Hagglund worked a variety of jobs, including porter, in New York. Taught to play organ by his devoutly religious mother, and self-taught on violin, guitar, and accordion, he played piano in downtown Manhattan saloons at night.

Moving on to Chicago, Hagglund found employment in a machine shop. Fired for attempting to organize workers, he was blacklisted. Changing his name to Joseph Hillstrom, shortened to Joe Hill, he continued to travel across the United States, arriving in San Francisco in time to cover the 1906 earthquake for a newspaper in his native city of Galve, Sweden.

After joining the IWW, in San Pedro, California, in 1910, Hill dedicated himself to the union's cause, writing songs to encourage solidarity and attract new members. Within four years, he had penned more than two dozen songs and parodies. "The Preacher and the Slave" borrowed its melody from S. Fillmore Bennett and Joseph P. Webster's "In the Sweet By and By," while "There Is Power in the Union" derived from Eddie Newton, Wallace Sanders, and T. Lawrence Siebert's "John Brown's Body." The melody of "Casey Jones—The Union Scab" came from James E. Greenleaf, C. S. Hall, C. B. Marsh, and William Staffe's "The Ballad of Casey Jones." Except for some fragments and rumored songs, they would be his only compositions.

In late 1913, Hill traveled to Utah to earn money as a mineworker. A few months later, on January 10, 1914, a grocer, John G. Morrison, and his son, Arlis, were killed in Salt Lake City. Ten days later, the songwriter/activist was accused of the murder and placed under arrest. Following an extremely controversial trial, he would be found guilty and sentenced to death. "The main thing the state had on Hill," said appeals lawyer Orrin N. Hilton to the BBC in 2002, "was that he was an IWW [member] and therefore sure to be guilty."

Despite the pleading of the Swedish ambassador to the United States, along with Helen Keller and President Woodrow Wilson, Utah governor William Spry denied Hill's final appeal, and a firing squad executed him on November 15, 1915.

Hill's spirit, though, did not die. With his songs sung on picket lines, his influence continued to grow. A decade after Hill's passing, Earl Robinson set a poem by British poet Alfred Hayes, "Joe Hill" (aka "I Dreamed I Saw Joe Hill Last Night"), to music. African American singer/activist Paul Robeson recorded the song in 1942 and performed it in Moscow in 1949 and in Carnegie Hall a decade later. Joan Baez, daughter of a Mexican American physicist and an MIT professor, would open her set at the Woodstock Music and Art Festival in August 1969 with it. Phil Ochs had commemorated Hill's legacy, a year before, including an original ballad, "Joe Hill," with Ramblin' Jack Elliott on rhythm acoustic guitar, on his album, *Tape from California*.

As the stock market crash, the displacement of the working class, and the proliferation of dust storms sparked a folk music revival in the 1930s and '40s, politics and folk music continued to intertwine. Little Rock, Arkansas–born Lee Elhardt Hays, the son of a Methodist preacher, had witnessed the suffering of sharecroppers (and seen the hope promised by the unions) while attending Commonwealth College, in Mena, Arkansas, during the Great Depression, and he had begun expressing what he felt in song. After moving to New York, in the mid-1930s, he, and his roommate, Patterson, New Jersey–born Millard Lampell, began singing together at union meetings. Joined by New York-born Pete Seeger, Hays and Lampell formed a singing group, The Almanac Singers, in February 1941, and performed at an American Youth Congress meeting, in Washington, DC. "I knew [Hays] was a very good song leader," Seeger told me, "and a very good singer. He said, 'your banjo could accompany me and we could make five dollars here and ten dollars there. We won't get rich, but we could sing some of these great union songs to these New York folks."

As the eldest son of folklorist/educator Charles Seeger, Seeger resisted his classical pianist mother Constance's suggestion that "it's all about the three B's—Bach, Beethoven, and Brahms." "My father was interested in all sorts of ideas," he remembered. "He came to the philosophical conclusion that, if you're going to make new music, you have to start with music that people knew already—whether it was jazz or different kinds of folk music."

Seeger's father had worked closely with Library of Congress folklorist Alan Lomax. "They tried to decide what had gone wrong with the attempts to revive folk music in Europe, where they had tried to arrange everything for chorus and piano. What my father and Alan did was to lay the basis for the revival. It let young people hear the music as it was recorded out in the fields."

Young Pete first heard folk music at a folk festival, in Asheville, North Carolina, that he attended with his father, in 1935. "That was my introduction to southern mountain folk music," he said. "It was right after my father met the Lomaxes. He'd known of folk music, but he started poring over books by Cecil Sharp and corresponding with Béla Bartók in Europe."

Aspiring to become a journalist, Seeger enrolled in Harvard University. "I'm a news-a-holic," he confessed. Formal education quickly disillusioned him, however, and he dropped out of school. "I was put off by the cynicism of the academics," he explained.

By then, Seeger had discovered politics. "I was sort of a closet Communist," he said. "I subscribed to *The New Masses*. My father, in 1929, started working with the Communist Party. He, Aaron Copeland, and some others, had a group that they called the Composer's Collective. It was partly the reason why my father had become intrigued by folk music. He brought Aunt Molly Jackson to one of the meetings of the collective and she had sung, 'I am a union woman/as brave as I can be/I do not like the bosses/and the bosses don't like me.' [People in the collective] said, 'Charlie, this is interesting, but this is music of our past. Our job is to create music of the future.' [My father] took Molly home and said, 'Don't feel badly that they don't understand you. I know some young people who would like to learn your songs.' I was one of them."

After a summer spent hitchhiking and riding freight trains across the United States, Seeger returned East and secured a job with Lomax at the Library of Congress. "There were stacks with thousands of old 78s," he recalled, "and [Lomax] told me, 'listen to each of these, weed out the worst ones, and make notes on which ones you think are interesting. That's where I first heard Uncle Dave Macon."

In 1940, Seeger met Okemah, Oklahoma–born singer-songwriter Woodrow Wilson "Woody" Guthrie. "He showed me how to sing in saloons and make a few quarters," he recalled. "I met him at a midnight benefit concert for the California agricultural workers. I sang one song very poorly and got off to polite applause, but Woody was one of the stars of the evening. No one had ever seen or heard him before. He stood on the stage and was so relaxed, spinning out story and after story. It was a remarkable evening. Burl Ives was there, Lead Belly, the Golden Gate Quartet, Josh White, and my wife, Toshi, was there, dancing with Margot Mayo's American Square Dancing Group. We weren't married then. We weren't even going together."

With Seeger joining them, Hays and Lampell released the Almanac Singers' debut album, *Songs for John Doe*, in May 1941. Speaking out against the war brewing in Europe and protesting the Selective Training and Service Act of the previous year, it became the victim of Germany's invasion of Russia (despite a nonaggression pact) a few weeks after its release. Keystone Records destroyed its entire inventory of the album.

Guthrie would soon join the Almanac Singers, along with Sis Cunningham and folklorist Alan Lomax's sister, Bess. Membership would continue to expand with the addition of Baldwin "Butch" Hawes (Bess's husband), his brother Pete (Joe Bowers), Sonny Terry, Brownie McGhee, Josh White, Tom Glazer, and Burl Ives.

Labor issues, however, continued to provide a theme for the Almanac Singers. Their six-song second album, *Talking Union*, included "Union Maid" by Woody Guthrie (based on "Red Wing"). The struggles of the United Mine Workers in Harlan County, Kentucky, provided "Which Side Are You On" by Florence Reece (the wife of a United Mine Workers organizer) and "I Don't Want Your Millions, Mister" by Jim Garland, younger half brother of United Mine Workers activist/songwriter Aunt Molly Jackson ("I Am a Union Woman," "Death of Harry Simms").

On July 7, 1941, the Almanac Singers gathered in the studio for a recording session, produced by Alan Lomax, in hopes of raising two hundred and fifty dollars to buy a car for a trip to California. The eighteen songs that they recorded released on two 78-rpm albums—*Deep Sea Chanteys and Whaling Ballads* and *Sod-Buster Ballads*. A fifth album of topical songs, *Dear Mr. President*, came out after the United States declared war following the Japanese bombing of Pearl Harbor in December 1941.

California seemed to rejuvenate the Almanac Singers. In February 1942, they appeared on *This Is War*, broadcast nationally by all four major radio networks. A radio contract and a major label record deal seemed to be on the horizon. Vermont-based folksinger Rik Palieri would retrace the Almanac Singer's journey, accompanied by George Mann, in July 2013, performing in twenty-eight union halls over five weeks. "Something about the idea of these four guys going from union hall to union hall and singing across the United States," he told Dan Bolles of Seven Days, "really appealed to the wanderlust that I've always had." The aspirations of the Almanac Singers had quickly dissipated, however, after newspapers began printing articles criticizing their political roots. Army Intelligence and the FBI interpreted their pro-union, and anti-draft, stance as a threat, and they continued to hound group members until they disbanded in 1945. Lampell would continue to write songs, novels, and screenplays (under fictitious names during the McCarthy era, and afterward). The recipient of an Emmy Award for his Hallmark Hall of Fame drama *Eagle in a Cage* in 1966, he would be responsible for a popular TV play, *The Adams Chronicles*, and a miniseries, *Rich Man, Poor Man*, a decade later.

Guthrie would become one of contemporary folk music's most influential songwriters—influencing everyone from Dylan to Bruce Springsteen. Seeger and Hays would become president and secretary, respectively, of People's Songs, an organization whose goals were "to create, promote, and distribute songs of labor and the American people," and published a quarterly magazine, *People's Songs Bulletin*, that served as a template for *Sing Out* and *Broadside*. "We wanted to help unions get new members," recalled Seeger. "We wanted to sing against Jim Crow and sing for peace. We were trying to carry on the New Deal ideas."

Seeger and Hays hosted People's Songs song circles in the Greenwich Village apartment that Seeger shared with his wife, Toshi. Two years later, in late November, the four folksingers agreed to pool their resources and form a quartet initially called The No-Name Group, and later The Weavers. "Pete and Lee made a natural duo," Gilbert told me in 1988. "I learned so much from them. I learned, from Pete, about music, and, from Lee, I learned all about the shape of the world. He was incredible. What the world lost from the blacklist was this amazing man with so many connections. He knew all about the South and tenant farmers. I met Fred at a summer camp. He was just learning to play the guitar. By the time that we were getting together, he knew what he was doing. His voice and mine blended well."

Building on the congregational sound of the Almanac Singers, The Weavers took folk music into a more commercially accessible direction. Unlike their predecessors, who were, according to Woody Guthrie, "the only group that rehearsed on stage," Seeger, Hays, Hellerman, and Gilbert took a serious approach to music, mixing a deeply rooted collection of string band classics, sea shanties, cowboy tunes, and a globe-spanning variety of folk songs.

A ten-day booking at Max Gordon's Greenwich Village club the Village Vanguard turned into a six-month engagement. One performance caught the ear of bandleader/arranger Gordon Jenkins, who helped The Weavers secure a contract with Decca Records and, according to some, "watered down" their recordings with string-laden orchestrations. "I had misgivings about the strings," admitted Gilbert, "but Gordon had respect for folk music. I am not ashamed about anything that we did with him. A lot of people heard us who wouldn't have had the chance."

A black Louisiana-born folksinger (and former Blind Lemon Jefferson accompanist) "discovered" in the Louisiana State Penitentiary by John and Alan Lomax in 1933, and, with their help, pardoned, Huddie "Lead Belly" Ledbetter provided the A-side of The Weaver's debut single, "Goodnight, Irene." He had sung it as early as 1908, but The Weavers turned it into one of the top tunes of 1950—selling more than two million copies and remaining on the *Billboard* charts for twenty-six weeks (including thirteen weeks in the top position). "It was the second biggest seller since World War II," said Seeger. "Only Bing Crosby's 'Sam's Song' sold more. It stayed at the top of the hit parade week after week after week. It was fantastic. All I could do was laugh." For the songwriter, who had died (at the age of sixty-one) on December 6, 1949, fame would come posthumously.

Despite their popularity, The Weavers' involvement with liberal causes, including the unsuccessful presidential run by progressive party nominee (and former FDR vice president) Henry Wallace, met with fierce opposition during the Red Scare of the 1950s. Both Seeger and Hays's names were included on a list of 151 "banned" performers published in *Red Channels: The Report of Communist Influence in Radio and Television* on June 22, 1950. Promoters canceled The Weavers' bookings and record stores stopped selling their recordings. Canceling its contract, Decca deleted their albums from its catalogue by 1953. By then, The Weavers had disbanded. "We were dissidents against the growing push for the cold war," recalled Gilbert. "We thought it was better to sit around a negotiating table and talk instead of building up armies and stockpiling weapons. It was a very unpopular stance with the powers-that-be. The Korean War was going on. It was an undeclared war, but American men were going to Korea to fight. Our message of peace was not welcomed."

When an FBI informant (who later recanted) accused them of Communist ties, in 1955, Lee Hays and Pete Seeger were among a lengthy list of musicians, artists, and writers summoned to testify before the House of Representatives' Un-American Activities Committee (HUAC). Some, including Burl Ives, a onetime Almanac Singers member (and later the voice of TV's "Frosty the Snowman"), provided the committee with the names of "suspected Communists." Hays pled the Fifth Amendment, remaining silent, while Seeger, refused to answer the committee's questions, claiming that they violated his freedom of speech. "Arthur Miller and I and a couple of others decided to challenge the Committee of Un-American Activity," he explained. "The Fifth, in a sense, is saying that 'you have no right to ask me this question.' The First is 'Nobody has the right to ask anybody these questions.' It's a much broader statement."

Charged with contempt, Seeger would be found guilty, after a quick trial, and sentenced to a year in jail (the conviction would be overturned in 1961). While waiting for bail, he spent four hours in a cell. "I learned a folk song while I was there," he said. "I was eating my lunch – two pieces of white bread, with a slice of bologna, and an apple – and the guy next to me was singing, 'If that judge believes what I say, I'll be leaving for home today'."

The Weavers would prove resilient. Brought together to perform at New York's Carnegie Hall on Christmas Eve 1955, they would go on to sign with Vanguard and continue to build on their legacy of song for another nine years (though Seeger would resign after the group agreed to sing in a cigarette commercial in April 1958).

Even without Seeger, The Weavers confronted political conflict. When they refused to sign an oath of political loyalty to the United States, NBC canceled their January 1962 appearance on the *Jack Paar Show* (later to become *The Tonight Show*).

Erik Darling, Frank Hamilton, and Bernie Krause attempted to replace Seeger, but The Weavers seemed to have run their course by 1964 and disbanded. "We tried to keep the group together," said Gilbert, "but there wasn't so much energy anymore."

Reuniting more than a decade and half later in 1980, The Weavers' original lineup proved (as demonstrated by Jim Brown's documentary film *Wasn't That a Time*) to be as magical as it had been more than a quarter of a century before. "Lee Hays had been ill for years," said Gilbert. "He was in a wheelchair, minus two legs. He had a severe heart condition and had to wear a pacemaker. He was never one to get much exercise anyway."

Hays's good-natured optimism drew people to him. "His neighbors loved him," said Gilbert, "and kids would always be hanging around with him."

One of the youngsters, Jim Brown grew up to become a prize-winning filmmaker. "When he saw that Lee was on his last legs," said Gilbert, "he decided that he wanted to film him at a party. He got all of Lee's friends together, including The Weavers. Pete [Seeger] did an annual Thanksgiving concert, at Carnegie Hall, and asked us to play with him. That was filmed, too."

In addition to releasing several solo albums, Gilbert would collaborate with singer/activist Holly Near—*Lifelines* (1983), *Singing with You* (1989), and *The Train Still Runs* (1997)—and, with Near, Seeger, and Woody Guthrie's oldest son, Arlo, participate in a folk supergroup, HARP (Holly–Arlo–Ronnie–Pete), in 1984. "HARP didn't last long enough," said Gilbert. "We only did six concerts."

One of folk music's great icons, Seeger would remain "banned" from commercial television until 1967, when he would appear (despite controversy over his antiwar song "Waist Deep in the Big Muddy") on CBS's *Smothers Brothers Comedy Hour*.

The Weavers' infectious harmonies and folk-rooted repertoire provided inspiration for a trio of folksingers—Dave Guard, Bob Shane, and Nick Reynolds—in Southern California. Forming the Kingston Trio in 1958, they would become one of the era's most successful pop artists, selling millions of copies of their recordings and inspiring similar groups including Glenn Yarborough's Limelighters and the Chad Mitchell Trio (who would later include John Denver, as Henry Deutschendorf). A folk revival was in full bloom—even humorist Allen Sherman released a parody album, *My Son the Folksinger*, in 1962.

The most successful of the folk trios, Peter, Paul, and Mary (Peter Yarrow, Noel Paul Stookey, and Mary Travers) represented the vision of music impresario Albert Bernard Grossman. The Chicago-born son of Russian Jewish immigrant tailors, Grossman (1926–1986) would serve as the thinly veiled model for Bud Grossman (portrayed by F. Murray Abraham) in the Caen Brothers's cinematic foray into Greenwich Village's late-'50s/early-'60s folk scene, *Inside Llewyn Davis*. Graduating from the University of Chicago, with a degree in economics, he worked briefly for the Chicago Housing Authority before becoming co-owner of the one-hundred-seat Gate of Horn in the basement of the Rice Hotel. One of folk music's first "listening rooms," it became a semi-regular home for African American folksingers Odetta, Josh White, Big Bill Broonzy, and Sonny Terry and Brownie McGhee, as well as Irish folksingers the Clancy Brothers and Tommy Makem, world music singer Theodore Bikel, and a twelve-string guitarist (Roger McGuinn) who would go on to form The Byrds. "I played the third night that the [Gate of Horn] was open," said Bob Gibson (a Brooklyn-born folksinger who shared an apartment on Chicago's north side with Grossman) to Rory O'Connor of *Musician* magazine in June 1987, "and I stayed for eleven months. There was nothing like it at the time. . . . If the audience wasn't attentive, if they really didn't listen to an act, they were asked to leave—this was unheard of at the time."

Meeting George Wein in early 1959, Grossman impressed the jazz pianist, club owner (of the famed nightspot Storyville in Boston), and Newport Jazz festival producer so much that he was brought on to help produce the first Newport Folk Festival a few months later. After the festival, Grossman relocated to New York. Briefly joining Wein (and a third partner) as Personal Artist Management Associates (PAMA), he soon launched his own company, Albert B. Grossman Management. Starting out with Gibson and Odetta as clients, the company would expand to include Peter, Paul, and Mary, the Butterfield Blues Band, Janis Joplin, Happy and Artie Traum, Gordon Lightfoot, and Todd Rundgren, as well as Bob Dylan and The Band.

Grossman first saw Peter Yarrow at a Greenwich Village club, Café Wha, in early 1960, but, needing to get to an appointment elsewhere, he had left before the end of the singer-songwriter's performance. Studying violin, and art, since childhood, New York–born Yarrow was one of a growing surge of teenagers playing folksongs on acoustic guitar. After graduating from Cornell University with a degree in psychology in 1959, he continued at the school as an assistant instructor to an English professor in a folklore and folk music course. "I did it for the money because I wanted to wash dishes less and play music more," he told former Warner Brothers promotion director Joe Smith in *Off the Record*, "but, as soon as I started teaching this course, something happened that altered my life. I saw young people, basically, very conservative in their backgrounds, opening their hearts up and singing with emotionality and a concern through this vehicle called folk music. It gave me a clue that the world was on its way to a certain kind of movement, that folk music might play a part in it, and that I might play a part in folk music."

A few months later, Grossman and Yarrow again crossed paths. The folksinger had come to a midtown club, The Baq Door, to audition for a folk music TV special, *Folk Sound USA*, as part CBS's *Kraft Television Theater*. Joan Baez, at the time managed by Grossman, also auditioned.

Impressed by what he heard, Grossman offered Yarrow a management deal. Quickly accepting, Yarrow advanced rapidly. Booked to perform at the second Newport Folk Festival in 1962, he continued to play at folk music clubs throughout the United States.

Louisville, Kentucky–born Mary Allin Travers had grown up in Greenwich Village as the daughter of journalists and organizers for a trade union, the Newspaper Guild. Gifted with a strong voice, she had been singing since earliest memory. "I was raised on Josh White, The Weavers, and Pete Seeger," she told the *New York Times* in 1994. "The music was everywhere. You'd go to a party at somebody's apartment and there would be fifty people there, singing well into the night."

Along with three classmates from the Elisabeth Irwin High School and four other singers, including ex-Weaver Erik Darling, Travers accompanied Pete Seeger in 1955 on seven tunes to supplement the Almanac Singers' 1941 album, retitled *Talking Union and Other Union Songs*. As the Song Swappers, they would go on to record three additional albums with Seeger—*Folksongs of Four Continents*, *Bantu Choral Folk Songs*, and *Camp Songs with Six to Eleven Year Olds*—before disbanding.

In April 1958, Travers appeared, as a member of a folk group, in a short-lived Broadway musical, *The Next President*, starring comedian Mort Sahl. "Folk music was a very integral part of the liberal Left experience," she told Joe Smith. "It was writers, sculptors, painters, listening to Woody Guthrie, Pete Seeger, and the Weavers. People sang in Washington Square Park on Sundays, and you really did not have to have a lot of talent to sing folk music. You needed enthusiasm, which is all [that] folk music asks. It asks that you care. Even if you're playing spoons, have a good time doing it."

Although she retreated from show business to focus on raising a daughter (and work in literary and advertising agencies), Travers's talents as a vocalist were impossible to ignore. Meeting Noel Paul Stookey, the resident emcee, comedian, and folksinger at the Gaslight Café, across the street from her apartment, in early 1961, they had begun singing together. "[Stookey] was a newcomer to town," Travers told *Goldmine* magazine, "and I sort of showed him the Italian fair and all that stuff because I grew up in the Village and I could be an official guide. . . . I would get up on-stage with Noel, sing two songs, and then go in the ladies room and think about throwing up."

Unlike Yarrow and Travers, Baltimore-born Stookey had grown up, not with folk music, but with rock and roll and R&B. Originally an electric guitarist, he had recorded an album, *The Birds Fly Home*, with a high school band, The Birds of Paradise, in the early 1950s. He continued with a similar group, The Corsairs, as a Michigan State University student.

Moving with his family to Philadelphia after graduating college, Stookey worked in a camera shop before continuing on to New York in 1959 and taking a job as a production manager for the Cormac Photocopy

Corporation. At night and on the weekends, he frequented Greenwich Village clubs, playing music and doing stand-up comedy. Within a year, he had left his job to become a full-time performer. "There was no booze at the coffeehouses," Stookey told me in 1989. "That meant there were ten places of entertainment that had listening crowds. They were not singles crowds. A performer could leave one place and go right down the hall to another coffeehouse to hear one of his friends. There was a great fraternity between all of the performers and a great exchange of ideas. There was a sense that we were holding hands, in a metaphysical sense, for a better world. We felt that we had seen the emperor's new clothes and that it was up to us to point it out. Much of our songs and much of our beatnik behavior was flying in the face of the Eisenhower era. The Baroque idea of American culture was caving in."

At the urging of Dave Van Ronk, a Brooklyn-born folk, blues, and ragtime guitarist/vocalist whose posthumous biography, *The Mayor of MacDougal Street*, written with Elijah Wald, would provide the inspiration for *Inside Llewyn Davis*, Stookey bought a Martin 0021 classical guitar and turned to folk music.

A number of folksingers auditioned for Grossman's new group. "They wanted someone who could carry a tune," Van Ronk told me in 1989, "sing harmony, and be reasonably strong as an instrumentalist. Peter wasn't facile on the guitar and Mary didn't play at all. They encouraged me, but I didn't want to do it."

When the trio's lineup coalesced, Yarrow was in the middle of a two-week stint at Folk City. Grossman approached the club's owner, Mike Porco. "[Grossman] came to me," recalled Porco in Robbie Woliver's *Bringing It All Back Home*, "and said, 'Mike, would you do me a favor? I just put together this group with Paul Stookey, Peter, and Mary Travers.' I knew them all. Grossman said, 'they're going to be very big, but if they don't get a gig, Peter is going to go to Chicago and the whole thing will fall apart. Will you hire them?' I said, 'Well, I have to hear them, and I'm not going to hire them if I have to pay extra money. I can't afford all three.' He said, 'Don't worry about the money. We'll just pay them twenty dollars extra and I'll cover it myself.' I hired Peter for another two weeks so he could work with the group and try it out."

When Porco balked at extending the trio's engagement after the initial two weeks, Grossman moved them to the Bitter End, where they continued to build an enthusiastic following.

Seeking a record deal, Grossman approached Warner Brothers Records, a subsidiary of the Burbank, California–based movie studio. Launched in March 1958, the label represented the studio's return to recording after a quarter of a century. Scoring their first hit with Bob Newhart's *The Button-Down Mind of Bob Newhart* (the first comedy album to reach number one on *Billboard*'s pop chart) in 1960, they continued their ascent after signing the Everly Brothers the following year and topping the charts with the brother's first single for the label, "Cathy's Clown."

Signing with Warner Brothers on January 29, 1962, Peter, Paul, Mary received a thirty thousand dollar advance while maintaining control over their music and its packaging. "[Grossman told Warner Brothers,] 'We'll make the whole thing,'" said Yarrow, "'we'll master it, [do the artwork], everything, and you'll just pay the bills.' It was more than anybody in the business got.... We had absolute control over what went on the album."

The label's trust paid off. With their debut album in March 1962, Peter, Paul, and Mary propelled to pop music's upper stratosphere. Selling more than two million copies, it would remain on the charts for 185 weeks, including eighty-five weeks in the top ten and seven weeks in the number one position, and again top the charts in October 1963—nineteen months after its release.

The album's first single, "Lemon Tree," based on a Brazilian folksong with English words by Portland, Maine–born folksinger/actor Will Holt, nearly missed the top forty, but the song would become a number one hit for Texas-born Trini Lopez.

Lopez would score an even bigger success by covering Peter, Paul, and Mary's second single, "If I Had a Hammer (The Hammer Song)." Written by Pete Seeger and Lee Hays, it had debuted at a testimonial dinner for Communist Party leaders at St. Nicholas Arena in New York on June 3, 1949. Recording it nine months later, The Weavers released it as a 78-rpm single (on Hootenanny Records). Although it would top the charts in thirty-six countries (peaking at the third position in the United States), Lopez's recording would have little impact on sales of Peter, Paul, and Mary's single (a top-ten hit), and the trio would score Grammy Awards for the year's "best performance by a vocal group" and "best folk recording."

Although not as striking as its predecessor, Peter, Paul, and Mary's second album, *Moving*, in January 1963 reached the *Billboard* pop chart's runner-up position, introduced the world to Yarrow's "Puff, the Magic Dragon," and helped to popularize Woody Guthrie's "This Land Is Your Land."

By the time Peter, Paul, and Mary began work on their third album (*In the Wind*), Grossman had taken over Dylan's management. Signing him to a songwriting contract with Warner Brothers–associated Witmark Publishing, he had begun shopping his tunes to other artists. Peter, Paul, and Mary agreed to record three songs. "Quit Your Lowdown Ways" and "Don't Think Twice, It's Alright" reflected on interpersonal relationships, but the album's title tune, and its first single, "Blowin' in the Wind," would provide the civil rights movement with one of its greatest theme songs. "Anybody who sang Bob's songs, at the time, was a big deal," said Bronx-born and Woodstock-based singer, songwriter, guitarist, banjo player, and founder of the music-instruction-oriented Homespun Recordings Harry Peter "Happy" Traum to me in May 2013. "Nobody knew his songs much, especially in the world outside of the folk scene in Greenwich Village."

As a member of the New World Singers, Traum had participated in the first recording of "Blowin' in the Wind"—included on a multi-artist, topical song compilation, *Broadside Ballads, Volume 1*, in 1963. "[*Broadside* magazine] was the focal point of the political songwriter movement," Traum explained. "It came out of the left, the communists of the '40's and '50's. There was a glorification of the labor movement, stemming from the Depression era. Woody Guthrie was a big part of it, along with the romanticism of hopping freight trains and being in hobo jungles."

For Traum, a former summer camp folksong counselor and a frequent presence at Washington Square Park jam sessions, folk music was tantamount to political causes. "I marched for Civil Rights, when I was in college, in the fifties," he said. "It was a natural chain of events."

The connection between music and politics intensified after Traum joined Robert "Bob" Cohen, Gil Turner, and Delores Dixon in the New World Singers. "We sang songs by Bob Dylan, Phil Ochs, Tom Paxton, and Pete Seeger," Traum remembered, "and played around the Village folk scene—Gerde's Folk City, the Bitter End, and places like that. We did benefit concerts with the Freedom Singers from Albany, Georgia, and shared stages with Ossie Davis and Ruby Dee. We were the northern wing of the Civil Rights movement, so we weren't beaten or thrown into jail; we raised funds and consciousness."

"They sing like the Ol' Almanacs used to sing," proclaimed Dylan in his liner notes for the New World Singers' debut album. "They sing like the Memphis Jug Band used to sing. They don' have no row to hoe. They got a new world to win. I got a new world to win. You got a new world to win."

The New World Singers' Bob Cohen (now cantor and music director at Temple Emmanuel in Kingston, New York) had been involved with political causes since the early 1960s, performing at benefit concerts for SNCC (Student Nonviolent Coordinating Committee) and others. Together with Gil Turner (a member of the editorial board of topical song magazine *Broadside*, an emcee at Gerde's Folk City, and a gifted songwriter whose "Carry It On" would become an anthem of political activism), he traveled to Edwards, Mississippi, in 1963 to organize and perform at freedom song workshops. The following summer, he returned to the southern state as director of the Mississippi Caravan of Music, accompanied by a group of folksingers including Pete Seeger, Theodore Bikel, Barbara Dane, and Phil Ochs, to promote voting rights.

Dylan frequented the New World Singers' performances in New York. During one Folk City show, he sat at the bar, nursing his glass of wine, as he listened to his sometimes-girlfriend Delores Dixon singing a song that originated with African American slaves before Emancipation,

"No More Auction Block for Me." "It was a very moving song of freedom written during slavery days," said Cohen, "insisting 'no more, no more,' and sadly reflecting on the 'many thousands gone.' She sang it with spirit and determination."

Including the song, as "Many Thousand Gone," in *Folksongs of North America* in 1960, Alan Lomax explained, "This is one of the spirituals of resistance (W. E. B. Dubois called them "Sorrow Songs"), whose antebellum origin had been authenticated. Runaway slaves who fled as far north as Nova Scotia, after Britain abolished slavery in 1833, transmitted it to their descendants, and it is still in circulation there. At the time of the Civil War, an abolitionist took it down from Negro Union Soldiers."

Dylan would use the song's melody for "Blowin' in the Wind." "In those days, we spoke of 'borrowing' tunes," said Cohen, "something Pete Seeger called 'the folk process.' Woody Guthrie, Joe Hill, and even J. S. Bach had done it. We thought it was great and started to sing it. We would bring Dylan up on that postage stamp of a stage to sing it along with us. It seemed to me then, as it does now, that his reworking or re-creation of that spiritual carried on its original message and was in itself a song of resistance to all the injustice in the world."

Broadside Ballads, Volume 1 featured the New World Singers on three tunes. In addition to "Blowin' in the Wind," they recorded "Bizness Ain't Dead," a topical tune that Woody Guthrie had adopted from a traditional folksong and recorded in 1951 but never released, and the more optimistic "I Can See a New Day."

Traum also joined Dylan for a duet rendition of an antinuke protest tune, "I Will Not Go under the Ground (Let Me Die in My Footsteps)." Dylan had come to the studio to record three songs—"John Brown," "Only a Hobo," and "Talkin' Devil"—as Blind Boy Grunt. "It was the first time that I was in a professional recording studio," remembered Traum. "It was a pretty heavy thing for me. [Dylan] loved the way that we had done 'Blowin' in the Wind' and told us that he had another song that he had brought to the studio. He turned to me and said, 'you sing this, and I'll back you up.' We took the sheet music, put it on a music stand, and did it in one take. It ended up on the record."

Dylan's song had personal meaning to Traum. "Gil Turner and I had been arrested (a year before) during a demonstration against compulsory air-raid drills," he explained. "We were fighting against nuclear warfare, as a part of the peace movement, and members of the war resistor's league. Bob knew that we had refused to go underground for that air-raid drill."

The New World Singers continued to extend their reach. "We got a contract with Atlantic Records," said Traum, "the home of Ray Charles, soul music, and jazz musicians like Herbie Mann. They brought us in as their folk group. They had seen the Kingston Trio and Peter, Paul and Mary becoming commercially successful. We had the good fortune of having Ahmet Ertegun producing us, but he tried to get us to be more pop and rock oriented. We were trying to be purists and stay acoustic, but there were some clashes."

The New World Singers' debut album included the first recorded appearance of Dylan's "Don't Think Twice, It's Alright." "It started to do something in the markets where they were promoting it," said Traum, "and, then, Peter, Paul, and Mary started doing their versions of Dylan's songs and wiped us off the charts."

Recorded on July 9, 1962, Dylan's version of "Blowin' in the Wind" would not be released until the following June. Covered by the Chad Mitchell Trio on their March 1963 album *In Action* (later retitled *Blowin' in the Wind*), Peter, Paul, and Mary's recording blew all others aside. Released on June 18, 1963 (the week that "Puff, the Magic Dragon," slipped off the charts), it would become the fastest selling single in Warner Brothers' first half decade, selling more than three hundred thousand copies in its first week. Peter, Paul, and Mary would receive "best performance by a vocal group" and "best folk recording" Grammy Awards for the second consecutive year. "[It] was the first time we ever made a song that was just a single," said Yarrow. "Before that, our singles were songs out of albums and they were successful, but with this one, we ran into the studio with this attitude, 'we don't really care whether this thing is a hit or not. We just want it to come out and be available.' What was important about 'Blowin' in the Wind' was that even though 'If I Had a Hammer' preceded it, it somehow became the first of the so-called protest songs. Everybody made a big thing out of that, but it was really an affirmation song. It was a song of caring and commitment and it was hopeful. It wasn't about teenage dating behavior."

Peter, Paul, and Mary would continue to be among Dylan's greatest boosters. They would cover "The Times They Are a-Changin'" and include a live version of "Blowin' in the Wind" on their million-selling double-album, *In Concert*, in 1964. "When the Ship Comes In" would be included on *A Song Will Rise* the following year; "Too Much of Nothing," a *Basement Tapes* tune, on *Late Again* in 1968; and "Forever Young" on *Reunion* in 1978. With the trio (and Joan Baez) hailing him as one of the generation's premiere songwriters, Dylan's second album, *Freewheelin'* broke into the top twenty-five.

Dylan's interests in politics were at their most acute while dating Suze Rotolo, the daughter of union organizers and a volunteer for the Congress of Racial Equality (CORE). He traveled to Mississippi to sing at civil rights rallies and began writing about the southern states' racial injustices. His first protest song, "The Death of Emmett Till," debuted at a CORE benefit concert in February 1962 and told of the Chicago-born black teenager brutally murdered for whistling at a white woman in Tallahatchie, Mississippi, nine years before. Another new song, "Oxford Town," addressed problems faced by James Meredith in September 1962 as the first black to attend the formerly all-white University of Mississippi.

The African American struggle for equality had been intensifying for more than a decade. Six days before a Washington, DC, protest against segregation (organized by Asa Philip Randolph, president of black labor union the Brotherhood of Sleeping Cars) in June 1941, President Franklin Delano Roosevelt issued an executive order demanding an end to discrimination within the defense industry and United States government, though it did not end military segregation (which would continue until 1948). Randolph called off the protest.

Forward strides toward desegregation came slowly. The Supreme Court ruling in *Brown v. the Board of Education* in 1954 struck down segregation in public schools, while Rosa Parks's refusal to move from her seat on a Montgomery, Alabama, bus the following year prompted a 381-day bus boycott and brought Rev. Martin Luther King Jr. and the civil rights movement to global attention. Sit-ins at segregated restaurants, and wade-ins at segregated beaches, brought further desegregation of public places. Freedom Riders (mostly white college students) traveled south in 1961 to help African Americans secure voting rights, but there was still a long way to go.

In the spring of 1963, Randolph and his deputy, Bayard Ruskin, renewed the call for a protest march on Washington, DC. President John Fitzgerald Kennedy responded by submitting a civil rights bill to Congress banning discrimination in public places, including restaurants, hotels, and retail stores, and planting the seeds of the Civil Rights Act that would be signed by his successor Lyndon Baines Johnson on July 2, 1964.

The August 28 March on Washington for Jobs and Freedom, as it was officially known, though, was unstoppable. More than a half century later, it remains one of the United States' most important milestones. Televised in its entirety by CBS, the daylong event drew a quarter of a million people to the nearly two-mile-long mall between the Lincoln Monument and the Capitol building. Rousing speeches were scattered throughout the program, while Martin Luther King Jr. left no one in doubt when he diverted from his prepared words (at the urging of Mahalia Jackson) and concluded the daylong protest with his still-riveting, nineteen-minute-long "I have a dream" speech.

A diverse range of musicians, black and white, performed throughout the day. Mahalia Jackson and Marian Anderson opened the morning with a gospel tune, "He's Got the Whole World (in His Hands)"; Dylan, Baez, and Peter, Paul, and Mary made their feelings known during seven-minute sets. Peter, Paul, and Mary performed "If I Had a Hammer (The Hammer Song)" and "Blowin' in the Wind," at the time in its sixth week in the top ten (in the fifth position). "If you could imagine singing in front of a quarter of a million people who believed they could make

America more generous and compassionate in a non-violent way," recalled Travers, "you begin to know how incredible that belief was."

Baez sang "We Shall Overcome" and "Oh, Freedom" and joined Dylan during his opening tune, "When the Ship Comes In." Written after a hotel clerk had denied him a hotel room based on his appearance in early 1963, Dylan would revive "When the Ship Comes In" during his 1985 *Farm Aid* set with the Rolling Stones' Keith Richards and Ron Wood. His second tune, "Only a Pawn in Their Game," addressed the assassination of NAACP field secretary Medgar Evers by white supremacist Byron de la Beckwith.

Dylan then joined Baez, African American folksinger Len Chandler, and others to sing "Keep Your Eyes on the Prize," one of the civil rights movement's most important songs. Based on a traditional tune, it had been included, as "Gospel Plow," in John and Alan Lomax's 1949 folksong collection *Our Singing Country*.

Civil rights provided only one hue in Dylan's topical palette. His early songs protested war and nuclear proliferation, and spoke volumes at a time of political turmoil. Standing up for what he believed in, he refused CBS-TV's request to substitute another song for "Talkin' John Birch Society Blues," his sarcastic diatribe against the ultra-right, and his appearance on the nationally broadcast *Ed Sullivan Show* in May 1962 was canceled.

Dylan's songs would remain political on his third album, *The Times They Are a-Changin'*. In addition to "Only a Pawn in Their Game," the album included "The Lonesome Death of Hattie Carroll," which recounted the murder of a black barmaid by a wealthy tobacco farmer, and "The Ballad of Hollis Brown," about a South Dakota farmer who kills his starving family. "With God on Our Side" delivered a powerful antiwar message.

Topical songs proved to be only a brief diversion, however. Whether it was the result of his breakup with Rotolo, a reaction to media coverage of the civil rights movement, or part of African Americans' discouragement of white participation is unclear, but Dylan veered from the cause. "*Harper's Bazaar* can feature it; you [can] find it on the cover of *Life*," he told Paul J. Robbin of the *Los Angeles Free Press*, "but when you get beneath it, like anything, you find bullshit tied up in it. The Negro Civil Rights Movement is proper, but there is more to it than picketing in Selma, right? There are people living in utter poverty in New York, and, then again, you have this big Right to Vote—which is groovy. You want Negroes to vote, [but they are only going to] vote for politicians—the same as the white people. I hate to say it like that, makes it sound hard, but it's going to boil down to that."

By his next album, *Another Side of Bob Dylan*, Dylan had exchanged politics for the personal introspection and surrealistic imagery of "My Back Pages," "I Don't Believe You (She Acts Like We Never Have Met),"

"It Ain't Me Babe," "Black Crow Blues," and "Motorpsycho Nightmare." Simultaneously writing a stream-of-consciousness book of poetry, *Tarantula*, that would circulate unauthorized in 1967 (with Macmillan and Scribner publishing it officially four years later), he had begun writing tunes that owed more to beat generation writers like Allen Ginsberg and Jack Kerouac than to southern folksongs and blues.

Dylan's shift from politics was upsetting to some longtime fans. *Sing Out* editor Irwin Silber criticized him in an open letter for "losing contact with the people" and selling out to the "paraphernalia of fame." "[Dylan] was the savior," said Happy Traum, "the guy that people looked to [for direction]. There were people writing topical songs, but nobody was writing the kinds of songs that he was writing. Songs like 'The Times They Are a-Changing',' 'A Hard Rain's Gonna Fall,' 'The Lonesome Death of Hattie Carroll,' 'The Ballad of Medgar Evers,' and 'Oxford Town' were transcendent. It restored your faith in humanity that anybody could write those songs, saying what was on everybody's mind, but he decided that he wasn't fulfilling his artistic vision, and wanted to move on, and speak in a more personal language."

"There were no politics [left in Dylan's music] at all," Traum continued, "and he wouldn't sing the old songs. People invested so much emotion and idealism, and built him up to be this demigod, but, whenever a god falls (for whatever reason), they turn against him. For a while, the animosity was horrible. It showed that people of any political stripe could be narrow-minded."

Many of his early fans saw him as a solo, acoustic guitar/harmonica-playing troubadour, but Dylan had been recording with other musicians from the beginning of his career. Spike Lee's father, William "Bill" Lee, played upright bass during an April 1962 session. Four months later, Dick Wellstood (piano), Bruce Langhorne (guitar), Howie Collins (guitar), Leonard Gaskon (bass), and Herb Lovelle (drums) accompanied the singer-songwriter on three tunes—"Corrina, Corrina," "Mixed Up Changes," and "That's All Right Mama," the Arthur "Big Boy" Crudup tune that Elvis Presley had recorded for his first single. The same lineup returned to the studio on November 14, 1962, to record "Mixed-up Confusion," the B-side of "Corrina, Corrina" (released a month later).

The musical experiments intensified after Tom Wilson replaced John Hammond as Dylan's producer in 1963. A Waco, Texas–born graduate of Fisk University and Harvard University, Thomas Blanchard "Tom" Wilson Jr. (1931–1978) had owned a small, independent label, Transition Records, in the late 1950s and produced embryonic albums by free jazz visionaries Sun Ra and Cecil Taylor. After briefly working for United Artists and Savoy (for whom he again produced Sun Ra), he had become a staff producer for Columbia Records. Assuming the reins from Hammond midway toward the album's completion, Wilson would produce (without credit) the final tracks of *The Freewheelin' Bob Dylan*.

As his first two full-length collaborations with the singer-songwriter (*The Times They Are a-Changin'* and *Another Side of Bob Dylan*) indicated, Wilson pointed Dylan toward a more contemporary direction. Planning to overdub a band onto three solo tracks, he scheduled a session (without the songwriter) in December 1961. Although he would cancel the session (and Dylan's solo tracks would be left as is), the producer would resurrect the plan four years later and add instruments to "Sounds of Silence," one of the songs from *Wednesday Morning, 3AM*, the scarcely noticed acoustic album that he had produced for Paul Simon and Art Garfunkel a year before. Released in September 1965, the revamped recording would top the pop charts and transform Simon and Garfunkel into a worldwide phenomenon.

Wilson and Dylan's vision would come into full bloom with *Bringing It All Back Home*. As far from the political messages as possible, Dylan's lyrics were aflame with post-beat stream-of-consciousness. A tongue-twisting rap precursor (later heard in the opening scene of *Don't Look Back*), "Subterranean Homesick Blues" set the pace from the start. Released as a single (with "She Belongs to Me" on the B-side), it would spend eight weeks on the United States' charts (peaking at number thirty-nine) and five weeks on the UK's top 50 (reaching number nine). "We had a lot of swinging cats on that track," Dylan told the *Sheffield University Press* in April 1965, "real hip musicians, not just some cats I picked up off the street, and we all got together and we just had a ball. Anyway, that's just one track off the album."

Four lengthy tunes ("Mr. Tambourine Man," "Gates of Eden," "It's All Over Now Baby Blue," and "It's Alright, Ma [I'm Only Bleeding]") infused Dylan's solo acoustic balladry with expressionistic wordplay, while the remaining songs, including "Maggie's Farm" and "Love Minus Zero/ No Limit," were flushed out by additional instrumentation. Bruce Langhorne and Kenny Rankin played guitar, Joseph Macho Jr. and Bill Lee played bass, Robert "Bobby" Gregg played drums, and Paul L. Griffin played piano. John Hammond Jr. made a guest appearance on guitar; John Sebastian (who would form the Lovin' Spoonful shortly afterward) played bass. *Rolling Stone* would place *Bringing It All Back Home* at number thirty-one on its list of the 500 greatest albums.

Dylan's sixth album, *Highway 61 Revisited*, featured full-band arrangements of "From a Buick 6," "Ballad of a Thin Man," "Queen Jane Approximately," "Just Like Tom Thumb's Blues," "It Takes a Lot to Laugh, It Takes a Train to Cry," and "Like a Rolling Stone." An eleven-minute-plus epic, "Desolation Row" concluded the album with the musical equivalent of Hieronymus Bosch's surrealistic fifteenth-century masterpiece *The Garden of Earthly Delights*. *Rolling Stone* would place *Highway 61 Revisited* at number four on its greatest albums list. "Articulate, poetic, and bitter songs," proclaimed *All Music Guide* critic William Ruhlmann.

"This is an album of brutality and innocence," said Hank Kalet of PopMatters.com, "an album that could only have been produced by an artist at the height of his powers, with a war raging overseas in the shadow of a presidential assassination. It is that rare album on which not only are there no weak cuts, but on which each song is a masterpiece, a classic rock and roll album."

Recording sessions for *Highway 61 Revisited* in mid-June 1965 were extremely fruitful. On the first day, Mike Bloomfield and Al Gorgoni (guitars), Joseph Macho Jr. (bass), Bobby Gregg (drums), and Frank Owens (piano) backed Dylan on "Sitting on a Barbed Wire Fence," a song that failed to make the album, and an early version of "It Takes a Lot to Laugh, It Takes a Train to Cry," listed as "Phantom Engineer Cloud."

Another song attempted the first day, "Like a Rolling Stone," transformed overnight from waltz time to the sharp-tongued, straight-ahead rock tune that Columbia would release as a single. Brooklyn-born Al Kooper (who had played guitar for the post–"Short Shorts" Royal Teens) attended the session as a guest of Tom Wilson. When keyboardist Paul Griffin (who had replaced Owens) switched to the piano, vacating the Hammond B3, Kooper pleaded with Wilson to give him a chance. Kooper's texturally heavy organ swirls would become essential to the finished recording. "It didn't matter that I knew next to nothing about playing the organ," he remembered in *Backstage Passes & Backstabbing Bastards*.

Concerned about its six–and-a-half-minute length, Columbia initially rejected "Like a Rolling Stone" as a single. When the label's release coordinator, Shaun Considine, brought a copy of Dylan's demo to a New York nightclub, however, the deejay flipped over it and played it repeatedly for the rest of the night. The label received so many phone calls about the tune that it reversed its previous decision and scheduled the single's release (with "Gates of Eden" on the B-side). Radio station copies split the song in half; deejays had to flip the disc to play the complete song.

Despite its length, "Like a Rolling Stone" would spend a dozen weeks on the American pop charts and reach the runner-up position (behind The Beatles' "Help!") on the *Billboard* pop charts. *Rolling Stone* would rank it at the top of its list of the 500 greatest songs of all time.

Inducting Dylan into the Rock and Roll Hall of Fame in 1988, Bruce Springsteen remembered hearing "Like a Rolling Stone" for the first time. "I was in the car with my mother, listening to [New York rock radio station] WMCA," he said, "on came that snare-shot that sounded like somebody'd kicked open the door to your mind. The way that Elvis [Presley] freed your body, Dylan freed your mind, and showed us that, because the music was physical, it did not mean it was anti-intellect. He had the vision and talent to make a pop song so that it contained the whole world. He invented a new way a pop singer could sound, broke through the limitations of what a recording could achieve, and he changed the face of rock 'n' roll for ever and ever."

"What a shocking thing," recalled Elvis Costello in an essay written for *Esquire*, "to live in a world where there was Manfred Mann, The Supremes, and Engelbert Humperdinck, and here comes 'Like a Rolling Stone.' That was a great world, a very exciting time."

Organized by Newport Jazz Festival producer George Wein in 1959, with a committee composed of folksingers Pete Seeger, Theodore Bikel, and Oscar Brand as well as Albert Grossman, the Newport Folk Festival was well on its way to becoming one of the folk revival's premier events. During its first year, in 1959, Bob Gibson had generously shared the spotlight with a folksinger from Boston who had appeared at the Gate of Horn—Joan Baez. When Baez returned in 1963 (there had been no festival in 1961 or 1962), she extended the folksinger's gesture to Dylan in the midst of her Friday-afternoon set. "I was moved by his youth," she told me in 1990, "and by his brilliance. The fact that he was a rebel was wonderful."

The following evening, Dylan stood on his own as he delivered a politically heavy set that included "Talkin' World War III Blues," "God on Our Side," "Only a Pawn in Their Game," "Talkin' John Birch Society Blues," and "A Hard Rain's a-Gonna Fall." The set's finale hammered it home. As Baez, Seeger, Peter, Paul, and Mary, Theodore Bikel, and the Freedom Singers (with future Sweet Honey in the Rock founder Bernice Johnson Reagon) joined him on stage, holding hands, the night climaxed with "Blowin' in the Wind" and civil rights anthem "We Shall Overcome."

The next day, Dylan presented three songs—"Who Killed Davey Moore," "Masters of War," and (with Pete Seeger) "Playboys and Playgirls"—at a topical song workshop, and again made a surprise appearance during Baez's evening set, joining for a duet version of "With God on Our Side."

By the time he returned to Newport a year later, Dylan radiated a much different aura, one reflecting changes sweeping through America. The assassination of President John Fitzgerald Kennedy eight months before on November 22, 1963, had dampened the country's optimism, while the war in Southeast Asia had continued to escalate. Three appearances by The Beatles on CBS-TV's *Ed Sullivan Show* in February 1964 had opened popular music to scores of British Invasion bands, including the Rolling Stones, The Kinks, the Dave Clark Five, Manfred Mann, Chad and Jeremy, Peter and Gordon, The Who, The Hollies, Freddy and the Dreamers, and The Yardbirds.

At a sparsely attended Saturday-afternoon workshop, Dylan performed "It Ain't Me Babe" (which he would reprise during Baez's mainstage set), a sarcastic kiss-off song later covered by The Turtles and Sonny & Cher. "Mr. Tambourine Man," which would become a massive hit for

The Byrds and help launch folk rock, debuted. The following night, he recoiled as main stage musical host Ronnie Gilbert introduced him (as the closing act) by telling the crowd, "You know him, he's yours: Bob Dylan."

"What a crazy thing to say," Dylan would later complain. "Screw that! As far as I knew, I didn't belong to anybody then or now."

Despite Gilbert's slight, Dylan delivered another unforgettable solo set, mixing topical tunes ("Chimes of Freedom" and "With God on Our Side") with more personal songs ("All I Wanna Do" and "To Ramona") and a reprise of "Mr. Tambourine Man."

It's unclear whether he had it planned, or made a last-minute decision after arriving in Newport a third time on July 24, 1965, but Dylan's decision to play with an electric band would impact the future course of contemporary music—folk and popular.

The first of the weekend's conflicts ignited during a Saturday-afternoon workshop ("Blues: Origins and Offshoots") that included appearances by African American bluesmen Willie Dixon, Mance Lipscomb, Memphis Slim, Sam "Lightnin'" Hopkins, and Reverend Gary Davis. Awed by such "authentic" bluesmen, the workshop's master of ceremonies, Alan Lomax, introduced the multiracial Butterfield Blues Band, led by Chicago-born harmonica player Paul Butterfield and featuring white guitarists Mike Bloomfield and Elvin Bishop, as mere "interpreters."

Albert Grossman, who managed the Butterfield Blues Band, was incensed by the folklorist's condescending remarks and tensions escalated. Grossman confronted Lomax and the two middle-aged, barely-in-shape men began rolling on the ground, physically brawling. It would be a harbinger of things to come.

Dylan gave no hint of what he had planned for his main stage set the following evening as he presented solo renditions of "All I Wanna Do," "If You Gotta Go, Go Now," and "Love Minus Zero/No Limit" at a Saturday-afternoon songwriter workshop. As night fell, however, he secretly joined Mike Bloomfield, Al Kooper, pianist Barry Goldberg, and the Butterfield Blues Band's African American rhythm section—Sam Lay (drums) and Jerome Arnold (bass)—in a Bellevue Avenue mansion and rehearsed. "[Dylan] felt that he could better express himself and reach more people by going electric," said George Wein in *Myself among Others*. "He felt it necessary to tap into the pulse of popular culture."

"I thought I'd get more power with a small group backing me," Dylan explained in the Martin Scorsese–directed documentary *No Direction Home*. "It was electric but that doesn't necessarily mean it's modernized just because it's electric. Country music was electric too."

"A lot of my songs were becoming hits for other people," he continued. "The Byrds had a big hit, some group called The Turtles had some hit; I didn't really like that sound—folk rock, whatever that was. I felt it didn't have anything to do with me."

There are conflicting views of what happened when Dylan (carrying an electric guitar) walked onto the stage, following a set by banjo player/folksinger Cousin Emmy (Cynthia May Carver) and an introduction by Peter Yarrow, but as soon as he, and his musical cohorts, launched into "Maggie's Farm," they met a reaction they had not anticipated. "People began booing," remembered Wein, "there were cries of 'sellout!'"

"There was anger, there was fury, there was applause, there was stunned silence," said music writer Greil Marcus, "there was a great sense of betrayal, as if something precious and delicate was being dashed to the ground and stomped. As if the delicate flower of folk music, the priceless heritage of impoverished black farmers and destitute white miners was being mocked by a dandy, with a garish, noisy, electric guitar, who was going to make huge amounts of money as a pop star by exploiting what he found from these poor people."

After struggling their way through two more songs—"Like a Rolling Stone" (which would reach number two on the pop charts within three weeks) and "Phantom Engineer" ("It Takes a Lot to Laugh, It Takes a Train to Cry")—Dylan turned to the musicians, said "let's go," and led the way off the stage. The crowd erupted even more. Many felt shortchanged by the sixteen-minute set. "Some had traveled thousands of miles and paid a lot for tickets," said Kooper. "What did they get—three songs? They didn't give a shit about us being electric; they just wanted more."

Recalling the riot that had broken out five years before when twelve thousand disappointed fans (unable to get tickets to the sold-out Newport Jazz Festival) had burst into uncontrolled frenzy (and forced the festival to end early), Wein convinced Dylan to return to the stage to play a couple of acoustic tunes. Borrowing a guitar from Yarrow and choosing one of the harmonicas tossed (at his request) onto the stage, the singer-songwriter struck back at the crowd with an exceptionally fiery rendition of "Mr. Tambourine Man" and a capping of his first era with "It's All Over Now, Baby Blue." "The old guard hung their heads in defeat," remembered Joe Boyd, the future record producer (Incredible String Band, Fairport Convention, and Toots and the Maytals) who was engineering the Newport festival's soundboard, in *White Bicycles*, "while the young, far from being triumphant, were chastened. They realized that in their victory lay the death of something wonderful. Anyone wishing to portray the history of the sixties as a journey from idealism to hedonism could place the hinge at around 9:30 on the night of 25 July 1965."

"I was kind of stunned," Dylan told Nat Hentoff of *Playboy*. "I can't put anybody down for coming and booing: after all, they paid to get in. They could have been maybe a little quieter and not so persistent, though. There were a lot of old people there, too, lots of whole families had driven down from Vermont, lots of nurses and their parents, and they just came to hear some relaxing hoedowns, you know, maybe an

Indian polka or two. Just when everything's going all right, here I come on, and the whole place turns into a beer factory."

Other electric bands had been on the bill, including the Butterfield Blues Band, Muddy Waters's blues band, and the Chambers Brothers, but Dylan and his overnight-assembled band roared with an intensity that was loud, intense, and unprecedented. The festival's sound system, accustomed to acoustic music, was unprepared for such an avalanche of sound. "The complaints weren't about the music," suggested Sam Charters. "My God, Dylan was the hottest thing going. People were yelling because all they could hear was noise."

"I was furious by the distortion," said Pete Seeger, the evening's musical host, to me in 1995, "and I couldn't understand the words. I went [to the sound booth] and said, 'Get rid of that distortion! Turn it down!' They said, 'No way, this is the way that they want it.' I said, "I wish I had an axe, I'd cut the cable.'"

"I don't believe people were booing because the music was revolutionary," Geoff Muldaur (who appeared at the festival with the Jim Kweskin Jug Band) told *New Republic* music critic David Hajdu in *Positively 4th Street*. "He had no idea how to play the electric guitar, he had very second-rate musicians with him, and they had not rehearsed enough. It just did not work. The musicians did not play good. There is no doubt, in my mind, [that] people were booing because it stank. [Dylan's] move into that music seemed so, 'okay, now I'm going to be a rock and roll star and sell a lot of records.'"

Boredom factored into Dylan's new direction. "I was doing fine, you know, singing and playing my guitar," he told Nora Ephron and Susan Edmiston. "It was a sure thing—don't you understand? I was getting very bored with that . . . I was thinking of quitting."

Dylan would not return to the Newport Folk Festival until 2002 (when he would appear onstage in a wig and fake beard and perform a career-spanning ninety-minute set), but, after debuting his new electric sound, he had a full itinerary of concerts ahead of him. There were concerts scheduled for the Forest Hills Tennis Stadium in Queens, New York, on August 28, with the Hollywood Bowl in Los Angeles, California, five days later.

Most of the musicians who had accompanied him at Newport went their separate ways immediately afterward. Sam Lay, Jerome Arnold, and Mike Bloomfield returned to the Butterfield Blues Band, while Barry Goldberg had gone back to Chicago, where he, Bloomfield, and drummer Buddy Miles would launch the Electric Flag two years later. Only Al Kooper remained. Dylan needed to regroup.

III

Three years of roadhouse performances and rehearsals had made Ronnie Hawkins and the Hawks extremely tight, but, having grown tired of the bandleader's over-the-top showmanship and harsh rules, Robbie Robertson, Levon Helm, Richard Manuel, Rick Danko, and Garth Hudson were ready to move on by late 1963. "There are a couple of ways of looking at it," said Danko. "I remember Ronnie firing me for something silly. He was the greatest discipline force in our lives, but he had a knack for picking on people. I watched him double the money that he was making and it didn't reflect in my paycheck."

The Hawks had grown away from Hawkins musically as well. "We were leaning even further away from rockabilly," remembered Bruce Bruno (who briefly sang with the group). "Richard [Manuel] liked to sing Bobby 'Blue' Bland material and those Ray Charles songs, and we all liked Sonny Boy Williamson's songs and anything by Jimmy Reed or Willie Dixon."

As Levon and the Hawks, they continued to perform weeklong residencies throughout Ontario and the northeastern United States. "We'd show up at a club that held two hundred or three hundred people," remembered Danko, "and there would be people lined up every night of the week. . . . The following Monday, we'd be in a new town and the same thing would happen."

The former Hawks recorded "Leave Me Alone" backed with "Uh-uh-uh" (credited to the Canadian Squires and released on Ware Records in the United States and Apex Records in Canada) in 1964 and "The Stones I Throw" backed with "He Don't Love You (And He'll Break Your Heart)" for Atlantic-distributed Atco a year later, but neither sold well. A third single in 1968 featured an updating of a New Orleans' brass band standard renamed "Go Go Liza Jane" and a reprise of Robertson's "He Don't Love You (And He'll Break Your Heart)." "Those records were just some people trying to sign us up," the songwriter told *Melody Maker*. "We didn't know what was going on; we didn't have any control over it. They just whipped us into the studio and we had to cut a few songs in an afternoon. . . . We didn't know that end of it at all, how you've got to be able to talk back a little bit, [and] you've got to say a few things if you want to do what you want to do. We were just doing what someone was telling us to do."

Whenever they were in Toronto on a Saturday afternoon, the former Hawks would perform alcohol-free shows for all-ages audiences. At one such matinee, they met John Paul Hammond (John Hammond Jr.), the son of the Columbia Records producer who had discovered Bessie Smith, Count Basie, Bob Dylan, and, later, Bruce Springsteen. The young bluesman was, according to Helm, "a solid blues singer and guitar player on the college and coffeehouse circuit, keeping the country blues of Robert Johnson and Son House alive."

A few months later, Levon and the Hawks reunited with the New York–born bluesman at the trendy Peppermint Lounge (where Ringo Starr had danced the twist a few weeks before). "I thought we had one of the best bands in the country," said Helm. "John knew his stuff, and was a hell of player, and we knew the stuff. We were having a hell of a time, but the guys at the Peppermint Lounge told us, 'this blues shit will never get you anywhere. It's a twist joint—play the twist.'"

In 1964, Hammond hired Robertson and Helm to play on his second album, *So Many Roads*, along with Jimmy Lewis (bass), Chicago blues guitarist Mike Bloomfield (on piano), and Charlie Musselwhite (harmonica). Garth Hudson played organ. A year later, Robertson returned for Hammond's intended debut for Red Bird Records, *I Can Tell*. Danko played bass, as did Lewis and the Rolling Stones' Bill Wyman. Not-yet-released when the label folded, the album waited two years before Atlantic Records issued it in 1967.

Levon and the Hawks were in the midst of a month-long engagement at Tony Mart's, a popular music club in Somers Point, New Jersey, southwest of Atlantic City, when they received a telephone call from Dylan. Helm, who answered, knew little about the tunesmith other than that he was "a folksinger and songwriter whose hero was Woody Guthrie." "I was into Muddy [Waters] and B. B. King," he explained, "and I thought Ray Charles had the best band."

As they spoke, Helm's fascination grew. "The phone call ended up," he recalled, "with me telling Bob that we were real interested in the project, that I'd talk to the other boys and get back to him the next day."

Dylan (who was actually just looking for a guitarist) had heard of the group from Mary Martin, the Toronto-born administrative assistant in Albert Grossman's New York office. Flying home to study typing and speed-reading on the weekends, Martin had become a regular attendee of Levon and the Hawks' Saturday-afternoon matinee performances. "They were a really mature and loving and dedicated bunch of boys who loved the music they were doing," said Martin (who would go on to manage Leonard Cohen, Van Morrison, Rodney Crowell, and Vince Gill), "and they executed it with passion. I would swoon when Richard (Manuel) would sing a Ray Charles song. I think we all would swoon."

Martin's friendship with the musicians remained mutually beneficial. "She turned us on to some of the people in Albert Grossman's stable," remembered Helm, "Gordon Lightfoot, Richie Havens, Peter, Paul, and Mary, and this guy called Bob Dylan."

On one Saturday afternoon, Martin and a girlfriend had come to the hotel where Levon and the Hawks were staying to escort Helm to a matinee. "She brought me Bob Dylan's *Highway 61 Revisited*," he recalled. "It was about to come out. It was the first time any of us had heard of him. Next thing I knew, Mary was calling me up to tell me that Bob was looking for a group, and she was telling him about the band."

Martin knew of Dylan's desire to play with a band, having listened to The Byrds' recording of "Mr. Tambourine Man" with him. "Never being shy about very much," she explained, "I suggested that it would be a good idea for him to check out these boys in the bars of Toronto."

After having his "scouts" check out Levon and the Hawks at Friar's Tavern in Toronto, Dylan summoned Robertson for a meeting in New York. "We didn't know very much about him," Robertson recalled. "I didn't even have time to get his records and become familiar [with his music]. I thought, 'why does he want me?' I didn't know what was going on.... At the time, I was a young, wailing, raging guitar player."

After a visit to a midtown Manhattan guitar shop, Dylan and Robertson returned to Grossman's office to play some tunes. "That was the first time I ever really heard Bob Dylan," said Robertson, "sitting on a couch with him singing."

Invited to join Dylan's band, Robertson thought immediately of The Hawks. "I told him that I played with these other guys," he remembered, "and I wasn't going to leave them. He said, 'How do we work this out? What if we just do two gigs?' I said, 'Okay, I'll do it, if Levon can come along.'"

Recalling his first impression of Dylan, Helm remembered, "Bob was wearing clothes he'd bought in England, a red op-art shirt, a narrow-waisted jacket, black pegged pants, pointed black Beatle boots."

The drummer asked about the booing at Newport. "We started having sound troubles," he remembered Dylan telling him, "and people down front tried to tell us about it because we couldn't hear ourselves, and the people behind them thought that the ones up front were booing, and they started to boo. They were yelling, 'get rid of the band and that electric guitar!' We had to leave the stage."

Dylan, Robertson, Helm, Al Kooper, and bassist Harvey Brooks rehearsed for two weeks at Carroll's Rehearsal Studio in Manhattan before playing Forest Hills Tennis Stadium. "In the beginning, I didn't know if it was ever going to be special," remembered Robertson. "Just making electric folk music wasn't enough, it needed to be much more violent than that, and I didn't know if [Dylan] was ever going to get it. There was a lot of strumming going on in this music, and for us anyone who strummed just seemed to take the funkiness out of it.... He was all folk songs—Big Bill Broonzy—and we were Jerry Lee Lewis."

Robertson remained skeptical. "I thought there were too many words," he recalled, "and, in the beginning, there were too many guitar solos—[Dylan] kept looking over and giving me the nod and I had to play another one. I would be like, 'we've got eight verses, and six solos, in this thing. I think we're dragging it out too long.' He was like, 'Really? You think that?'"

Before the Forest Hills show, Dylan and the musicians went over the entire set during a lengthy sound check. Gathered backstage, Dylan spoke to the musicians. "We talked about remembering the music," recalled Brooks, "and having a good time with it. Bob said, 'If they don't like it, too bad. They'll have to learn to like it.'"

"We don't know what's going to happen," Helm remembered the singer-songwriter saying. "It may be a real freak show out there. I want you to know this up front. Just keep playing, no matter how weird it gets."

On the morning of the concert, Dylan spoke to Robert Shelton of the *New York Times*. Addressing the audience resistance, the singer-songwriter condemned those who "can't understand green clocks, wet chairs, purple lamps, or hostile statues."

After the fifteen thousand people entering the stadium settled into their seats, Murray "The K" Kaufman did the introductions. "It ain't rock, and it ain't folk," announced the New York–based rock-and-roll deejay who referred to himself as "the fifth Beatle." "It's a new thing called Dylan, and it's what's happening, baby!"

The concert split into two forty-five minute sets. During the first half, Dylan appeared onstage alone, accompanying himself on acoustic guitar and racked-harmonica. As a barely audible bootleg demonstrates, the audience's hostility calmed as Dylan delivered heartfelt renditions of "She Belongs to Me," "To Ramona," "Love Minus Zero/No Limit," and a chilling "Gates of Eden." The crowd seemed eager to listen to the songwriter's wordplay as he launched into "Desolation Row," for the first time in concert, but as its imagery grew increasingly ominous, uneasiness took over. The set finished with the two acoustic tunes that Dylan had played at Newport—"It's All Over Now, Baby Blue," and "Mr. Tambourine Man."

As soon as Helm (and road manager Bill Avis) started setting up the drums and Robertson began tuning his guitar, things turned ugly. They only got worse. "The lights went up and we were into 'Tombstone Blues' full force," remembered Kooper, "but the audience got quiet—too quiet. The wind churned around the stadium and blew Dylan's hair this way and that, as if reprimanding him for this electric sacrilege."

When the song ended, the crowd erupted, recalled Kooper, with "the booing that all these kids had read so much about and probably felt obliged to deliver. Of course, the barrage was peppered with 'Dylan, you scumbag! Get off the fucking stage!' and other subtle pleasantries characteristic of our generation."

The mayhem continued to increase. "Even the hero worshippers were unusually aggressive on this particular evening," remembered Kooper. "They'd try to claw their way onto the stage to make contact with Dylan and the police were sparing no tactic to keep them back. One kid chased behind me and as he flew by, he hooked his leg on my stool, taking me with him as he went down. I was on my ass and not the least bit pleased about the situation."

"People were being thrown out," said Helm. "People were cursing, but not at Bob. They were mad at us, the band. People were throwing fruit at us!"

Despite the crowd's continuous booing and yelling of obscenities, Dylan and the five musicians maintained their assault with "I Don't Believe You," "From a Buick 6," and "Just Like Tom Thumb's Blues." After a particularly dynamic version of "Maggie's Farm," the tune that had opened Dylan's Newport set, "someone yelled out, 'Scumbag,'" Helm recalled, "and all hell broke loose."

Moving to the piano, Dylan repeated the introduction to "Ballad of a Thin Man" for nearly five minutes. As the crowd started to settle down, he directed his ire at those unwilling to accept changing times, singing, "There's something happening, and you don't know what it is, do you, Mr. Jones?" It wasn't a far jump from "The Times They Are a-Changin'."

Segueing into "Like a Rolling Stone" (the pop chart's number-one hit), Dylan and company concluded the set on an upswing. "I looked out [at the crowd]," recalled Helm, "and saw [that] the younger kids—not the old folksters—knew all the words and were singing along."

Kooper walked to the post-concert party (at Grossman's apartment) with Harvey Brooks. "Neither of us had the slightest clue as to what Dylan had thought of the concert," he said. "All we knew was that we [had] played what we were supposed to play and that the sound had been excellent."

Arriving at the party, Dylan was waiting to welcome them. "[Dylan] bounded across the room," said Kooper, "and hugged both of us."

The organist was anxious to hear what the singer-songwriter had thought of the show. "It was fantastic," Kooper recalled Dylan telling him, "a real carnival."

The Hollywood Bowl, five days later, was next. With a star-studded audience that included Gregory Peck, Johnny Cash, Dean Martin, Tuesday Weld, and members of The Byrds, the vibe was less confrontational than Newport or Forest Hills. "[The audience] listened attentively to the new Dylan," remembered Kooper, "and, after polite initial applause, got caught up in the electric feeling."

After the show, Helm mentioned the more pleasing conditions to Dylan. "I wish they had booed," he remembered the singer-songwriter telling him. "It's good publicity, sells tickets—let them boo all they want."

Not all of the musicians were as accepting of the harsh reception. "I began to give serious consideration to making my exit from this traveling circus," said Kooper, who resigned after learning that a concert in Dallas, Texas, was included on the band's itinerary. "Look at what they had just done to [President John Fitzgerald Kennedy] down there, and he was the leading symbol of the establishment. What was going to happen when

Bob Dylan, the most radical vision of the counterculture, paid them a visit? I wasn't sure I wanted to find out. Besides, what musician enjoys being booed on a consistent basis?"

Asked to remain, Helm and Robertson's thoughts returned to their longtime band mates (Danko, Manuel, and Hudson), who had continued to perform together in their absence. "Robbie told [Dylan] that he had a band," remembered Danko, "and that we'd been playing together for a long time. Bob said, 'OK, I'll send my plane to pick all of you up. We'll start touring in November.'"

Dylan's first meeting with the former Hawks, which *Time* called "the most decisive moment in rock history," occurred on September 15 after he had flown to Toronto (where the group was playing at the Friar's Tavern). For the next two nights, he and his new backup musicians rehearsed (after their shows) into the wee hours of the morning. "I have to give [Dylan] all the credit," said Helm, "because he worked hard with us. He was turning around from being a solo performer and teaching himself how to lead a band. We went through his songs once, trying to strobe those guitars together, and Bob gave us some tapes to listen to."

"The wonderful thing in working with Dylan," said Hudson to Bob Doerschuk of *Keyboard* magazine, "was the imagery in his lyrics and I was allowed to play with these words. I didn't do it incessantly; I didn't try to catch the clouds or the moon or whatever it might be every time, but I would try and introduce some little thing at one point a third of the way through a song, which might have something to do with the words that were going by."

Setting Dylan's lyrics to R&B/rockabilly arrangements created intensity previously unparalleled in popular music. "[Dylan] had a feeling of a surge of power and volume," said Robertson. "He wasn't just flipping these songs out there; he was drilling them into the audience."

"It's very complicated to play with electricity," said Dylan. "Most people don't like to work with other people, it's more difficult. It takes a lot. Most people who don't like rock and roll can't relate to other people."

Dylan and the former Hawks rehearsed for only two nights before their debut shows on September 24 at Austin's Municipal Auditorium (now Palmer Auditorium), and the next night at Southern Methodist University's Moody Coliseum in Dallas. "We went out into the world prematurely," admitted Robertson in 2011. "We were used to honing our skills and having a deeper understanding of the music. We had to figure out how to make it work musically for all of us. Rather than rehearsing, we went out and experimented in front of audiences. I'll be doggone if they didn't boo and throw shit. Some people were offended. I thought it was understandable. We should have gotten our stuff together, and, then, they wouldn't have had a reason to boo, but that wasn't the case."

Dylan jokingly addressed his changing direction at a press conference at the Villa Capri Motor Hotel in Austin the day before the first concert in

Texas's capital city. "I plan to get into classical music," he claimed, "that was the plan all along. Why hide it—strings, violins, and a band."

The next night, more than four thousand people, cramming into Municipal Auditorium, witnessed one of the strongest concerts in rock-and-roll history. After a four-song solo set that included "Gates of Eden," "It's All Over Now, Baby Blue," "Desolation Row," and "Mr. Tambourine Man," Dylan and the former Hawks kicked off the second set with a take-no-prisoners rendition of "Tombstone Blues." They didn't let up as they roared through "Maggie's Farm" (with Dylan on piano), "Ballad of a Thin Man," "Just Like Tom Thumb's Blues," and "Like a Rolling Stone." As an encore, Dylan resurrected "Baby, Let Me Follow You Down," a traditional song taught to him by the dean of the Boston/Cambridge folk scene, Eric von Schmidt, that he had recorded solo for his 1962 debut album. With the former Hawks setting the pace, the tune took on a new dimension. "It was so in-your-face," said promoter Angus Wynne to Michael Corcoran of the *Austin American-Statesman*. "You couldn't really understand the words—quality concert sound systems were nonexistent back then—but you could feel the energy. It was like being knocked over by this huge burst of sound."

Audiences in Austin and Dallas seemed open to Dylan's new music. Although there were scattered boos, most people remained reverent throughout the shows, giving the singer-songwriter and his band a chance. The Lone Star state remains one of Dylan's favorite stops. "Texas might have more independent-thinking people," he told *Rolling Stone* in 2009, "than any other state in the country."

Retreating to Dylan's home in Woodstock, New York, after returning from Texas, the six musicians settled into a schedule of intense rehearsals. By the time that they appeared at Carnegie Hall on October 1, they were ready. "It was just a resounding standing ovation," recalled Mary Martin of the audience's response. "I remember going to Dylan and saying, 'well done' and 'hurray for you,' because all he really wanted to do was continue to get his music out in a new form, because that's what artists do. He had this wonderful smile; I had never seen him smile like that. There were crinkles by his eyes that were crinkles of joy. It was fabulous."

Dylan and the former Hawks kept the momentum going in the studio—recording "Can You Please Crawl out Your Window" and "I Wanna Be Your Lover"—but the booing picked up as soon as they got back on the road to tour the East Coast. "We were booed everywhere," remembered Helm, "it became a ritual. People had heard they were 'supposed' to boo when those electric guitars came out."

"We'd go from town to town," Robertson said in the liner notes of *Biograph*, "from country to country, and it was like a job. We set up; they booed, and threw things at us. Then, we went to the next town, played, they booed, threw things again, and we left again. I remember thinking, 'this is a strange way to make a buck.'"

The booing confounded the musicians. Listening to tapes of the shows after returning to the hotel, Helm said, "We couldn't believe it was that bad that people felt they had to protest, the tapes sounded good to us. It was just new."

Even in The ex-Hawks' former home base in Toronto, fans made their opposition felt at the sold-out Massey Hall on November 15. Audience hostility ranked among the most severe of the tour. "It was like a different planet," recalled Robertson. "People were horrible—as bad as anywhere else."

Margaret Steen reviewed the concert for the *Toronto Star Weekly*. "[Dylan] does the first half of the show by himself with guitar and harmonica," she wrote, "the social-comment songs that first won him renown and—mostly—the more recent love songs, but then he brings on Levon and the Hawks, with their array of electric guitars, electric Fender bass, electric organ and piano and drums. Dylan plays an electric guitar—himself—and they do the New Sound. The words are as brilliant, surrealistic, and meaningful as ever, but it's harder to hear them, and quite a few folkniks have been booing their one-time idol."

"If they like it or don't like it, that's their business," Dylan told Steen after the show. "You can't tell people what to do at a concert. Anyway, paying out four dollars for a ticket to come and boo—is anyone groovy going to do that anyway? Four years ago, I used to sing in Village coffee houses, and they were packed, fire inspectors all over the place, you know? Then I knew my real fans. Now, these concerts, I don't know them, I don't know why they're there. I don't know what they think about when they go away."

With a world tour on the horizon, Helm hated the thought of another eight months of booing. Handing in his resignation, he headed to Mexico (where he lived on a beach), then to Florida, and finally to New Orleans (where he worked on an Aquatic Engineering and Construction Company oilrig). "I wasn't made to be booed," he told Larry Getlin of the *New York Post* in 2000. "It's funny, it doesn't sound like much when you're talking about it, but when you're playing a song, and you get through it, and everybody goes 'boo,' you just can't imagine. It sounds awful. It made me crazy after a little bit. I was laughing on the outside, but crying on the inside."

Replacing Helm with Bobby Gregg (the drummer on *Bringing It All Back Home* and *Highway 61 Revisited*), Dylan and his cohort continued to the West Coast. In San Francisco, the singer-songwriter consented to a press conference in the studios of educational television station, KQED. "[Dylan] arrived early for the press conference," recalled Ralph Gleason, who organized the conference, "accompanied by Robbie Robertson, and several other members of the band, drank tea in the KQED office, and insisted that he was ready to talk about 'anything you want to talk about.' His only request was that he be able to leave at 3 PM so that he could rehearse in the Berkeley Community Theater where he was to sing that night."

Addressing the recent audience hostility, Dylan said, "Oh, there's booing—you can't tell where the booing's going to come up, can't tell at all. It comes up in the weirdest, strangest places and when it comes, it's quite a thing in itself. I figure there's a little 'boo' in all of us."

Asked if the booing had surprised him, Dylan responded, "Well, I did this very crazy thing [at Newport]. I didn't know what was going to happen, but they certainly booed, I'll tell you that. You could hear it all over the place. I don't know who they were though, and I'm certain whoever it was did it twice as loud as they normally would. They quieted down some at Forest Hills although they did it there, too. They've done it just about all over except in Texas—they didn't boo us in Texas or in Atlanta, or in Boston, or in Ohio. They've done it in just about—or in Minneapolis, they didn't do it there. They've done it other places. I mean, they must be rich to be able to go someplace and boo; I couldn't afford it if I was in their shoes."

Returning to New York, Dylan hung out at Andy Warhol's Factory, while Robertson, Danko, and Hudson settled into the Chelsea Hotel. "There were poets and a lot of friends," Robertson remembered of the ill-fated hotel. "It was wonderful in a way . . . the streets were so vivid, the parties were so much fun, and so much was being developed day by day."

Robertson spent hours reading, especially screenplays. "I was a junior film buff," he said. "I got into it so deep that I would go to the Gotham Book Store, in New York, where you could buy these little books with the scripts for all these movies. I tried to read all the scripts from John Ford's movies, Fellini, Bergman, Kurosawa, Luis Bunuel. . . . I was always a big admirer of the person who sat down with a typewriter and wrote the maps of what these movies were going to be. I'd think, 'How could anyone possibly sit down and write, say, 8½.' It was mysterious, so I read and read, and perhaps I got some good ideas along the way."

Returning to the recording studio to start work on his next album, *Blonde on Blonde*, on January 21, Dylan and the former Hawks recorded two versions of "She's Your Lover Now" (working title: "Just a Glass of Water"). A rendition with Dylan on piano remains unreleased, while a full-band version surfaced on *The Bootleg Series—Volumes 1–3* in 1991.

Dylan and the former Hawks released very few official recordings together. "Can You Please Crawl out Your Window" waited until 1976 for release (in Japan and Australia) on *Masterpieces*. Two songs—"Jet Pilot" and "I Wanna Be Your Lover"—also appeared on *Biograph* in 1985. Early versions of "Temporary Like Achilles" and "Medicine Sunday" (also known as "Midnight Train") were included on an interactive *Highway 61 Revisited* CD-ROM. "(Seems Like) a Freeze-Out," featuring Dylan on piano and Richard Manuel on harpsichord, appeared on *The Genuine*

Bootleg Series, Volume 1. Although Columbia recorded the entire 1966 world tour, the only official release (before the *Bootleg Series*) was the B-side of "I Want You," "Just Like Tom Thumb's Blues," recorded in Liverpool. An instrumental, "Number One," remains unreleased.

Dylan returned to the studio on January 24, accompanied by Robertson and Danko, and cut "One of Us Must Know (Sooner or Later)" and "I'll Keep It with Mine." Al Kooper played organ, Paul Griffin piano, and Sandy Konikoff (replacing Gregg) drums.

Resuming their tour on the East Coast in early February, Dylan, the ex-Hawks, and Konikoff concluded a whirlwind two weeks with concerts in the South. Afterward, Dylan and Robertson flew to Nashville to continue working on *Blonde on Blonde*. Danko, Manuel, and Hudson remained in New York. Although most of Dylan's album wound up being recorded with Nashville session musicians, including guitarists Joe South and Wayne Moss, Robertson got to apply his guitar harmonics to "Pledging My Time," "Visions of Johanna," "Leopard Skin Pill-Box Hat," and probably "Most Likely You Go Your Way (And I'll Go Mine)," "Temporary Like Achilles," "Absolutely Sweet Marie," and "Obviously Five Believers." Danko played bass on "One of Us Must Know (Sooner or Later)," recorded in New York.

As his first two full-length collaborations with the singer-songwriter (*The Times They are a-Changin'*, and *Another Side of Bob Dylan*) indicated, Wilson pointed Dylan toward a more contemporary direction. In a March 1966 interview, he explained how working with the group had shaped his music. "The songs used to be about what I felt and saw," he said, "but nothing of my own rhythmic vomit ever entered into it. I used to think songs were supposed to be romantic, but vomit is not romantic."

As Dylan and the former Hawks pushed on to Australia and Europe, Houston-born drummer Mickey Jones (who had played with Johnny Rivers and Trini Lopez) replaced Konikoff. An avid filmmaker, he would later release footage from the tour as *Bob Dylan — World Tour 1966: The Home Movies*.

After a show in Copenhagen, Denmark, on April 19, Dylan and the former Hawks did not play their next concert, in Stockholm, Sweden, until ten days later. On a Swedish radio station, Dylan discussed the evolution of contemporary music. "[When I was younger], all you heard was rock 'n' roll, country and western, and rhythm and blues music," he told deejay Klas Burling. "Now, at a certain time, the whole field got taken over into some milk, you know—into Frankie Avalon, Fabian and this kind of thing.

"Folk music came in as some kind of substitute for a while," he continued, "but it was only a substitute, don't you understand—that's all it was. Now it is different again because of the English thing. . . . They proved that you could make money, you know, at playing the same old kind of music that [we] used to play, and that's the truth . . . but you know the English people can't play rock 'n' roll music."

Inquired about The Beatles, Dylan answered quickly, "The Beatles are great, but they don't play rock 'n' roll."

Pressed further, he explained, "Rock 'n' roll is an extension of twelve-bar blues; it's white, seventeen-year-old, kid music . . . rock 'n' roll is a fake kind of attempt at sex, you know."

Filmmaker D. L. Pennebaker, who had produced *Don't Look Back* during Dylan's solo acoustic United Kingdom tour a year before, arrived in Sweden with a film crew, but this time the singer-songwriter was in control. The resulting film, *Eat the Document*, would leave critics bewildered by its disjointed editing (by Dylan and Howard Alk) and drug-infused montage of backstage chatter, press conferences, and fan interviews. Musical highlights include a pair of tunes played on acoustic guitars by Dylan and Robertson, sitting on hotel beds facing each other, and close-up footage of Dylan's breathtaking harmonica solo during a concert performance of "Mr. Tambourine Man." Johnny Cash pays a backstage visit and, with Dylan playing piano, revives "I Still Miss Someone," the B-side of his 1958 country hit "Don't Take Your Guns to Town." Most of the songs in the film, however, were limited to brief snippets.

In one of *Eat the Document*'s most playful scenes, Dylan and Richard Manuel stroll through a park in Sweden. Spying a young couple on a bench, Manuel offers his jacket in exchange for the blonde female and goes on to increase his offer with a can opener, ChapStick, his shirt, cigarettes, and cash (in Australian currency).

Commissioned for national broadcast by ABC's *Stage 67*, *Eat the Document*'s drug-fueled frenzy was too much for network executives, who rejected it. Screened at the Academy of Music and the Whitney Museum of Contemporary Art in New York in the early 1970s, it became available as a widely circulated bootleg in 2003.

Arriving in London on May 2, Dylan and the ensemble spent two days in England's capital city. As America's leading musical voice, the singer-songwriter joined the royalty of British rock—Paul McCartney, Brian Jones, and Keith Richards—at Dolly's Nightclub in the heart of London's most historic and fashionable district, St. James.

Dylan's absurd behavior continued the next day during a press conference at the London airport. Questioned about the message that he was trying to convey with the giant light bulb that he held in his hand, he replied, "Keep a good head and always carry a light bulb," jokingly adding, "I plugged it in my socket and my house exploded."

Returning to England, after performances in Dublin on May 5 and in Belfast the next night, Dylan and his musicians performed in The Beatles' hometown, Liverpool, on May 14. Audience hostility remained fierce three nights later, as evidenced by a live recording of their concert at Manchester's Free Trade Hall released as the mislabeled double-CD *The*

Bootleg Series, Vol. 4: Bob Dylan Live 1966: The "Royal Albert Hall" Concert. As the crowd settled down following a scorching rendition of "Ballad of a Thin Man," a voice accusingly crying out, "Judas," punctuated the quiet. Responding with a snide, "I don't believe you, you're a liar," Dylan is heard turning to the band (heeding Robertson's suggestion that he stop talking), commanding "Play it fucking loud," and launching into the most defiant "Like a Rolling Stone" that he had ever played. Speaking to *Rolling Stone* in 1997, he reflected, "Judas, the most hated name in human history, and for what—for playing an electric guitar. As if that is in some kind of way equitable to betraying our Lord, and delivering him up to be crucified; all those evil mothers can rot in hell."

"[The mislabeled live recording was] at once an historical document of unparalleled significance in rock and simply the greatest live rock 'n' roll album ever released," claimed Seth Rogovoy of the *Berkshire Eagle*. "With clarity that defies the lapse of decades, it captures a moment when rock musicians and audiences alike were struggling over the role folk, rock and popular music would play in the greater culture. It also contains some of the most shocking, urgent, incendiary rock music ever made."

Members of The Beatles, the Rolling Stones, and The Who attended the tour-concluding concerts (on May 26 and 27) at London's Royal Albert Hall. "I remember it well," said George Harrison. "Bob did his set at the beginning . . . his usual thing with guitar and harmonica. In the second half, he came out with the band. We knew this was going to happen, but Bob came out, 'some of you may know this song, it used to go like that, it goes like this now.'"

After the show, The Beatles visited Dylan and the former Hawks backstage. "We were still basically scroungy street kids," remembered Robertson, "and we were astonished at how naïve they were, how very sweet, and nice, and everything. They all had on matching boots and matching clothes, and they talked about mystical things that were very corny."

Robertson recalled when the collaboration with Dylan had begun to gel. "I could really see this thing blending together in a beautiful way," he said, "that was the saving grace. It wasn't improvising with people flailing along to the words. It started to have dynamics that built, and, then, went down quietly. We were able to say, with confidence, 'We don't care what anyone says; this [music] is good. We can be proud of this.'"

"It's very exciting to hear somebody singing so powerfully, with something to say," continued the guitarist, "but what struck me was how the street had such a profound effect on him, coming from Minnesota, setting out on the road, and coming to New York. There was hardness, toughness, in the way that he approached his songs and the characters in them. [It] was a rebellion against the purity of folk music. . . . This was the rebel rebelling against the rebellion."

TWO

Ronnie Hawkins and the Hawks

As the former Hawks toured the world with Bob Dylan without him, Levon Helm remembered when, at the age of seventeen, he had found space for himself (and his drums) in Ronnie Hawkins's station wagon and headed to Canada. "My dad had told me the Eskimos were violent and would kill us if they had a chance," he recalled. "We thought we were going to igloos and dogsleds."

Plenty of great musicians had emanated from the Great White North, including Guy Lombardo, who sold more than 250 millions copies of his albums (with his big band the Royal Canadians), jazz pianist Oscar Peterson, and Grand Ole Opry member Hank Snow. Buffy Sainte-Marie, Neil Young, Joni Mitchell, Bruce Cockburn, and Leonard Cohen would experience international success. British-born and Canadian-raised vocalist David Clayton Thomas would replace Al Kooper in Blood, Sweat, and Tears in 1968. Manitoba-born Randy Bachman and Burton Cummings would score top-ten hits with the Guess Who in the '60s and with Bachman-Turner Overdrive in the '70s, and the Cowboy Junkies would successfully combine ethereal vocals and alt-rock/blues/folk-rooted songwriting in the '90s. Before Hawkins and the Hawks' arrival, though, rock and roll had been almost exclusively restricted to late-night radio shows from the United States.

Even before the first of their weeklong series of shows (booked by rockabilly-singer-turned-country-music-crooner Conway Twitty's Canadian agent, Harold "The Colonel" Kudlets) at the Golden Rail Tavern in Hamilton, Ontario, Hawkins and the Hawks faced resistance. As they rehearsed for opening night, the club's bartenders (more accustomed to acoustic duos, solo pianists, and lounge bands) threatened to resign.

There was, however, plenty of support for Hawkins and his group (temporarily christened the Sun Records Quartet). A Canadian songwriter that Hawkins had befriended in Arkansas (Dallas Harms) put the word out, drawing more than sixty people to the club for the band's debut. The attendance continued to double every night for the rest of the week. By weekend, Ronnie Hawkins and the Hawks were stars. It became a pattern. "We played some real tough places," Hawkins told *Rolling Stone*. "The people didn't come to hear [you]; they came to mess with you. They'd flick cigarette butts, throw coins, steal your gear, and if you still kept playing, well, they'd sit right down and listen."

Ronnie Hawkins and the Hawks' home base, Le Coq d'Or, was one of many clubs lining Yonge Street in downtown Toronto. Now a respected theater district, Yonge Street (named after late-eighteenth-century British secretary of war Sir George Yonge) was a much different place in the late 1950s and early 60s, challenging, according to Hawkins, "the sleazy best Montreal could offer as the Canadian epicenter of all that was dubious, certainly illicit, potentially immoral (we hoped) and possibly illegal."

"Toronto was the best I've ever seen," remembered Helm. "There were more places to play [than anywhere else]. If you went up to North Yonge, [you could hear] Oscar Peterson, Ed Thigpen, and people like that, in the jazz clubs. If you [came down the street], you would come by the Zanzibar [where] you might have Billy Riley from Memphis, you would come to the Edison Hotel and Carl Perkins would be there. We would be with the Hawk, next door, at Le Coq D'Or. Ray Charles and his orchestra might be at Massey Hall. Cannonball Adderly and his band might be at the Colonial, and Harry Belafonte at O'Keefe Center."

In a land fascinated with anything American, especially music, Hawkins and the Hawks became the most popular band in Ontario. They enjoyed monthlong stints in Toronto, Hamilton, London, Kitchener, Windsor, Oshawa, and Kingston and performed as far to the east as Montreal. For Robertson, Helm, Manuel, Danko, and Hudson, it would be a time of apprenticeship. "They were boys when they started," Ronnie Hawkins told Ritchie Yorke of *Rolling Stone*, "but they were men when they finished. They had seen damn near everything there is to see. They practiced, played, and fucked, in every town you care to name—real dudes, man."

"Most of it was pretty funny," remembered Helm in *The Big Beat: Conversations with Rock's Great Drummers* by Bruce Springsteen drummer Max Weinberg. "My attitude at the time was the same that it was in high school: the goofier, the happier it is. At all costs, let us laugh. That's why life was everything from aggravating the desk clerk in the hotel to throwing a cherry bomb in a car when someone was sleeping."

Born two days after Elvis Presley on January 10, 1935, Ronald Cornett "Ronnie" Hawkins had been a dropout of the University of Arkansas physical education department, an ex-army sergeant, and a former alcohol runner. The ex-leader of one of the first integrated R&B groups in the American South (The Blackhawks), he rehearsed The Hawks relentlessly.

"We worked day and night trying to get better," he remembered in *Last of the Good Ol' Boys*. "Goddamn, we practiced more than any band in the world."

"It was the kind of thing that if you didn't do something, you got fined," said Robbie Robertson, who joined The Hawks in 1960, "or if you were late, you got fined.... There was a certain respect for discipline and Ronnie pushed really hard."

Hailing from the Ozark Mountain city of Huntsville in northwest Arkansas, Hawkins had grown up amid contradiction. His mother was a deeply religious schoolteacher, while his father was a fast-living, hard-drinking barber who had barely attended school. "All the men on the Hawkins side were drinkers, smokers, fighters, and boozers," he remembered, "and all the women they married were religious fanatics. These women didn't drink, didn't smoke; they worked day and night."

The people of the Ozark Mountains were some of the most stereotyped in America. Misrepresented as simple-minded, moonshine-drinking, and inbreeding hicks, they had been derogatorily called "hillbillies," "rednecks," "crackers," and "white trash." "They're sensitive to being stereotyped as rubes and yokels," University of Arkansas English professor and author Robert Cochran told me in May 2013. "If you're from Arkansas, you make jokes about it, but, if you're from outside the state, and you do it, you're resented. They refuse to be subordinated."

"To them, a hillbilly doesn't represent a toothless, overall-wearing, barefooted, whisky runner, with a banjo on his knee," said Jill Henderson on her *Show Me Oz* blog, "nor does it hint of an uneducated backwoods people with no class or character. Rather, a hillbilly is someone with rugged tenacity and common sense, someone who can live on the land and provide for their self. A hillbilly is someone who can make something out of nothing and laugh when all else fails."

The plaintive strains of country harmonica playing had long been a familiar sound in the Ozark Mountains, with many radio stations employing harmonica orchestras. Lonnie Elonzo Glosson, whose 1936 tune "Arkansas Hard Luck Blues" was an early example of the talking blues popularized by Woody Guthrie and Bob Dylan, often collaborated with Wayne Raney, a Wolf Bayou, Arkansas–born harmonica player/vocalist. Appearing regularly on KARK in Little Rock in 1938, and later on WCKY in Cincinnati, Ohio, Glosson and Raney sold millions of harmonicas via mail order.

For a while, Raney toured with William Orville "Lefty" Frizzell (1928–1975). A hard-edged Corsicana, Texas–born and southern Arkansas–raised country singer, Frizzell's hits included "The Long Black Veil" in 1959, a haunting tune by Danny Dill and Marijohn Wilkin that The Band would cover on *Music from Big Pink*. "We liked the story of the young man who goes to the gallows for a murder he didn't commit," said

Helm, "because his alibi was that he was 'in the arms of my best friend's wife.'"

A member of the Delmore Brothers from 1946 to 1952, Raney was cowriter (with record producer/songwriter Henry Glover) of one of their best-selling singles, "Blues Stay Away from Me." The Band would cover it as the closing tune on *Jericho*, their first release since reuniting in 1993.

Hot Springs, Arkansas–born Henry Glover (1921–1991) had gone from playing trumpet, cornet, and piano in Buddy Johnson's Big Band and Lucky Millinder's Orchestra to a staff producer position with Cincinnati-based King Records by the mid-1950s. After producing R&B hits for the Millinder Orchestra's vocalist/saxophone player, Benjamin "Bull Moose" Jackson, he branched out to country music with recordings by Grandpa Jones, Moon Mullican, Cowboy Copas, and the Delmore Brothers, becoming one of the first African Americans to integrate southern country music. "[There was] never a big deal about it," he said. "They took it as something altogether different, not me trying to integrate. They saw that I had something to offer, that I knew what I was doing, and that [I was there] because I could be of benefit to the artist."

Glover increasingly focused on R&B, producing groundbreaking recordings by Hank Ballard and the Midnighters and James Brown, and composing Ray Charles's 1956 hit "Drown in My Own Tears." He became instrumental in the crossover success of "Little" Willie John (William Edward John), a soulful crooner who would influence George Benson, Donny Hathaway, Jeffrey Osborne, and the Four Tops' Levi Stubbs. John's music was especially inspirational for Robbie Robertson. In addition to referencing the singer in his 1987 song "Somewhere Down This Crazy River," Robertson hired British rocker Robert Palmer to reprise John's "My Baby's in Love with Another Guy" for the soundtrack of Martin Scorsese's 1986 flick *The Color of Money*.

With Glover producing, John scored hits with "All around the World (Grits Is Groceries)," in 1955, and "Need Your Love So Bad," and the R&B chart-topping (top-ten pop) "Fever," the following year. Although he continued to record after he and the producer went their separate ways in 1958, his career and personal life increasingly spiraled out of control. "He was drinking and carrying on from an early age," said Susan Whitall, author of *Fever: The Fast Life and Mysterious Death of Little Willie John, and the Birth of Soul*, to me in January 2012. "He was a charmer, the life of the party."

John's problems peaked in 1964. While attending an after-show party, following a club performance in Seattle, he was involved in an altercation. "This ex-railroad worker/ex-con had been picking fights with everybody," said Whitall. "He insulted a woman in Willie's group; that was the big thing. Willie told the guy to cut it out. The guy punched him in the face, which for a singer was the worst thing anyone could do. At that point, a knife came out and the guy was knifed by somebody."

John was accused of the murder and arrested. Posting a $10,000 bond, he briefly resumed touring before returning to stand trial in 1965. Found guilty, he was sentenced to eight-to-twenty-years in the Walla Walla, Washington, State Penitentiary. "The defense was really bad," said Whitall. "The defense attorney didn't even file an appeal. There was very little evidence to link him except for the unreliable witnesses who kept changing their stories." Testifying for himself, John added little to his defense. "He bragged that he had had an affair with Ava Gardner," said Whitall, "and he spoke in a British accent. The prosecuting attorney told me that it was one of the weirdest cases of his entire career. He came off as this cocky, little guy from Detroit. People in Seattle didn't know what to make of him; they thought he was a bit of a weirdo."

Entering prison on July 6, 1966, John died in the maximum security faculty, nearly two years later, at the age of thirty-one. "The prosecutor felt that Willie's death was due to him being a loudmouthed little guy," explained Whitall. "He was beaten to death, probably, by a prisoner. It's a tragedy. He was due to come up for his probation hearing in July 1968, but he died on May 26th."

James Brown would record a tribute album, *Thinking of Little Willie John and a Few Nice Things,* while The Beatles's previously unreleased 1964 recording of John's "Leave My Kitten Alone" would be included on *Anthology* thirty years later. John would be posthumously inducted into the Rock and Roll Hall of Fame in 1996.

As a producer for Morris Levy's Roulette label, Glover would work with Sarah Vaughn, Dinah Washington, Sonny Stitt, and Bobby "Blue" Bland, as well as Ronnie Hawkins and the Hawks. After their split from Hawkins, he would remain involved with the former Hawks, producing their debut single (credited to the Canadian Squires)—"Uh Uh Uh" backed with "Leave Me Alone," in 1964. Eleven years later, he would join Helm to create RCO Productions and coproduce Paul Butterfield's *Put It in Your Ear* and the Grammy-winning *The Muddy Waters Woodstock Album.* He would also help arrange the horn section for *The Last Waltz.*

Music had been essential to Hawkins's life from infancy. "All the Hawkinses were musical," he remembered. "They played all the time. I can't remember ever not being able to pick up the guitar. The rest of the family, they'd have guitars and fiddles and banjos."

Hawkins's father, uncles, and cousins had toured Arkansas and Oklahoma in the 1930s and '40s. Relocating to California around 1940, his uncle Delmar "Skipper" Hawkins had joined cowboy singer Roy Rogers's band, the Sons of the Pioneers, and become a star. "He'd come home for a week or two," recalled Hawkins, who was five or six when his uncle left for California, "driving a brand new Cadillac and wearing brand new clothes and I knew that's what I wanted to be."

As he watched his uncle, however, Hawkins witnessed life's darker side. "He spent every penny he made on whiskey," he remembered, "and he was divorced because he was running around with all sorts of women. His wife left Arkansas and went to Louisiana."

Hawkins remained in touch with Delmar Allen "Dale" Hawkins, his cousin (and one of Skipper Hawkins's sons). The first white artist to sing at the Apollo Theater in Harlem and the Regal Theater in Chicago, Dale Hawkins would become the host of a popular *American Bandstand*–like TV dance party, *The Dale Hawkins Show*, for WCAU-TV in Philadelphia in the late 1950s. Among the forty songs that he would record for Chess Records and its subsidiary Checker was "Susie Q," a top-ten R&B hit (that reached the twenty-seventh slot on *Billboard*'s Hot 100), in May 1957, featuring soon-to-be Ricky Nelson guitarist James Burton. The Rolling Stones, Creedence Clearwater Revival, Jose Feliciano, Suzi Quatro, and Roy Buchanan (who toured with Dale Hawkins in the late 1950s) would cover it.

Singing at local fairs from the age of eleven, Ronnie Hawkins was still a preteen when he shared a stage in Fort Smith, Arkansas, with country music superstar Hank Williams. "Old Hank was so drunk he couldn't do anything on stage," he recalled.

With its frontman unable to perform, Williams' band, the Drifting Cowboys invited volunteers to come to the stage to sing. "I got up and did the Burl Ives songs I knew," remembered Hawkins.

Hawkins also performed two Stephen Foster songs—"Beautiful Dreamer" and "Camptown Races"—popularized, in the mid-nineteenth century by black-faced minstrel troupes. "Even back then I knew that every important white cat—Al Jolson, Stephen Foster—they all did it by copying blacks. Even Hank Williams learned all the stuff he had from those black cats in Alabama. Elvis Presley copied black music; that's all that Elvis did."

Hawkins's musical talents were balanced by business savvy. As soon as he had his first car (a 1929 Model A), he found a way to generate income. "I ran liquor," he confessed. "It wasn't moonshine exactly, just bottles of booze. I went to Missouri to get the whiskey. The state line is only about sixteen miles from Fayetteville"—where he moved before his twelfth birthday—"and, just across the Missouri line, gas was half price, cigarettes were half price and whiskey was half price. I started when I was only fourteen and I kept at it until I was nineteen or twenty. That's how I made my money for the clubs I bought into."

Although enamored of Hank Williams, Lefty Frizzell, and Jimmie Rodgers's country music, Hawkins gravitated more to the blues. Buddy Hayes, the shoeshine boy in his father's barbershop, introduced him to the music of John Lee Hooker, Howlin' Wolf, B. B. King (who was still doing a radio show in Memphis), and Muddy Waters. "Buddy had a blues band," he recalled, "and they used to practice in the back of the barbershop. They were into a sort of Louis Armstrong–New Orleans kind of blues and jazz."

A black twelve-year-old street performer named Half Pint, inspired by tap dancer/actor Bill "Bojangles" Robinson, provided another influence. "I learned a lot of steps off of him," admitted Hawkins. "He was doing the duck walk way back then, before Chuck Berry did it. Vaudeville people called it the 'camel walk.' It's like you're standing still and you're moving."

Starting out as a guest of as many bands as he could convince to let him sing, Hawkins formed his first group while still in high school. "We played everywhere," he recalled. "We played garage parties and the Huntsville Festival. . . . Hell, we'd play anywhere they'd let us."

Although he consented to his mother's wishes and enrolled in the University of Arkansas, Hawkins's attention remained elsewhere. "There was too much action around the university," he remembered, "what with the fraternities and sororities, and all those opportunities to play dances—and meet girls."

"I met [Hawkins] at the University of Fayetteville," said rockabilly singer/guitarist Albert Austin "Sonny" Burgess when we spoke in April 2013. "My band [The Pacers] and I did a show for a fraternity and we saw this kid standing beside the bandstand. A feller came up [to the bandstand], pointed at him, and said, 'Ronnie likes to sing—get him up there to sing something,' so we did. All of the songs were by Carl Perkins and Roy Orbison."

Dropping out of the university a few credits short of graduation, Hawkins enlisted in the United States Army—having completed ROTC training, he would be required to serve for only six months. Shortly after his arrival at Fort Sill in Lawton, Oklahoma, he was nursing a drink at the Amvet Club when a quartet of African American musicians began to play. As soon as they hit their first notes, he could feel his future beckoning. Setting his drink aside, he leaped onto the stage and began singing. "It sounded like something between the blues and rockabilly," he remembered. "It sort of leaned in both directions at the same time, me being a hayseed and those guys playing a lot funkier."

Hawkins and the group (renamed The Blackhawks) may have created some of the South's most dynamic music, but he would later admit, "I wanted to sound like Bobby 'Blue' Bland but it came out sounding like Ernest Tubb."

Although they had previously been playing "really good blues—the older style—the jazz-pop kind of blues like Cab Calloway might've done back in the forties," Hawkins brought contemporary influences to the group, expanded by the arrival of Missouri-born saxophone player Aaron Corthen "AC" Reed. "They had to start playing as close as they could to my material," recalled Hawkins. "It came out like the original tunes, only funkier. So instead of doing a kind of rockabilly that was closer to country music, I was doing rockabilly that was closer to soul music, which was exactly what I liked."

Not everyone in the American South of the 1950s, however, was ready for an integrated band. "One strike we had against us was being in the South," Hawkins remembered, "where the prejudice against blacks was the strongest. Even if you had the law on your side, everyone and everything was against you. The music was the second strike. Playing rock 'n' roll or rhythm 'n' blues was playing the music of the devil.

"People in the South did not want white kids dancing to sinful 'nigger music,' as they called it," he continued, "yet there we were, trying to play black music, but it was coming out differently because we weren't doing it right. It was coming out like country rock. We were taking the old rhythm 'n' blues songs and playing them country-style with a black beat. We were doing that with Hank Williams stuff, too."

After his six-month enlistment completed, and the Blackhawks disbanded, Hawkins headed back to Fayetteville. Two days after his arrival, the telephone rang. Sun Records was calling. "They were going to give me one hundred dollars a week," Hawkins recalled, "and a place to stay for fronting the session band. That was big time to me."

Located at 704 Union Avenue in downtown Memphis, Sun Records had become the epicenter of the rockabilly boom. An adjunct of the Memphis Recording Service, founded by Alabama-born cotton-picker-turned-radio-deejay-and-engineer Samuel Cornelius "Sam" Phillips in 1952, the label had originally focused on southern black bluesmen. Early releases included career-launching tracks by B. B. King, Howlin' Wolf, James Cotton, and Bobby "Blue" Bland.

Sun Records reached unprecedented heights after the arrival of Elvis Presley in August 1953. "Elvis came along and changed everything," said Sonny Burgess, who remembered seeing the future "King of Rock and Roll" in March 1955 at Newport, Arkansas, nightspot Porky's Rooftop. "I thought he was the greatest ever. He could really sing. He was everything that they said he was—a true star—and Scotty [Moore] was creating stuff that guitarists were not playing before. I've always wished that I could play like Scotty and sing like Elvis."

Sam Phillips sold Presley's contract to RCA for $35,000 in late 1955, but Sun Records' success continued with groundbreaking rockabilly hits by Jerry Lee Lewis, Carl Perkins, Roy Orbison, Charlie Rich, and Johnny Cash.

Hawkins's enthusiasm was quickly dashed. By the time that he arrived at the Sun Studios, the group he was intending to join had disbanded. Although he used the studio to cut demos of Lloyd Price's "Lawdy Miss Clawdy" and Hank Williams's "Mansion on the Hill," the label's focus remained on its more successful roster, and the recordings went unnoticed.

As he waited to hear from Sam Phillips, Hawkins was unsure of his next step. He had bragged to friends and family about the job offer, and he was hesitant to return without a record deal. When the demo session's guitarist, Jimmy Ray "Luke" Paulman (who had played with Conway Twitty, Roy Orbison, and Billy Lee Riley), suggested that he accompany him to his home in Helena, Arkansas (now Helena–West Helena), Hawkins jumped at the chance.

Seventy miles downriver from Memphis, in the heart of the Mississippi Delta, Helena offered a much different setting than the Ozark Mountains. "Cotton fields, groves of pecan trees, canebrakes, bayous, pump houses, kudzu vines, sharecroppers' cabins, tenant farmhouses, flooded rice fields, the biggest sky in the world, and the nearby Mississippi," remembered Levon Helm, who had grown up in Turkey Scratch, a small, unincorporated community outside Marvell, Arkansas, about a half hour west of Helena, "like an inland sea with its own weather system. Think one hundred and ten degrees in the shade in the summertime."

Inhabited originally by Choctaw, Chickasaw, and Natchez Indians, Helena was settled by North Carolina's Sylvanus Phillips, Abraham Phillips, and William Patterson in 1790. Because of its rich soil and dire need for farmworkers, the city became a center of the slave trade, and the birthplace of three Confederate generals (though it would be occupied by Union forces from the early days of the Civil War).

Like the entire Mississippi Delta region, Helena resonated with music. "The sound of the blues, rhythm and blues, and country music is what we lived for," remembered Helm, "black and white alike. It gave you strength to sit on one of those throbbing Allis-Chalmers tractors all day if you knew you were going to hear something on the radio or maybe see a show that evening."

"Even in slavery times," said Robert Cochran, "African Americans performed at parties attended by white people. It was never separate. They influenced all types of music. Radio and phonograph records certainly accelerated it, but it was there from the beginning."

Among the white musicians who made their home in Helena was Friar's Point, Mississippi-born Harold Lloyd Jenkins (1933–1993). Moving to the Arkansas city at the age of ten, Jenkins formed a string band, the Phillips County Ramblers, while still in his preteens, and soon afterward became the host of a popular Saturday-morning radio show.

Adopting the name Conway Twitty (combining the names of Conway [Faulkner County], Arkansas, and Twitty, Texas), Jenkins continued to sing. Scoring his first number-one hit, in 1959, with a rockabilly tune, "It's Only Make Believe," written with Jack Nance, he would appear in youth-oriented flicks, *Sex Kittens Go to College* (with Mamie Van Doren) and *Platinum High School* (with Mickey Rooney). His greatest success, however, would come after switching to country music. Accumulating an astounding fifty-five chart-topping country hits, he sold more than fifty million copies of his albums, and was inducted into both the Country Music Hall of Fame and the Rockabilly Hall of Fame.

The Mississippi River provided a gateway for musicians from New Orleans in the South; Indianola, Mississippi, and Memphis, Tennessee, in the East; and St. Louis and Chicago in the North. With plenty of opportunities to play at levee camps and juke joints, the region was a hotbed of soulful music.

The diverse soundtrack provided a welcoming sound for Ronnie Hawkins. As soon as he and Luke Paulman arrived in Helena, they tracked down Paulman's brother, George (who played standup bass), and their cousin Willard "Pop" Jones (who played piano), and put together a band—The Hawks. "[Jones] was an amazing pianist," recalled Sonny Burgess, "a real wild man, a forerunner of Jerry Lee Lewis."

"I [had] never heard anyone amplify a piano as loud as Pop Jones," said Hawkins. "He was a big guy, with incredible thrust, and he could do all those Jerry Lee Lewis glissandos in his sleep."

The Hawks' drummer, Mark Lavon "Levon" Helm, the son of Jasper Diamond "JD" Helm, a cotton farmer and amateur musician, and the former Nell Wilson, first played with the group at the Delta Supper Club in Helena in early 1957. George Paulman had noticed the blonde-haired teenager intently watching the band, recognized him as the youngster who had played snare drum for him a few weeks before in Forrest City, and invited him to sit in during The Hawks' closing set.

Shortly afterward, Helm was doing chores on the farm when he noticed a Model A Ford "moving fast up our road, leaving a tornado of yellow dust in its wake." When the car pulled to a stop, Luke Paulman and Ronnie Hawkins (whom he remembered as "a big ol' boy in tight pants, sharp shoes, and a pompadour hanging down his forehead") stepped out.

After greetings were exchanged, Helm brought the musicians into the house to meet his family. Once inside, Hawkins, who was preparing for his first club dates in Toronto, made his pitch. "Lavon, we're starting a band," Helm remembered him saying, "and there aren't any drummers around. They tell me [that] you're a good guitar player and that you play drums too—do you wanna join the band?"

This was the moment that Helm had dreamed of ever since he had attended a concert by "Father of Bluegrass" Bill Monroe and the Bluegrass Boys at the age of six. He had progressed from an imaginary instrument ("I took a broom, held it sideways, and made believe it was a guitar") to playing harmonica by the age of eight. Soon after placing first in a school talent contest at the age of ten, with what he recalled as "my hambone act, slapping my hands against my legs, and rapping out 'Little Body Rinktum Ti-mee-oh,'" one of the songs that he had learned during "family musicales around the supper table," he acquired a guitar. Within two years, he and his sister (who played washtub bass) had formed a duo, "Lavon and Linda," and were playing at "every Kiwanis Club, Farm

Bureau, Lions Club, Rotary Club, Future Farmers of America, and 4-H Club meeting in Phillips County."

Helm seemed to have unlimited energy. In addition to playing with his sister for five years, he played drums in the high school band and with a rock and roll band, The Jungle Bush Beaters. "[Music was the] only way to get off that stinking tractor," he recalled, "and out of that one hundred and five degree heat."

Folksongs and country music provided his earliest roots, but the blues captured Helm's soul. Since 1941, Helena had been the home of *King Biscuit Time*, a daily blues radio show on KFFA featuring blues harmonica player/vocalist Sonny Boy Williamson and his band, the King Biscuit Boys—Robert Lockwood Jr. (guitar), Dudlow Taylor (piano), and James "Peck" Curtis (drums). As soon as he was old enough (ten or eleven), Helm began catching rides to the WFFA studios. "They'd let me sit in the corner," he remembered, "and watch the King Biscuit Boys do their show."

On Saturday afternoons, Williamson and the King Biscuit Boys would come to Marvell to perform. Helm would be there, watching their every move. "The first thing you noticed about Sonny Boy was his size," he remembered. "This was a big man. He would lie out a tarpaulin on the ground and set his mike on it. Then he would open the back door of the bus, and there'd be an upright piano. His drummer would set up his cymbals, a big wooden snare, and a wooden bass drum hand-lettered 'King Biscuit Time/King Biscuit Entertainers/J. P. Curtis/KFFA/Monday thru Friday.'"

Mississippi-born Aleck or Alex "Rice" Miller (1912–1965) was the second bluesman to assume the name Sonny Boy Williamson. The first—John Lee Curtis Williamson (1914–1948), born near Jackson, Tennessee—had been one of the pioneers of modern blues harmonica playing. According to Robert Lockwood Jr. (1915–2006), whose mother lived with bluesman Robert Johnson for a decade, "Rice Miller could play Sonny Boy's stuff better than he could play it."

Adopting Williamson's name, Miller made his recording debut with "Nine below Zero," and "Eyesight to the Blind" (covered by The Who on their 1969 rock opera *Tommy*) in 1959 and continued to release influential blues singles including "Fattening Frogs for Snakes" (later covered by John Hammond Jr.) and "One Way Out" (later covered by the Allman Brothers Band). He was elected to the Blues Hall of Fame in 1980, and the Arkansas Entertainers Hall of Fame inducted him in 2008.

The King Biscuit Boys' drummer, Peck Curtis (who incorporated a cowbell into his playing), had a profound impact on Helm's drumming. "As good as the band sounded," said Helm, "it seemed that [Peck] was definitely having the most fun. I locked into the drums at that point. Later, I heard Jack Nance, Conway Twitty's drummer, and all the great drummers in Memphis—Jimmy Van Eaton, Al Jackson, and Willie Hall—

the Chicago boys (Fred Belew and Clifton James) and the people at Sun Records and Vee-Jay, but most of my style was based on Peck and Sonny Boy—the Delta blues style with the shuffle. Through the years, I've quickened the pace to a more rock-and-roll meter and time frame, but it still bases itself back to Peck, Sonny Boy Williamson, and the King Biscuit Boys."

Helm renewed his connection to Williamson shortly after recording Levon and the Hawks' second single in April 1965. Booked to perform at a junior/senior prom at Marvell High School, he and his band mates heard the bluesman on the radio and tracked him down. After introducing themselves, they escorted Williamson to a neighborhood bar where they drank moonshine (at one dollar a pint) and listened to tales about the bluesman's recent trip to England (where he had been backed by The Yardbirds and The Animals).

Retreating to the Rainbow Inn Motel in West Helena, where Levon and the Hawks kept a drum set and several amplifiers, they jammed long into the night. "Sonny Boy worked his harmonica like a damn brass section," remembered Helm, "backwards and inside out. He played it sticking out of his mouth like a cigar."

The sound of Williamson's harmonica playing and singing—accompanied by one of the all-time great backup bands—must have been formidable. As they shared a post-jam feast at a barbeque joint, the six musicians discussed combining forces and going out on tour. Their conversation ended abruptly with the arrival of three police cars with sirens flashing. Stepping into the restaurant, one of the police officers approached the musicians' table. Asking if there was a problem, Helm remembers being told, "There ain't no problem, not as long as you don't mind sitting here eating with a bunch of niggers, there ain't no problem."

Attempting to defuse the hostility, Helm mentioned his uncle, a deputy sheriff in Marvell. The officer's response was not what he expected. "Well, I guess Deputy Cooper'd be real proud of you down here in Niggertown," Helm remembered being told, "eating with a bunch of goddamned niggers."

Realizing that they were not going to make progress against such overt racism, the six musicians decided to call it a night. Promising to get in touch again, everyone headed off to catch some sleep. "The plan when we shook hands goodbye," recalled Helm, "was that we would be back in touch and we'd try and get [Williamson] fixed up so he'd come up to New Jersey and join us before the summer was out. We didn't know how to pull that off, but we had some big plans."

It would be the last time that the musicians would be together. On May 25, 1965, Williamson succumbed to tuberculosis, at the age of fifty-three.

Aching to play music (and escape the farm), Helm listened as Hawkins pleaded his case. His parents remained insistent that he graduate high school. After three hours of negotiation, they agreed that he could join The Hawks following his graduation and head to Canada. "Where Levon came from, in Phillips County, they're ignorant mothers," said Hawkins. "They were still in the Civil War there. It was really rural."

As he waited for school to finish, Helm spent hours practicing on a makeshift drum kit (that included a snare drum that had to be heated and retuned between sets), strengthening his drumming skills. By his graduation in May, he was ready.

With Helm on board, Ronnie Hawkins and the Hawks thrived in Canada. Tiring of waiting to hear from Sun Records, they continued to pursue a record contract elsewhere. On April 13, 1959, they auditioned for Morris Levy, owner of New York–based Roulette Records. Four hours later, they were rushed into the studio to record their first tracks. They hit pay dirt with their debut single, "Forty Days," a thinly masked takeoff on Chuck Berry's "Thirty Days," backed with "Mary Lou" by Dallas-born Young Jessie (Obediah Donnell "Obie" Jessie). The A-side would reach number forty-six on the American charts, but "Mary Lou," recorded at the suggestion of Roy Orbison, would just barely miss pop's top twenty-five (peaking at number twenty-six) and become Hawkins's biggest hit. Wisconsin-born Steve Miller would cover it on his 1973 album *The Joker*.

Promoting the single's release, Hawkins and the Hawks appeared on several high-profile television shows, including the *Steve Allen Show*. "They'd never seen anything like us," remembered Hawkins. "We had the fiddle pickup we put on that piano, which made it ten times as loud as an ordinary piano. It did not sound electric, but that didn't make any difference. It was loud. Of course, I was doing double backflips. The cameras stopped and all of a sudden, everybody in the building was watching us play. They'd never seen a monkey act like that."

Hawkins and the Hawks followed with an appearance on Dick Clark's *American Bandstand*, lip-synching to "Mary Lou" and "Bo Diddley" (Hawkins's second single).

One of early rock and roll's most controversial figures, Harlem-born Moishe "Morris" Levy (1927–1990) was, according to the *All Music Guide*, "a notorious crook who swindled artists out of their owed royalties."

Going from an impoverished childhood in the East Bronx to great wealth, Levy owned nightclubs (including Birdland) in midtown Manhattan, held profitable copyrights to scores of popular songs, and was the power behind Alan Freed's rock-and-roll shows at Brooklyn's Paramount Theater. Heavily tied to organized crime, he continued to build on his musical empire. Acquiring gambler/record producer George Goldner's labels (End, Gee, Gone, and Rama), he made his entry into recording in February 1956 with Frankie Lymon and the Teenagers' "Why Do Fools Fall in Love" (sharing in the songwriting credits)—the single reached number one on the R&B charts and number six on the pop charts. Launching Roulette Records in 1957, Levy continued his success with

Buddy Knox's "Party Doll," Jimmy Bowen's "I'm Stickin' with You," and Jimmie Rodgers's chart-topping folk-pop hit "Honeycomb."

Implicated in the payola scandal (accused of paying for radio airplay) in 1959, Levy managed to sidestep the career-ending turmoil that befell Alan Freed (the most influential of the accused deejays). Remaining active until the mid-1980s, Levy would never mellow. He would successfully sue John Lennon in 1970 for using the phrase "here comes old flattop," from Chuck Berry's "You Can't Catch Me," for which he held the copyright, in "Come Together." As part of the settlement, the ex-Beatle agreed to record three songs published by Levy on his 1975 Phil Spector–produced album of oldies, *Rock and Roll*. Levy released a mail-order bootleg of the demo tapes of the not-yet-released album and more lawsuits resulted. Although the judge awarded Levy with $6,795, for damages, it would be more than one hundred and thirty thousand dollars less than awarded to Lennon, Capitol, EMI, and Apple in their countersuit.

Levy's fall from grace continued. He sold Roulette Records (and his publishing holdings) for twenty-two million dollars in 1986, and Strawberries (the chain of record stores he had started in the northeast in the 1970s) for forty million two years later, but his troubles had just begun. Convicted in a federal trial on October 28, 1988, of conspiring to extort a record distributor in Philadelphia, he received a prison sentence of ten years and a fine of two hundred thousand dollars. Although he lost the appeal, no date had yet been set for his surrender when he succumbed to liver cancer on May 21, 1990. "I don't care what Morris was supposed to have done," said Hawkins. "He looked after me and he believed in me. I even lived with him in his million-dollar apartment on the Upper East Side. That was when showbiz was really rocking, with the pit orchestras and the chorus girls. He'd take us to his clubs and invite all the chorus girls home for breakfast."

Robbie Robertson (born Jaime Royal Klagerman on July 5, 1944) was fourteen years old when he first heard Hawkins and the Hawks at Le Coq d'Or. An infant when his father (a Jewish gangster) had been killed in a shootout, he had been raised by his mother (who had grown up on the Six Nations Reserve near Hagersville, Ontario, north of Lake Erie) and James Patrick Robertson, a jeweler that she married shortly after his birth.

Spending most of his formative years amid the inner-city squabble of Toronto's Cabbagetown, Robertson's experiences on the Six Nations Reserve helped to balance his worldview. "I've read things that talk about me spending my summers there," Robertson told me in 2012, "but it was much more than my summers. We went all of the time. Every holiday, we would go there or our relatives would visit us in Toronto."

Robertson's mother instructed him to be proud of his Native heritage, but she suggested that he keep it hidden. "When my mom was growing up on the Six Nations Indian Reserve," he said, "it was a period when schools were trying to dismiss and wash away the Indian-ness. When we think about it now, it seems so horrible, just distasteful. My mom's mother died when she was quite young, and she had gone on to live in Toronto with her aunt. Before she left the reserve, it was 'good luck' and everything, 'just remember and be proud that you're an Indian, but be careful who you tell.' She passed that on to me, but the times had changed. It wasn't like I had to think about wondering if they would let me in here, but, for her, it was a reality."

Relatives on the Six Nations Reserve sparked Robertson's connection to music. "All my cousins, all my uncles, everybody played a guitar, a mandolin, a fiddle, or something," he remembered. "It thrilled me to see and hear them play. I wanted to do what they did."

Robertson's mother encouraged his passion for music. "I remember one day I was coming home from school," he said, "and a guy came up and handed me a piece of paper that was for guitar lessons; I took it home and told my mother."

Robertson quickly discovered that the guitar teacher viewed music differently. "Instead of holding it like a guitar, he put it on my lap," he recalled, "and started teaching me [Hawaiian guitar playing]. I did not want to play Hawaiian music. I had Hank Williams in my mind and the music to 'The Hawaiian War Chant' in front of me."

Country music had a more positive impact. "Hank Williams, Lefty Frizzell, and Hank Snow were big on the Rez," he recalled. "Sometimes, someone would sing Slim Whitman's 'Indian Love Call.' Sometimes, it would be a hybrid—country music and some kind of chanting. It sounded like it was right in the middle of those two worlds."

Radio provided a link to blues and rock and roll. Tuning into stations from Nashville, Tennessee, and Buffalo, New York, Robertson would spend hours listening to the music that would forever change his life. "Link Wray had the rawest sound," he remembered, "just dirty and up to no good, [but] dirty, to me, also meant Bo Diddley and Hubert Sumlin, Howlin Wolf's guitarist. They put me over the top. I had no choice but to play guitar."

An avid concert attendee, Robertson continued to build on his love of rock and roll. "I went to shows by Chuck Berry, Lavern Baker, Little Richard, and Fats Domino," he recalled, "and I saw a couple versions of the Alan Freed shows. I met Buddy Holly. [I remember that the sound of] his guitar blasted out of his amp; there was something about it beyond the normal. All these little pieces fit into the puzzle perfectly for me. Each thing taught me more."

Between gigs with Robbie & the Robots, Thumper & the Trombones, and Little Caesar & the Consuls, Robertson hung out at Yonge Street clubs, listening to groups like Ronnie Hawkins and the Hawks. "[They] played the fastest, most violent rock and roll I'd ever heard," he remembered. "It was exciting and exploded with dynamics. I knew [that] the majority of the music [that] I liked and felt connected to was from the South and they represented that to me."

Enchanted by Hawkins and the Hawks, Robertson did everything to ingratiate himself with the band. "I wanted to be the nicest guy they ever knew," he remembered. "I was trying to do what Ronnie would later phrase as 'swindle my way in.'"

The effort began to pay off. "[Robertson] was just hanging around, like a roadie," remembered Hawkins, "but I could see he was smart and hungry, and [that] when the chance came, I knew I had to do something with him."

The opportunity came soon enough. In search of songs for his second album, *Mr. Dynamo* (released in January 1960), Hawkins wanted to hear what the fifteen-year-old had written. In addition to choosing two of Robertson's songs to record—a Latin-tinged rocker ("Hey Boba Lou") and a Buddy Holly–like ballad ("Someone Like You")—he brought the young songwriter (as his consultant) to New York's Brill Building, where they auditioned tunes by Otis Blackwell, Doc Pomus, and Leiber & Stoller. "[Hawkins] told me, 'Son, I've got to get more songs,'" remembered Robertson. "Maybe, if you can write those songs, you've got a good ear."

As soon as Hawkins's album released, Robertson rushed to get a copy. Looking at the credits for the songs he had written, he was startled. "[They] had another name, besides my name, for some writer named Morris Levy," he told Andy Tennille of Jambase.com. "I said to Ronnie, 'there was nobody [with me when] I wrote these songs, who is Morris Levy?' Ronnie just tapped me on the head and said, 'there are certain things about this business that you just let go and don't question.' That was one of my early music industry lessons."

The Hawks' personnel continued to change. Jimmy Ray "Luke" Paulman had gone on to play with Dale Hawkins's band, and future Nashville-based session guitarist Fred Carter Jr. had replaced Jimmy "Lefty" Evans. For a while, Ozark, Arkansas–born Roy Buchanan played guitar for The Hawks. The son of a Pentecostal preacher, and a former protégé of white R&B bandleader Johnny Otis, Buchanan had been one of the earliest to replace James Burton in Dale Hawkins's band, appearing on Hawkins's hit cover of Willie Dixon's "My Babe" in 1958. A master at sculpting harmonic textures with his Fender Telecaster guitar, Buchanan radiated mystique. He would regale Robertson with tales of his being a werewolf. Although he would go on to record an impressive series of solo albums, his limited vocals and inability to attract a memorable lead singer would hold him back and depression would haunt him his entire life. Arrested for intoxication near his home in Reston, Virginia, in February 1988, Buchanan would hang himself (in a jail cell) while in police custody.

Robertson never stopped trying to break into The Hawks. When Pop Jones returned to Arkansas (to be with his wife and kids) in December

1959, Hawkins phoned pianist Scott Cushnie, who was staying at Robertson's apartment, and invited him to audition. Hitchhiking more than one hundred and twenty miles in bitter, zero-degree weather, the pianist, accompanied by Robertson and Pete the Bear (Peter Derimigis), arrived at the Brass Rail in London, Ontario, (where Hawkins and the Hawks were preparing for that night's show). Tracking down the bandleader, Cushnie threatened that he would play only if his traveling partners were also hired. Hawkins quickly rebuffed his demand, and the pianist and his friends returned to the frigid cold and hitchhiked back to Toronto.

Soon afterward, Cushnie accepted Hawkins's invitation and joined The Hawks. Robertson would follow a few months later when The Hawks needed a new bass player. Cushnie had convinced Hawkins that Robertson could play the four-stringed instrument. Telephoning the sixteen-year-old in Toronto, the bandleader told him to get down to Arkansas, where The Hawks were playing. Robertson wasted no time. After a week spent sharpening his bass skills and raising enough money for a bus ticket, he headed south. "I had to hock my 1957 Stratocaster," he remembered. "I got on a bus and trusted that [the bus driver] knew where [we] were going."

Though he would later tell Oprah Winfrey that traveling to the Mississippi Delta was like "going to the holy land of rock and roll," Robertson seemed out of place when he arrived. "[Hawkins and the Hawks] looked at me as if I was a Martian," he remembered. "I looked very city-ish; greasy hair, baggy pants, and an overcoat. [Hawkins] has always said that I was this little street kid on his way to jail. He's convinced that if he hadn't hired me, I would have ended up in prison."

The South enchanted the young guitarist. "I remember when I got off the bus," he said in a Findlay Bunting–directed documentary, *Going Home*, in 1995, "and smelled the air and looked around, the way people talked, it was in rhythm. Sitting on the edge of the Mississippi River was poetic by itself, but the river going by, and the riverboats, everything seemed to move in rhythm. You could hear music coming from somewhere at night, always. It would be leaking out of somewhere, or the wind would change, and all of a sudden, you'd hear a harmonica in the distance and think, 'You never hear anything like this up north.'"

Ensuring that he had an appropriate haircut and wardrobe, Hawkins took Robertson under his wing. When he and Helm flew to England for a TV appearance, they left the teen with instructions to practice the bass. Instead, guitarist Fred Carter Jr. brought him across the Mississippi River to Memphis, where he sought out a Beale Street record shop, the Home of the Blues, and spent the hundred dollars that Hawkins had advanced him on blues albums.

Hawkins had been considering hiring Buchanan to play lead guitar, moving Helm to rhythm guitar, and having Robertson play bass. "I listened to [Buchanan] play this *Louisiana Hayride* sort of style," he recalled, "like Fred [Carter Jr.] and James Burton do—but with a different twang to it—and I thought he was fantastic."

When they returned from England, Hawkins and Helm discovered that Robertson had practiced nearly nonstop and was playing at an incredibly proficient level. "I really only gave him nine days to learn guitar," claimed Hawkins. "He had to learn because he wasn't worth anything when he first took it over."

Robertson had to rely on his own resources. "When I first heard bottleneck guitar [played] by Muddy Waters or Elmore James," he told *Rolling Stone*, "I didn't know they were playing a bottleneck. They would take a bottle, cut the neck off, sand it down, and play it like a slide. I'd never seen or heard of it, so I thought that it was just someone playing a guitar in a particular way. I worked so hard, trying to get that sound down—for months; I worked on it day and night. When I found that they were using a bottleneck, I said, 'Oh, Jesus.' My fingers were bleeding from trying to get it."

The persistence paid off. When a guitar battle with Buchanan erupted in Grand Bend, Ontario, Robertson (whom Dylan would later call "the only mathematical guitar genius I've ever run into who does not offend my intestinal nervousness with his rear guard sound") was ready. "[Buchanan] was much more advanced than I was," Robertson recalled. "I'd been playing a year and a half, two years. He had been playing many, many years, and had more tricks than I did, but I could play more excitingly. I could [make the guitar] scream like hundreds of birds."

Flourishing under Hawkins's mentorship, Robertson grew into one of Canada's most talked-about young instrumentalists. "Guitar players were coming from all around," he remembered, "just to hear this thing that I was doing, but, because it was new, they didn't know how I was doing it, how I made that sound. They did not know how I bent the strings. There were no light gauge strings, back then. You had to use a banjo string for the first string and move all the other strings down one. People were mystified by this."

Robertson yearned to be more than a mere guitar slinger, however. Though he had barely attended school, he had continuously sought new avenues of learning. "I started reading—all kinds of things," he said. "I was reading Zen and I was reading Faulkner, Hemingway, and just about anybody who wrote about the South. I had a view of what that whole situation there was like. It was very enlightening to me."

Hawkins took a harsh view of Robertson's literary pursuits. "Ronnie didn't like this at all," recalled the guitarist. "To him, it was, first you're reading, the next thing, God knows what you're going to be doing."

As the 1950s transcended into the '60s, rock and roll was experiencing its roughest days. Elvis Presley and the Everly Brothers were in the army. Eddie Cochrane had died in an automobile accident, Buddy Holly, Ritchie Valens, and J. P. "The Big Bopper" Richardson in a plane crash. Jerry

Lee Lewis's career was in turmoil (after marrying his thirteen-year-old cousin), Chuck Berry was in jail for violating the Mann Act (by transporting an underage white woman across state lines), and Little Richard had traded rock and roll for religion. In their place was an emerging crop of clean-cut, formulaic singers, including Fabian, Bobby Rydell, Frankie Avalon, and Annette Funicello. The blues-meets-country rockabilly of artists like Ronnie Hawkins and the Hawks rarely aired on the radio anymore.

Another factor in Hawkins's relative obscurity in the United States was his reluctance to leave Canada. Although he and the Hawks performed occasionally in Arkansas and surrounding states, he spent most of each year in the Great White North, playing music, co-owning nightclubs, and (as a big fish in a small pond) having the time of his life.

Helm played an important role in shaping Robertson's musical vision. "I thought Levon was the most talented person that I'd ever met," said the guitarist. "I was maybe fourteen or fifteen years old when I met him, and I looked up to him tremendously. Ronnie Hawkins was terrific and a great showman and a great character and all of that, but Levon was the ace in the hole. . . . He had music running through his veins, you know. It was the real deal."

As the lineup of The Hawks evolved, the pieces that would grow into The Band continued to fall into place. The third of four brothers, Richard Clare "Rick" Danko (1942–1999) arrived in early 1961, replacing Rebel Payne on bass. "I thought Rick Danko was the leader of The Band," Amy Helm (Levon Helm and Libby Titus's daughter) confessed to Peter Crowley of the *Adirondack Daily Enterprise* in July 2013, "and [that] my dad played drums for Rick Danko's band."

Hailing from the tobacco farmlands of Simcoe in southwestern Ontario, Danko had grown up without electricity, listening to music on a windup Victrola and a battery radio. "Hank Williams was like a healing power to me," Danko told me. "My dad played mandolin and piano, as did my Uncle Spence, who dressed like a cowboy. His wife was my mother's sister. It was always the greatest party when they would show up. I also had three aunts on my mother's side, and they sang harmony. By the time I was seven, I was singing on stage at a Christmas party."

Playing stringed instruments from the age of five, Danko taught himself to play mandolin, banjo, violin, and guitar. "They're all tuned the same," he explained. "I [convinced] my older brother to buy a guitar that I couldn't afford but really wanted. By the time that I was seven, I could accompany myself on the guitar."

Like Robertson, Danko knew that he wanted to join Hawkins's band from the moment he first heard them at a local dance in Simcoe. He had been serving an apprenticeship to be a butcher, but his dreams had remained focused on music; he had been performing (with his older brother) at local venues like the Teenage Club. "I was so engrossed with Ronnie Hawkins," he recalled, "that I got us booked as his opening act in Port

Dover. He hired me after the first night. I played rhythm guitar, but I ended up learning the bass because his bass player was leaving."

"When we first saw Rick," recalled Robertson, "he was playing with a group that wasn't too hot, but they made him stand out. . . . You could tell that he was very musical. He had soul in his voice; [it was] somewhere between the tobacco-belt sound and Sam Cooke."

"[Danko] had a unique [vocal] style," said Elvis Costello. "It was kind of nasal and had a little bit of what I now realize is country in it, but at the same time, it was just so unusual, such a lovely and relaxed sound."

"The Danko boys have really weird ears," said Hawkins, who included the bassist's younger brother, Terry Danko, in a later incarnation of The Hawks. "That made it sound distinctive. That's what The Beatles had, too: their distinctive voices and the drive they put on it."

Danko's bass playing added a further dimension. "I was mostly influenced by the great Motown bass players, like Phil Upchurch and James Jameson, and Edgar Willis from Ray Charles's band," he told Kevin Ransom of *Guitar Player*, "and some tuba players, as well. I just tried to listen and play in the spaces, hook up with the bass drum, and leave some space for the backbeat to hit. . . . I tried to play in front of the beat in a way that didn't rush it, or behind the beat in a way that didn't drag it. The Band was very good at listening to each other, and working out the arrangements in a very economical way, and making it add up so that you could not only hear the sum of the parts, but feel it as well. . . . Sometimes, it's not what you [play], it's what you leave out."

No one in The Hawks had a vocal tone as emotionally rich as that of Richard George "The Beak" or "The Gobbler" Manuel (1943–1986). Briefly considered The Band's lead singer, the Stratford, Ontario–born pianist/drummer left listeners in awe whenever he opened his mouth. His high, weary vocals could tear at the heart of a tune like "I Shall Be Released," while his singing of "The Shape I'm In" and "King Harvest (Has Surely Come)" proved that he could rock. "[Manuel] had this amazing power to move you with his music and his voice," said Eric Clapton, "with his presence, even. If he came into a room, you felt drawn to the amount of energy. He was very shaky, very fragile, and scared, but, in some reverse way, that had a power that attracted you. For me he was the true light of the Band. The others were fantastic talents, of course, but there was something of the holy-madman about Richard. He was raw. When he sang in that high falsetto, the hair on my neck would stand on end. Not many people can do that."

"[In] the hurt in his voice," said Robertson, "there was a certain element of pain. You didn't know if it was because he was trying to reach for a note, or if it was that he was a guy with a heart that had been hurt."

"There was only one Richard, without a doubt," remembered Danko. "I met him, in 1959, before I started playing with The Band. He was a party kind of a guy and he sure was one of my favorite singers."

Manuel's interpretation of Hoagy Carmichael and Stuart Gorrell's "Georgia on My Mind" nearly surpassed Ray Charles's 1960 hit. Performing it since his teens, he would record a version for *Islands*, the final album by the original Band, in 1977. "I learned [singing] from Ray Charles," he told British English professor and music journalist Peter Viney, "and people think I sound just like Ray Charles, but I don't sound like Ray Charles—I imply, I make the same implications, I infer the same kind of things, you know what I mean?"

Manuel grew up singing with his three brothers in a church choir, while a variety of R&B vocalists provided further inspiration. "Bobby Bland and Ricky Nelson probably influenced me," he said. "Howlin' Wolf, Muddy Waters, and Jimmy Reed—nearly all of the singing influence is black."

A gifted songwriter, Manuel would pen "In a Station," "We Can Talk," "Lonesome Suzie," and (with Dylan) "Tears of Rage" for *Music from Big Pink*, and cowrite (with Robertson) "Whispering Pines," "Jawbone," and "When You Awake" for *The Band*, as well as "Sleeping" and "Just Another Whistle Stop" for *Stage Fright*.

The son of a Chevrolet dealership mechanic and a schoolteacher, Manuel had taken some piano lessons at the age of nine, but formal training had ended when the piano teacher slammed the lid of the piano on his fingers. "I played a note that wasn't on the paper," he told Ruth Albert Spencer of the *Woodstock Times*, "[but] it wasn't wrong; it was a different voicing; same chord, different voicing, like I put the E in a C chord on the top instead of in the middle."

Teaching himself a rhythmic style of piano playing, Manuel began performing (along with John Till, the future guitarist of Janis Joplin's Full Tilt Boogie Band) in The Rebels (or Rockin' Revols) by his sixteenth birthday. "[Manuel] did teen-idol songs like 'Eternal Love' and 'Promise Yourself,'" recalled Helm, who saw the Rockin' Revols when they opened for The Hawks in Dover, Arkansas, "and he played a mean rhythm piano on a boogie-woogie version of Franz Liszt's 'Lieberstraum.'"

After the two groups again crossed paths at a battle of the bands in the Stratford Coliseum in 1961, Manuel's rendition of "Georgia on My Mind" impressed Hawkins so much that he booked the Rockin' Revols to perform at his nightclub in Fayetteville. For Manuel and his teenaged band mates, traveling south represented unabashed freedom. Partying nonstop from the moment that they hit Arkansas, they demolished Hawkins's trailer, where they were staying. For the pianist, it would be a hint of darker times to come.

The final piece of the puzzle that would become The Band was its most musically proficient. Already a veteran of London, Ontario's rock and big band jazz scene when he joined The Hawks at the age of twenty-four in December 1961, Eric Garth "The Bear" Hudson brought an instrumental dimension that propelled Hawkins's group, and later The Band, to unprecedented heights. "[Hudson] heard all sorts of weird things in his head," said Hawkins. "I didn't know what he was doing musically, but it worked. Every band needs someone like Garth. Every band needs a genius musician; the way The Beatles had George Martin as their genius musician-producer to help them—that is why I hired Garth Hudson. You have to have somebody who has been to school and knows how to do arrangements and all that. You need him to teach the rest of the guys."

"Garth is beyond question the most brilliant organist in the rock world," proclaimed *Time* magazine. "[His] improvised variations, drawn from a vast knowledge of popular and classical music, provide both the decorative scroll-work and depth of The Band's total impact."

"Few people have been able to bring songs to life with such exciting and unexpected tone color blends," said Bob Doerschuk of *Keyboard* magazine, "or develop as original an approach to phrasing rock keyboards solos, as Hudson, the first true rock keyboards virtuoso."

"Anybody who gets a chance to play with Garth Hudson, they'd be a fool not to," Helm told the *San Francisco Chronicle*. "As far as The Band is concerned, he's the one who rubbed off on the rest of us and made us sound as good as we did."

"Garth was far and away the most advanced musician in rock 'n' roll," Robertson said to Joshua Baer of *Melody Maker*. "He could just as easily play with John Coltrane as he could play with the New York Symphony Orchestra as he could play with us as he could play with Minnie Pearl. He was just remarkable. He could listen to a song and tell us the chords as it went along, I mean, songs with complicated chord structures. It widened our scope and it was just a lot more fun. We could do things. If we picked up something we wanted to do like the version we had heard, [with] the same harmony that they did in the horn section or background, we could do it."

Preferring the Chicago-manufactured Lowrey organs to the more-common Hammond B3 (for their ability to slide and sustain notes), Hudson conjured some of popular music's most distinctive textures. "The Lowrey had enough bite," he explained, "and I could make it distort enough, to fit in with what we were doing. The early Lowries had a nice little growl. I began with a Lowrey Festival organ, which had something like ninety or a hundred tubes in it, and that gave it a distorted sound when you turned everything up."

Hudson was more than a keyboardist, though. He played accordion on "Rockin' Chair" (*The Band*), "When I Paint My Masterpiece" (*Cahoots*), "Ain't No More Cane (On the Brazos)" (*Basement Tapes*), and Bobby Charles's "Down South in New Orleans" during *The Last Waltz*. The saxophonist on "Tears of Rage" and "Unfaithful Servant," he also played all of the brass and woodwind instruments on "Ophelia" from *Northern Lights—Southern Cross*.

Born in Windsor and raised in London, Ontario, Hudson inherited his passion for music from his parents. His mother played piano and accordion and sang, and his father (a farm inspector who had been a World War I fighter pilot) played drums, C melody saxophone, clarinet, flute, and piano. "I took private lessons in theory, harmony, and counterpoint with Thomas Chattoe," Hudson told *Keyboard* magazine, "composition with John Cooke, and piano with Clifford von Kuster. I would recommend reading a Bach chorale every other day, and continuing on to improvise to maintain an awareness of four-part voice leading. I am continuing to devise my own exercises, a whole study in illegitimate techniques, and techniques that are not [usually] taught."

Hudson's father helped to spark his fascination with the keyboards. "My dad bought a reed pump organ," he recalled, "and began fixing it, and then I began to get into it and repair things. All these little wooden parts were always breaking, and the reeds needed cleaning. When you buy an antique . . . there will always be dirt in the reeds, so you have to go through and clean all of them to begin with. Then you wait till one stops sounding, go in, pull that one, clean it out, and so on. They need repair constantly."

By the age of twelve, Hudson was playing the squeezebox in country bands and piano in jazz big bands. "We did all the old charts," he remembered. "I saw 'em all, from 'In the Mood' to 'Paradiddle Joe.'"

Hudson's approach to the keyboards incorporated a wide variety of influences. He spent a summer as an organist in an Anglican church in the Diocese of Huron. "The Anglican Church has the best musical traditions of any church I know," he told *Time* magazine. "It's the old voice leading that gives it the countermelodies, and adds all those classical devices which are not right out there, but they add a little texture."

Hudson also gained experience by playing organ in his uncle's funeral parlor. " My aunt played in the funeral home too," he recalled. She helped and advised me with the collection. One nice hymn we discovered that was a little different and that had that emotional quality, that basic melodic quality, and was less Germanic than most hymns, was 'Dear Lord and Father of Mankind, Forgive Our Foolish Ways.' We would play 'Abide with Me' and that was the signal for the preacher to come in. I think I had twenty or thirty of those hymns."

Hudson became a master at improvisation. "I could transcribe [a score]," he told the *Woodstock Times*'s Ruth Albert Spencer, "but I couldn't memorize it. I would memorize shapes and forms. I had encouragement, from a teacher in high school who played in a big band, who asked me to transcribe scores. I used a record player and wrote down what I heard; then my teacher played the transcriptions with his band. I worked in the high school variety show playing for the choirs and got a little group together called the Three Blisters. We got the most applause of any of the acts. The trumpet player's father was Don Wright, who had the Don

Wright Chorus in Canada, and they had a weekly show on CBC. He was also a good trumpet player; at one point, Louis Armstrong asked him to go on the road. His son Timothy picked up the trumpet and we formed the Three Blisters. The next year it became the Four Quarters."

Hudson began tuning into Alan Freed's Cleveland-based *Moondog Matinee* radio show in 1952. Five years later, he helped to form a rock band (The Silhouettes) that would evolve into Paul London and the Kapers. After opening for "Guy Lombardo–like big bands" throughout Southwest Ontario, they expanded to Detroit and Chicago and recorded two singles—"Sugar Baby" and "Big Bad Twist." "We played teen hops and similar things," remembered Hudson. "I originally wanted to play piano in the band, but it turned out to be more fun to play the saxophone. We played 'Mr. Lee' [The Bobbettes' 1957 hit featuring saxophonist Jess Powell] and 'Honky Tonk,' which was [originally] played [on the tenor saxophone] by Clifford Scott of the Bill Doggett Band. I still like to proclaim, 'I know who the hero is—go and dig Clifford, man.' In that era, he was the crowned prince. He was the best—on alto as well."

Hudson was still in his teens when he began earning a substantial living in music. "I was working with songwriters, doing demos," he remembered. "This one fellow wanted to know about ear training. He had progressed to the point where he wanted me to tell him if it was possible to hear something, know what it is, and write it down. I had some [manuscript] notepaper lying in the hot sun that recommended that you assign numbers to notes instead of do-re-mi. It was very simple."

Hawkins had been attempting to recruit him since 1959, but Hudson had continued to turn him down. Finally, in December 1960, at Robbie Robertson's pleading, the keyboardist agreed to attend a show by The Hawks (who were seeking to replace Pop Jones). He was not impressed, and Richard Manuel took the job instead. "The whole thing was too loud," recalled Hudson, "too fast and too violent."

The Hawks extended a second invitation a few months later when Hudson attended their show at the Legion Hall in Ingersoll, Ontario. He again turned them down. "I wasn't interested in that kind of music at the time," he insisted. "I liked chord changes and music that was a little more 'uptown.'"

Hudson was also concerned about going against his parent's feelings about rock and roll. "My family thought 'rock and roll musician' was a déclassé occupation," he said, "especially after my conservatory background, and they were already upset with me for dropping out of college after only a year."

When The Hawks extended a third invitation, in 1961, Hudson began to soften. "I saw they were making big money," he said, "because they worked seven nights a week, every week."

After telling his parents about Hawkins's offer and experiencing the opposition he had dreaded, Hudson had the bandleader speak to them.

"I have a band of talented young men who are being held back by their lack of musical education," Hudson remembered Hawkins telling his parents. "I want to hire your son to come along and teach them music. I want them to learn how to read notation properly."

With his parents' reluctant consent, Hudson became a member of The Hawks—paid an additional ten dollars a week to provide the group with music lessons, and presented with a new Lowery Festival organ.

The combination of Hudson's organ and Manuel's piano recalled the gospel sounds of the southern African American church. "[Manuel is] great at organizing, very good with chords," said Hudson, explaining how he and the pianist figured out their parts. "He works closer, at the beginning, with the guitar players and the bass. Then, later on, I come in and do whatever I can; I come up with a riff or a sound that suits a tune after I've heard it a few times."

Hudson's saxophone brought an additional sound to The Hawks, expanded with the addition of saxophonist Jerry Penfound. "With [Penfound's] baritone and Garth's alto," remembered Helm, "we had a soul-band horn section when we needed one. That really changed our sound toward a more R&B feel from the rockabilly we'd been playing for almost four years."

With the final pieces of what would become The Band assembled, Hawkins put the musicians to work—performing or rehearsing nearly every hour they were awake. During the three years that they were together, they played six or seven nights a week, because, as Rick Danko explained, "We didn't know any better. That was kind of our dues-paying time. We really got our chops together."

THREE

Voices from the Mountain

After the world tour with Dylan ended in London on May 27, 1966, the former Hawks returned to New York. Planning on a couple of months of unwinding before reuniting with Dylan for a sixty-show tour set to begin in August, they settled back into the Chelsea Hotel, where Robertson and his wife, Dominique, spent time with Edie Sedgwick, an actress, socialite, fashion model, and Andy Warhol superstar managed by Grossman. "[Sedgwick] would come and hang out in my room in the hotel," he told Robert Everett-Green of the Toronto *Globe and Mail* in April 2011. "[Warhol] was so fascinated with her; he would come looking for her. She would be [whispering to me], 'Tell him I'm not here.'"

Dylan, meanwhile, had been going through personal changes, secretly marrying Sara Lownds (Sara Nozinsky) on November 22, 1965. The singer-songwriter had met the fashion model, actor, and Playboy Club bunny three years before at the wedding of Albert Grossman and Sally Anne Buehler (a server she had befriended).

The former Mrs. Lownds, immortalized in Dylan's songs "Sad Eyed Lady of the Lowlands" and "Sara," had been born to Jewish parents in Wilmington Delaware on October 28, 1939. After her mother suffered a stroke when she was still a child, a great aunt, Esther, had helped to raise her. Her father (a scrap-metal dealer) died after being shot in 1956; her mother died five years later.

Although she was married to photographer Hans Lownds (with whom she had had a daughter, Maria) when she met Dylan, their marriage had fallen apart soon afterward. By 1964, she and the singer-songwriter had become romantically involved and had moved into separate rooms at the Chelsea Hotel to be closer together.

During a break from touring, Dylan and Sara secretly married on the lawn of a judge in Mineola, Long Island—Sara was seven months pregnant (with their son Jesse Byron Dylan). They would go on to become the parents of Anna, Samuel, and Jakob, and Dylan would adopt Sara's daughter. After honeymooning in Spain, Dylan moved his new family into a house on Camelot Road in Woodstock's Byrdcliffe artist colony.

Plans for another world tour came to an abrupt end when Dylan sustained a severe motorcycle accident on July 29. After picking up his motorcycle at Grossman's home in West Saugerties (where it had been stored), he had been heading to have it serviced (with Sara following in her car). There are several stories about what happened next. The *New York Times* reported, "[Dylan] was buzzing along on his Triumph 500 near Woodstock, N.Y., when the rear wheel froze, flipping him off and onto the pavement. Dylan was rushed to a doctor and will spend at least two months in bed, recuperating from a neck fracture, a concussion (he wasn't wearing a helmet), and severe face and back cuts."

Dylan told biographer Robert Shelton that an oil slick had sent his motorcycle out of control. He had a different tale for Sam Shepard, who turned it into a one-act play for *Esquire* magazine. "I was blinded by the sun for a second," he told Shepard. "I just happened to look up right smack into the sun with both eyes and, sure enough, I went blind for a second and I kind of panicked or something. I stomped down on the brake, and the rear wheel locked up on me and I went flying."

Researchers have debated the extent of his injuries, but Dylan reportedly wore a neck brace, underwent ultrasound treatment, and suffered from chronic back pain. His six-week stay in the home of internal medicine physician Dr. Edward Thaler fifty miles from Woodstock led some to postulate that he had actually been in drug recovery—a charge denied by Thaler's widow, Selma. "He did not come here regarding any situation involving detoxification," she told the *Woodstock Times*. "He had some kind of anonymity here. As it turns out, the people next door had a teenaged daughter who recognized him, [but] nobody bothered him and they certainly would have in [Woodstock]. The house was peaceful [and] he felt comfortable here. His friends could visit him. Nobody stalked anybody. He could be alone. I don't know whether he was writing or thinking or what he was doing, but he was away from [his] ordinary daily life—and I think that provided some peace of mind."

In *Chronicles, Volume One*, Dylan discussed the accident. "I'd been hurt," he wrote, "but I recovered. Truth was that I wanted to get out of the rat race. Having children changed my life and segregated me from just about everybody and everything that was going on. Outside of my family, nothing held any real interest for me and I was seeing everything through different glasses.

"When I woke up and caught my senses [following the accident]," he continued, "I realized I was just working for all these leeches. I didn't want to do that, plus, I had a family, and I just wanted to see my kids."

Whatever the truth behind his retreat from public view, Dylan was definitely in need of a break. In a brief fourteen months, he had recorded three of his most important albums (*Bringing It All Back Home, Highway 61 Revisited*, and the double-disc *Blonde on Blonde*) and toured the world. He still had to complete the editing of *Eat the Document* and had last-minute work to do on his long-overdue book, *Tarantula*, after reading the galleys and requesting time to revise it. Macmillan had given him two weeks. "I was straining pretty hard," he remembered, "and couldn't have gone on living that way much longer. The fact that I made it through what I did is pretty miraculous."

For the ex-Hawks, the layoff was costly. "New York was expensive," remembered Robertson, "and we were just these road musicians with no road to go on. We had no place to work on our music. People would say that we could play at their places, but [neighbors] would be banging on the wall. It was very frustrating."

Albert Grossman knew little about the former Hawks beyond their involvement with Dylan. When Robertson told him that working with the singer-songwriter had been a "sideline," and that the ex-Hawks' focus had remained on their own music, Grossman was taken aback. "Interestingly, neither Bob nor anybody around had any idea of what we were going to do," recalled Robertson. "Albert said, 'Have you thought of doing a record of Bob Dylan instrumentals?'"

Invited to help Dylan and folk-club-owner-turned-filmmaker Howard Alk finish editing *Eat the Document*, Robertson relocated to Woodstock, paving the way for Danko, Manuel, and Hudson, who soon followed. "We couldn't find a place [in New York City] where we could work on our music without it being too expensive or it bothering people," Robertson told Bluesmobile.com, "so we went up to Woodstock. Albert Grossman said, 'Up there, you could find a place where there're no people around. You could do whatever you want.' We desperately needed that."

"The reason that [Grossman] first came to Woodstock," explained Milton Glaser, who painted the poster that was included with Dylan's *Greatest Hits*, "was because my wife, Shirley, was told about a fabulous house that was available but cost fifty thousand dollars. Albert was the only person we could think of, amongst our friends, who could afford that. Afterwards, Shirley managed to find a house for Dylan. You could say the future of Woodstock was set by these two events."

Nestled in the scenic Catskill Mountains, straight up the New York State Thruway, about two hours north of New York City and northwest of Kingston (New York's first state capitol), the Ulster County town of Woodstock (established in 1787) had enjoyed an extensive involvement with aesthetic culture.

British art critic, draughtsman, watercolorist, Oxford University professor, and pioneer of the Arts and Crafts Movement, John Ruskin (1819–1900) planted the seeds that would inspire Woodstock's artistic transformation in his five-volume work *Modern Painters*. Although his utopian artist colony in England, St. George, failed, Ruskin's students continued to spread his beliefs in the power of the individual, the importance of a connection with nature, and the expression of arts and crafts for personal and professional fulfillment.

A Yorkshire-born former student of Ruskin's, Ralph Radcliffe Whitehead, brought these teachings to America. Arriving in the United States in 1892 and marrying Jane Byrd McCall of Philadelphia (who had also studied with Ruskin), Whitehead (who had inherited a fortune when his father, a mill owner and industrialist, died) longed to create a utopian community based on "the brotherhood of artistic collaboration." Purchasing fifteen thousand acres in Woodstock, Whitehead and his wife, along with Iowa-born and Kansas-raised novelist and poet Hervey White (1866–1944) and painter/lithographer Bolton Brown (1864–1936), founded the Byrdcliffe Arts and Crafts Colony in 1902. The serene, art-centered life attracted artists of every ilk to the colony. Poet Wallace Stevens, novelist Thomas Mann, educator John Dewey, and dancer Isadora Duncan spent time there. In the late '60s and early '70s, Dylan and his family lived in the colony, in what the *Woodstock Times* described as a "rambling house in the woods."

Although the strict rules by which Whitehead governed the colony led many residents to leave by the mid-1920s, the Byrdcliffe Arts and Crafts Colony continued to operate until his death in 1929. After his widow's death in 1955, much of the property was sold to pay for taxes and the maintenance of the remaining land, which remains dedicated to "the continuing study, practice, and development of skill in the fine arts and crafts."

One of the first artists to leave, Hervey White (1866–1944) started an even more radical artist's colony, Maverick, in 1905 on the south slope of Ohaya Mountain, just over the town line in Hurley, New York. Initially conceived as a getaway for White and his partners, it grew into the hub of a thriving intellectual scene with a publishing company, Maverick Press (established in 1910), issuing a series of monthly art journals.

White was a hippie decades ahead of his time. Building simple cabins (where artists paid very little rent or lived free), he shaped a community that lived by artistic exploration—one of America's first communes. Parties at Maverick were outrageous experiences with costumed partygoers guided by an anything-goes morality. Erecting a "musical chapel in the woods," White began hosting concerts featuring the many classical musicians who spent their summerlong off-season at the colony. When he needed to raise fifteen hundred dollars for a new well in 1916, he launched the Maverick Music Festival and began charging for tickets. It would evolve into the longest-running summer chamber music event in the United States. "Nearly everybody said I couldn't put this over without money," White told the *New York Times* before the premiere Maverick

Music Festival in 1916. "High finance is a great discovery. We are living in a remarkable age. When I invested in this farm, ten years ago, I did it with the idea of gathering some good musicians during the summer months and giving chamber music in a rustic music chapel among tall trees at the foot of a hill. The farm cost two thousand dollars and I happened to have two hundred dollars in cash at the time, so I turned that over to the owner. I suppose a good high financier would have kept his two hundred dollars, but I was just beginning, you remember."

Creativity prospered in Woodstock. Operating from 1906 to 1922, the Art Students League of New York was resurrected in 1947 and continued for another thirty-two years before the Woodstock School of Art absorbed it in 1980. Both the Woodstock Artists Association and Museum (WAAM), which launched in 1919, and the Woodstock Guild, founded by Byrdcliffe students in 1939, remain active.

Music was very much a part of Woodstock's lore. Peter Yarrow had arrived in 1942, at the age of five, after he and his mother (following his parents' divorce) moved into his aunt's house within walking distance of the village's center. Studying painting from the age of seven or eight (with Louise Brock, wife of renowned portrait painter Frank T. "Brock" Brokenshaw), he sold his first painting to Art Students League instructor Sigmund Menkes. "When I was a teenager, I studied with [Menkes]," he told the *Hudson Valley Times Herald Record*. "I was mainly focused on art, not music, at the time."

Yarrow claims to have brought Dylan to Woodstock in 1963. "It was a scorcher in New York City in June and July," he recalled. "Prior to the march on Washington, in which Peter, Paul, and Mary were to sing, I called up Bobby and said, 'Let's get out of the city. Come on up here with Suzie Rotolo.'"

Dylan wasted no time in taking the folksinger up on his invitation, settling into a routine after arriving in Woodstock. While he and Rotolo attended daily art classes, Yarrow remembered that Dylan "plunked away on a typewriter and came out with these unlikely songs like 'Only a Pawn in Their Game' and 'Masters of War.' We would come home with a painting and he would greet us with a new song. It was quite a time."

One of the earliest folk musicians to reside in Woodstock, Brooklyn-born banjo player William "Billy" Faier (1930–) arrived with his parents and siblings a few months before his fifteenth birthday. He had felt like an outcast in Brooklyn and at Kingston High School, but he found himself at home in Woodstock amid the community's musicians and artists. "There was a camaraderie among these folks that was new to me," he recalled. "Not only did they seem to like and understand each other but they included me in that communal umbrella of feeling, even though I was new to them and just a fourteen-year-old kid. In Brooklyn, most of my classmates patronized, ignored, or abused, me. In Kingston High, where I now went to school, the same was true, but, in Woodstock, there was this other group of people who accepted me. It gave me, for the first time in my life, an intense feeling of belonging to something bigger than myself."

Going on to become a regular participant at Washington Square Park jam sessions in New York, Faier recorded his debut album, *The Art of the Five String Banjo* (with Frank Hamilton), in 1957, followed by *Travelin' Man* the following year. A performer at the 1959 Newport Folk Festival, he produced the first Woodstock Folk Festival in 1962.

Bernard and Mary Lou Paturel approached him afterward. They had purchased an ice cream and sandwich shop and transformed it into a bistro, Café Espresso, where they planned to present local and national folk acts. With Faier hired to book performers, Ramblin' Jack Elliott, John Sebastian, Dave Van Ronk, Joan Baez, and her brother-in-law and sister, Richard and Mimi Farina, became regulars. For a few months in 1963, Dylan lived in an upstairs studio.

Libby Titus worked as a server at Café Espresso. The Woodstock-born daughter of an Earl Carroll dancer, Titus (born Elizabeth Jurist) balanced motherhood with a career as a pop singer, having briefly married novelist Barry Titus and given birth to their son, Ezra, at the age of nineteen. Releasing a self-titled debut album on the Hot Biscuit label in 1968, she would become romantically involved with Levon Helm a year later. Their daughter, Amy, was born on December 3, 1970. Helm and Titus would remain together until the late 1970s, with the songstress going on to be briefly involved with Dr. John before marrying Steely Dan's Donald Fagen in 1993. Together with Fagen, she would coproduce shows by the New York Rock and Soul Revue (Dr. John, Fagen, Phoebe Snow, and Bonnie Raitt) at the Lone Star Café from 1989 to 1992.

Titus experienced her first success as a songwriter when Bonnie Raitt covered her song "Love Has No Pride," written with Eric Kaz, on Raitt's 1972 debut album, *Give It Up*. A year later, Linda Ronstadt included a rendition on *Don't Cry Now*. Titus's own interpretation would be included on her second self-titled album, released by Columbia Records in 1977.

For the same album, Robbie Robertson produced two tracks, "The Night You Took Me to Barbados in My Dreams" by Titus and Girth Martinez, with Garth Hudson on keyboards, and "Miss Otis Regrets" by Cole Porter, with Robertson playing guitar. Hudson was reportedly the subject of "Can This Be My Love Affair," written by Titus and Carly Simon.

Another influence on Woodstock's roots music scene was Greenwich Village–born John Herald (1939–2005). Dubbed "the Stevie Wonder of country music" by Dylan, Herald had come to Woodstock in 1964 looking for a weekend writing retreat, fallen in love with the area, and stayed. "The thing I like most about Woodstock, to this day," explained the son of an Armenian poet in the liner notes of his 2005 album *Just another*

Bluegrass Boy, "is the surrounding [environment]. If I had not become a musician, I would have been something in the wild, the naturalist world. . . . I moved to Woodstock and became what I call a 'forage ranger.' I know a lot about eating and hunting for wild plants, and then I became an amateur mycologist, one who specialized in eating mushrooms—fifty different kinds. I really lived for the summer because I know all the best swimming holes, and follow all the streams for miles around. I go swimming at one of the towns up here—I won't name it—but there will be hundreds of trout all around your heads—you might be diving off a reef—and that is my big love for Woodstock to this day."

A Buck County, Pennsylvania, boarding school student in the mid-1950s, Herald had immersed himself in bluegrass from the moment that he first heard it on the radio. At the University of Wisconsin, he had joined similarly bitten classmates Eric Weissberg and Marshall Brickman on a lifelong exploration of the music of America's hill country. "I was going to be an entomologist," he said, "then, I discovered the guitar, and that was the end of my academic pursuits."

Returning to New York in 1959, Herald formed a bluegrass trio, the Greenbrier Boys, with Weissberg on mandolin (soon to be replaced by Ralph Rinzler) and Bob Yellin on banjo. The first northern group to win the Union Grove Fiddlers' Convention in Union Grove, North Carolina, they would back up Joan Baez on her second album as well as record a pair of albums for Vanguard, and one for Elektra, on their own. In a *New York Times* review of their show at Gerde's Folk City (that mentioned Bob Dylan's appearance as opening act), Robert Shelton applauded the Greenbrier Boys for whipping up "some of the fastest, most tempestuous bluegrass music this side of Nashville. They join Mr. Herald, a leather-lunged tenor whose athletic, high-range country yodeling is a thing of wonder."

A gifted, though far from prolific, songwriter, Herald would write "Stewball" (covered by Peter, Paul, and Mary) and "Jon the Generator" (covered by Maria Muldaur). Linda Ronstadt and the Stone Poneys would turn his arrangement of pre-Monkees Mike Nesmith's "Different Drum" into a top-thirteen *Billboard* pop hit in 1967.

Happy Traum first came to Woodstock in the 1950s. "The Arts Students League was here," he told me, "and friends of mine, who were painters, would come up to spend their summers. I would visit them. There was a small, burgeoning folk community even before [Dylan]. I played at the Woodstock Playhouse and the Café Espresso, which later became known because Bob hung out there a lot. John Herald, who was a dear friend and a great singer and guitar player, was the one who convinced [my wife, Jane, three kids, and I] to move there."

With the presence of Dylan and his manager, Albert Grossman (who would build an empire that would include two restaurants and the world-class Bearsville Recording Studios), Woodstock became the hub for a thriving folk and roots-oriented music scene. "People from the folk world in Boston and New York were moving here," remembered Traum. "Eric Andersen, John Sebastian, Jim Rooney, Bill Keith, and Geoff and Maria Muldaur moved to Woodstock, and, then, Van Morrison, Richie Havens, and Paul Butterfield. Charles Mingus and Jimi Hendrix spent some time here. Frank Zappa and the Mothers of Invention rented a house. Muddy Waters came. You wouldn't be surprised to see anybody walking down the street."

As editor of *Sing Out*, Happy Traum was the first journalist to interview Dylan following the motorcycle accident. "He was very communicative," he remembered. "I was trying to push him in the interview because we were at the height of the Vietnam War, and I was antiwar, but he wasn't willing to say anything politically revealing against the war. John Cohen [from traditional folk group the New Lost City Ramblers] turned out to be the main interviewer and he asked artistic and almost abstract questions. I kept trying to bring it back to the war and politics."

During the interview, Dylan shared his view of popular music. "Rock and roll is dance music," he said, "perhaps an extension of the blues forms. It is live music; nowadays they have these big speakers, and they play it so loud that it might seem live, but it has rhythm. I mean, if you are riding in a car, rock and roll [radio] stations playing, you can get into that rhythm for three minutes—and you lose three minutes . . . you do not have to think about anything. . . . It's just pleasant music."

Traum's friendship with Dylan extended to members of The Band, especially after his brother, Artie, and he signed with Grossman. "I remember [Manuel] being a very funny, very offbeat kind of guy," he said. "He had a slightly sarcastic sense of humor and always seemed to be chuckling about something, always coming up with some wry comment. I liked that about him. Obviously, he had a much darker side, but I didn't see much of it."

"[Danko] was thoroughly into music," he continued. "It was everything. He gave his complete heart and soul to it and there was a joy in his playing. Anytime that he was on a stage, with a bass or a guitar in his hands, he was having fun. [Hudson] could talk for hours about accordion reeds. He was all about the music, too. [Helm], the one I got to know best, wasn't particularly political, but he had a certain sensibility towards injustice, even in his later years, when he sang about a farmer who had to grow pot because he couldn't make it with the normal crops. That is powerful stuff—political on a very grassroots level, not what you would usually hear from northern intellectuals."

After following Robertson north, Hudson, Manuel, and Danko rented a house (for $125 a month) on one hundred acres of land that Danko found in nearby West Saugerties. Pink asbestos shutters marked the three-bedroom house as "Big Pink." With the three musicians settled into the house, work resumed on their music. Robertson (who continued to live with his wife in one of Grossman's cabins) proposed setting up a recording studio in the basement. "[I called] a friend of mine who knew about acoustics, recording, and microphones," he remembered, "and I said to him, 'Take a look at this place.' At the time, nobody was recording outside of a studio. Les Paul did it, but, for everybody else, if you were going to make a record, you [went to a studio] where they made records."

Robertson was caught off guard by his friend's assessment. "He said, 'This is a disaster, the worst situation,'" he recalled. "[He told me,] 'You have a cement floor, cinder block walls, and a big, metal furnace. Your music will sound so bad that you'll never want to record again.'"

With the house already rented, Robertson felt that "we had no choice, we had no flexibility."

"We cleaned out the basement," remembered Danko, "and Garth put together a couple of microphones and connected them to a little two-track reel-to-reel tape recorder—that was our studio. For ten months [March to December 1967], we all met down in the basement and played for two to three hours a day, six days a week. That was it, man."

They were not alone for long; Dylan had seen what the four musicians were doing. "I was thinking, 'We have to work on our music,'" said Robertson, "but he would come out every day. It became like a clubhouse. It was like the Dead End Kids.

"[Dylan] needed to make up some songs for the publishing company for other people to record," he continued, "and we owed it to him to do something. We were going to do another tour, but he broke his neck. We were still on the payroll. It was a way to do a gesture back. I said, 'Okay, we'll do these things and work on our stuff, too.'"

The informal setting lent the recordings a unique quality. "They're like field recordings," said Robertson; "they sound fantastic. There's something [enriching] about bringing the recording experience to your comfort zone, as opposed to going into somebody's studio with a huge clock on the wall and the guys from the union saying, 'It's dinner break.' You make your own atmosphere. There's something creative about this."

"That time really opened the door for us into the recording and songwriting world," explained Helm. "That's what the *Basement Tapes* were about—Bob's songwriting lessons for us. We would get together and Bob and Richard would swap lyrics on typewriter, and the rest of us would be hunting chords on little patterns and stuff. We wrote a lot of songs in that basement; it was incredible.

"We would record something, Garth would tape it, and we'd hear ourselves back," he continued. "When you first start that stuff, it's a hell of a hard lesson to take, 'cause you sound like hell; you just can't help it. We had to listen for a while in order to stop doin' that stuff that didn't sound so good. I've had [bassist] Duck Dunn tell me that being in the house band for Stax Records made him a much better player. . . . They'd cut something with Otis [Redding] or Sam & Dave, or whoever, listen to it back, and try and better that performance. Otherwise, you just work and sleep and work and do a song, and you're just producing all the time, so, in Woodstock, for the first time we could kind of sit back and take our medicine with it. After a while, we'd get it going and record it, then tear it up and start all over with it and re-record it. If you do that three or four times, you can finally shake the dust out of 'em, if it's got any kind of a hook or little thing that calls on you at all—that's the only way we've been able to come up to what I would call record quality."

Inspiration permeated through the entire house. "Up in the living room, there were four tables," recalled Robertson, "with two typewriters with paper ready to go. On the other tables there were checkerboards, and there was this strange competition going on. People would get so frustrated that they would go to the typewriters and type something. Bob came up with some wild things—like 'bottle of bread.' He'd say, 'That's how I feel.'"

For Robertson, the setup was ideal. "It was the first time in my life," he said, "where I thought, 'I can write and build what I'm looking for.' The feeling of the music was not as neurotic as it had been when I was living in the city. It was the first time I'd ever really lived in the country and liked it."

The scenic environment, and influence of Dylan, did wonders for Robertson's songwriting. "It's about incorporating all these musical impressions that come before your eyes," he explained, "just because you're influenced by those things. We had been through the musical revolution with Bob and come through the storm alive. Now, we were holed up in a basement, in the mountains, in upstate New York, looking at where we were, where we came from, what we brought with us, and finding out through songwriting."

With the completion of *Eat the Document* in early 1968 and Dylan's continued retreat from live performance, the ex-Hawks turned back to their own music, signing a management contract with Grossman, who began shopping their demo. A potential deal with Warner Brothers fell through, but the manager was met with an enthusiastic reception at Capitol.

The West Coast's first record label, Capitol had grown considerably since its founding in 1942 by songwriter Johnny Mercer, with financial backing from songwriter/filmmaker Buddy DeSylva and record store owner Glenn Wallichs. Within a year after being acquired by London-based Electric and Musical Instruments Ltd. (EMI) in 1955, it had built a state-of-the-art studio (to match EMI's Abbey Road Studios) at the intersection of Hollywood Boulevard and Vine Street in Los Angeles. Capitalizing on the studio's pristine sound (and the echo chamber below the parking lot), the Kingston Trio used the studio to transform folk songs into chart-topping country charts, while Merle Haggard and Buck Owens used it to craft country music's Bakersfield sound.

Although its roster included Gene Vincent and the Bluecaps (whose debut single "Be Bop a Lula" was a top-five hit in June 1956) and The Jodimars, consisting of ex-members of Bill Haley and the Comets, Capitol resisted rock and roll until signing the Beach Boys in 1962. Possessing first right of refusal of EMI artists, they passed on The Beatles (who were signed to EMI's sister label, Parlophone) before reluctantly agreeing to release their records in late November 1963, and they subsequently passed on other British Invasion bands including the Dave Clark 5, Gerry and the Pacemakers, The Hollies, and Manfred Mann.

The Brooklyn-born, and Levittown, Long Island–raised son of a police officer, Arthur Lawrence "Artie" Kornfeld was brought in to direct Capitol's rock music division in 1966. He had not yet reached his twenty-fourth birthday. Playing guitar from the age of fourteen, he had acquired a booking agent (GAC) and was recording for Broadway Sound by sixteen. As a songwriter, he had worked in New York's Brill Building, writing or cowriting (with Carole King and Gerry Goffin, Burt Bacharach and Hal David, Ellie Greenwich and Jeff Barry, and Barry Mann and Cynthia Weil) more than two hundred demoed tunes.

Meeting Jan Barry at an Alan Freed Concert in 1963, Kornfeld had gone on to cowrite "Drag Strip City," "Hot Sticker," and the tragically prophetic "Dead Man's Curve" (written with Berry and the Beach Boys' Brian Wilson) for Jan and Dean. As a songwriter for Screen Gems in Hollywood, he had met Steve Duboff, a Miami-born singer, songwriter, and producer, with whom he would write more than five-dozen songs. "Follow Me, I'm the Pied Piper" became an international hit for British pop singer Crispian St. Peters. As a folk-pop duo (the Changing Times), Kornfeld and Duboff appeared as the opening act of Sonny & Cher's first national tour in 1964.

Kornfeld's ascent continued as he produced and cowrote songs such as "The Rain, the Park, and Other Things" for Rhode Island–based family group The Cowsills. He made such a favorable impression that Capitol president Alan Livingston hired him as the label's first vice president and director of rock music. He would remain in the position until shortly before the release of The Band's second album, when he turned his focus to coproducing the Woodstock Music and Art Festival with Michael Lang, John Roberts, and Joel Rosenman.

After Capitol agreed to sign them to a ten-albums-in-ten-years contract, the ex-Hawks tracked Helm down in Memphis and asked him to return. "I was certainly lonesome for the band," he remembered. "I guess I believed that, at some point, we would get back together. I didn't figure that they would give up their dreams just to be Bob's backup band. Nor did I have any false ideas about becoming a troubadour and thumbing my way through life with a set of drums strapped to my back."

Arriving in Woodstock, Helm was encouraged by how far Dylan and his band mates had grown since he had left. "I could tell that hanging out with the boys had helped Bob to find a connection with things we were interested in," he said, "blues, rockabilly, and R&B. The boys had also discovered how to write songs—Bob Dylan had opened it up for them."

Among the more than 150 songs that Dylan and the future Band would record in Big Pink's basement (with or without Helm) were tunes by Johnny Cash, the Carter Family, Hank Williams, Eric von Schmidt, and Elmore James and traditional folksongs. Tongue-in-jowl ditties ("See You Later, Allen Ginsberg," "Give Me Another Bourbon Street Please," "Teenage Prayer") balanced with masterfully penned ballads. Several songs—"Million Dollar Bash," "Lo and Behold," and "Please Mrs. Henry"—were to be included on an album to satisfy the singer-songwriter's contract with Columbia Records and allow him to sign a long-term deal with MGM, a plan that failed to materialize.

It would take another nine years before the tracks recorded by Dylan and the ex-Hawks became commercially available on the 1975 double-album *The Basement Tapes*, but the songs spread quickly. Peter, Paul, and Mary covered "Too Much of Nothing." Manfred Mann recorded "Quinn the Eskimo." The Byrds recorded "You Ain't Goin' Nowhere," and the Dylan-and-Danko-penned "This Wheels of Fire." The Band would include their version of "This Wheel's on Fire," along with Dylan's "I Shall Be Released" and Dylan and Manuel's "Tears of Rage," on *Music from Big Pink*. "Down in the Flood" would be redone live for *Rock of Ages*. Rerecorded during sessions for *Music from Big Pink*, The Band's rendition of "Bessie Smith," Dylan's tribute to the Empress of the Blues, would be included as a bonus track on the remastered CD edition of *Cahoots* in 1995. Happy and Artie Traum would include their version on their debut duo album.

As word leaked out about the basement recordings, public curiosity intensified. In a June 1968 cover story about the tapes, *Rolling Stone* called it "the missing Bob Dylan album." Thirteen months later, Los Angeles–based bootleg record label Trademark of Quality released *The Great White Wonder*. The first notable rock bootleg, it introduced seven tunes recorded in the basement of Big Pink, along with tracks that Dylan had recorded in a Minnesota hotel room in 1961, studio outtakes, and his summer 1969 *Johnny Cash Show* performance of "Living the Blues," an original tune that would resurface on *Self Portrait*. "What we were doing seemed so 'inside,'" Robertson told *Rolling Stone* in 1998. "We would do these songs and fall on the floor laughing, or we would say, 'Boy, this sounds like it could turn into something.' There were even things that were embarrassing. It was private, and when they got out in the beginning, everybody was uptight. It was like somebody got your diary."

Additional bootlegs with tunes from the sessions, including a two-disc set, *Blind Boy Grunt and the Hawks*, and two five-CD collections, *A*

Tree with Roots and *The Genuine Basement Tapes*, continued to circulate. "It looks like they got it all," said Garth Hudson in the early 1990s.

Officially released by Columbia in 1975, *The Basement Tapes* were deceptive, according to British musicologist Clifton Heylin, author of *Bob Dylan: The Recording Sessions, 1960–1994*. Of the eight songs featuring The Band, two were demos recorded in New York in September 1967; two tracks were recorded at Shangri-La in Malibu, California, in 1975; and two were piano demos (recorded at Big Pink) with drums and guitar added in 1975. Three tunes composed by Manuel—"You Say You Love Me," "Ferdinand the Imposter," and "Beautiful Thing"—were missing from the double-album, according to Heylin, "possibly because they highlighted how Manuel, not Robertson, was the first to pen original Band material."

The break from touring provided Dylan with a respite from rock-and-roll stardom, a retreat from the hostile reaction to his electric music, and an opportunity to reinvent his musical direction. Embracing a softer country-rock sound with *John Wesley Harding* (1968), *Nashville Skyline* (1969), and *New Morning* (1971), he would set the stage for his chart-topping masterpiece, *Blood on the Tracks* (1975).

Returning to the stage, accompanied by The Band, for the first time in two years on January 20, 1968, Dylan performed "I Ain't Got No Home," "Dear Mrs. Roosevelt," and "The Grand Coulee Dam" at a memorial concert at Carnegie Hall for his one-time role model, Woody Guthrie. "I don't think Pete Seeger was too thrilled to see us at first," said Helm, "but the audience was warm, and our evening show brought down the house. Bob tore it up!"

It would be Dylan and the former Hawks' last appearance together until the Isle of Wight, more than a year and half later.

FOUR
The Band

Dylan's former backup band had not yet taken a name when *Music from Big Pink* debuted on July 1, 1968. They had thought of calling themselves The Crackers, but learning that some people considered it to be an offensive slur, on the level of "hillbilly," executives at Capitol had nixed it.

With the label insisting that they take a name, the group finally settled on The Band. "When we were working with [Dylan], people just called us 'the band,'" Robertson told *Rolling Stone*. "When we were living in Woodstock, we'd go to the bakery and people would say, 'Oh, that's one of the guys in the band.' We got used to it, and we wanted to represent ourselves as five [musicians] who did something very, very unique and special in their own way, and that is what would make up a real definitive band. This was not a singer, a guitar, and some other guys—this was really five people and everybody played a very, very important part."

Everyone but Robertson was proficient on a variety of instruments. Danko played bass guitar, upright bass, fiddle, and trombone; Helm played drums, mandolin, and guitar; and Manuel played piano, drums (when Helm was otherwise occupied), and baritone saxophone. Hudson split his time between keyboards, accordion, and soprano and tenor saxophones. Someone might sing lead on a song and background harmonies on the next. "We worked so hard on that music," said Helm, "that no matter what the song credits say—who supposedly wrote what—you'd have to call it a full-bore effort by the group to show what we were all about."

"We liked stuff that had a timeless quality to it," explained Robertson. "We gathered all these pieces of music and pulled them together, not talking about it. It was a natural procedure and the depth that we were looking for, and the type of storytelling. All these things had an opportunity to be seasoned in a way that, when we were writing and working on music, you could feel that it had years and years of being in a wine keg."

Robertson's experiences with Dylan further strengthened his songwriting. "[Dylan showed me] how to tell a story in a short form without necessarily having to go from point A to point B," he remembered, "[and] he broke down a whole lot of the tradition of songwriting right before my very eyes. With all the rules broken, [I] could go ahead and tell the truth without having to do some kind of fancy dance, [but] I never thought that I was writing poetry; I was writing songs."

Robertson avoided political commentary in his songs. "We're musicians," he told John Poppy of *Look* in August 1970; "we don't know about American politics. Besides, who can write songs about all this garbage that's happening now—wars and revolution and killing—I can't—words for that stuff don't work right in songs."

The Band's precise arrangements, soulful vocals, and ultra-tight musicianship contrasted with the heavily electric, psychedelic sounds dominating the hit parade. "The trend at the time was the acid rock phase," remembered Helm. "That was the new trend, the new fad that was going on, and tune in, turn on, and drop out—hate your mom and dad, don't trust anyone over thirty, and a bunch of other stuff that didn't make a lot of sense. We steered clear of all that and tried to keep it on musical terms. We got away with it, pretty much, for the most part, anyway."

"The Band was rebelling against the rebellion," Robertson reminded Nashville-based musician/producer/music journalist Paul Burch. "The rebellion had gotten too trendy. It was our choice to get off the bandwagon—no pun intended."

"We didn't like psychedelic things," Robertson told Edward Kiersch. "I wasn't interested in wearing paisley pants. When we played with Bob Dylan, we wore jackets and ties. He hated it [and he] kept telling us, 'You've got to do something with your clothes'."

The Band's songs sparkled with harmonies rarely heard in pop music. "[Manuel] had an otherworldly voice, ethereal, and legitimately spooky in the best possible way," said Elton John's songwriting partner, Bernie Taupin. "Rick Danko, with whom I spent some questionably manic moments, and cerebral hours, and whom I loved dearly, was like an unfettered young buck, all tremulous beauty and with poignant longing. . . . Then there was Levon: a voice birthed from the land from which he sprung. Rich as Arkansas soil and raw as a plug of tobacco, gnarly as knotted pine and so expressive, it seemed like he was chewing on the words before they left his mouth."

"I didn't like [the kind of] singing when everybody came in perfectly together," Robertson explained. "I thought that was a bad rule; it didn't seem real to me.

"[I thought of when I was] in school, singing a song," he continued, "and somebody would come in a little early or a little late. I always thought that it stood out and made something nice happen against the music—a little call-and-response feeling, almost. It wasn't like an orchestra playing together—these were human voices—and when they wove in and out of each other—that's what was the most interesting to me."

"[They were] somewhere between real harmonies," said Danko, "and, because of our lack of education in music, things that sounded interesting, or the only [pitch] that a person could hit. It was sometimes the limitation of the instrument that provided the originality."

"We discovered a whole new vocal thing that we weren't aware that we had," explained Manuel to Nora Ephron and Susan Edmiston. "I remember listening to playbacks after sessions and thinking, 'I really like this stuff and I don't have anything to compare it to.'"

Robertson sang lead on the oddly syncopated "To Kingdom Come," the first of three Band songs spotlighting his vocals. "Robbie was always one of my favorite singers," said Danko, "but he was always shy of the microphone, might have been an element of stage fright there. He would sing the parts for us and we would reproduce them."

"I thought the guys were great singers," Robertson explained, "and [having them sing] gave me an opportunity to stand outside of it a little bit, and be able to look at the cast of characters, like a director should be looking at these things, and really helping to shape it."

Music from Big Pink represented a sharp diversion from the ex-Hawks' previous work. "[It was about] telling a story and getting across what I was trying to write about in a song," said Robertson. "It had nothing to do with what we had done as kids with Ronnie Hawkins and the Hawks, nothing to do with what we did as [Levon and the Hawks], nothing to do with what we did with Dylan. These were precise stories and emotional experiences. Discovering the soul of the music was what was important, getting a song across with as much emotion as we could—that was the objective, not flailing away, and blasting the walls down. That had nothing to do with it any longer."

"We wanted *Music from Big Pink* to sound like nothing anyone else was doing," agreed Helm. "This was our music, honed in isolation from the radio and contemporary trends, liberated from the world of bars and the climate of the Dylan tours."

"I'm not a good enough musician to understand all that stuff," said Hawkins when a *Rolling Stone* writer asked about *Music from Big Pink*. "I do understand the lyrics, though, and better than most people. . . . They're writing about true things, the things that happened to us all along the way."

Emphasizing ensemble playing over soloing, Robertson explored a more textural approach to the guitar. "By the time we made our first record, it seemed like everyone knew [how to bend strings]," he explained. "I did it like mad in the beginning, with Ronnie Hawkins, and I did it with The Hawks, and I did it with Bob Dylan, but it was no longer exciting to me. I wanted to do things that were so tasteful and discreet and subtle, like Curtis Mayfield and Steve Cropper."

"[Robertson] plays guitar like a songwriter," said Eric Clapton. "He'll put together in his head, and then through his fingers, the series of phrases and melodic lines that make sense to him, and make sense to you."

"There are guitarists who could play ten thousand notes a second," pointed out George Harrison, "but it doesn't mean anything. Robbie was the type of guitarist who was more concerned with the overall song and structure than with his own personal prowess."

Although he did not appear on the album, The Band commissioned Dylan to paint the front cover of *Music from Big Pink*. The singer-songwriter's primitive watercolor included an elephant, a sitar player balancing a cup on his head, a Native American upright bass player, a guitarist in a yellow sweater, and a pianist playing the keys, from behind a piano, boosted up by an unidentifiable, seated man. The contemporary art Gagosian Gallery offered the painting (still owned by Dylan) for sale in 2010 at a price of eighteen million dollars. "The art world is crazy and magical at the same time," said Robertson.

Music from Big Pink's centerfold featured Elliot Landry's black-and-white photograph of The Band in the wooded grounds of Big Pink, and a larger color photograph taken at Terry Danko's farm near Simcoe, with The Band and members of their extended families (Helm's parents, unable to make the shoot, were included in a separate photograph). At a time when the generation gap was at its widest, this constituted a bold move. "There was a very strong thing going on about how, if you were fucked up, it was because it was somebody else's fault," said Robertson to Joshua Baer of *Musician* in May 1982. "It was your mother, or your father, or the last generation. It got obnoxious. We never had that relationship with our parents. . . . We would talk about our parents—we missed them and we would laugh about the funny things they did. We took the picture with all of our mothers and fathers as a nice gesture—it [may have] had something to do with the kind of songs [on *Music from Big Pink*], I do not know. Not very much of it was consciously clever or rebellious or against the grain; it was just where we were at."

Robertson's wife, Dominique, wrote the brief liner notes: "Big Pink—a pink house seated in the sun of Overlook Mountain in West Saugerties, New York. Big Pink bore this music and these songs along the way. It's the first witness of this album that's been thought and composed right there inside its walls."

Recorded at CBS Studio (Studio E) and A&R Recorders (Studio A) in New York, and Goldstar Studios (Studio B) and the Capitol Studios in Los Angeles, *Music from Big Pink* marked The Band's first collaboration with producer John Simon. The Norwalk, Connecticut–born son of a country doctor and amateur violinist, Simon had studied violin and piano as a youngster, written songs by the age of ten, and spent his teenage years leading a rock band. As a music student at Princeton University, he had penned two musicals and written music for school productions. Columbia Records recruited him immediately after his graduation. "I had two job offers," he remembered on his website; "one was to write Anacin commercials for the Ted Bates Advertising Agency and the other one was to be a trainee for Columbia Records (at a salary of eight-five dollars a week)."

After working on box-set documentaries about the Irish Rebellion, doctors, drugs, diseases, and the Senator Joseph McCarthy hearings as a junior producer under Columbia's president, Goddard Lieberson, Simon produced albums by jazz flutist Charles Lloyd, polka accordionist Frankie Yankovic (Weird Al Yankovic's father), and communication theorist Marshall McLuhan. His first success as a producer came with a 1966 cover of the Paul Simon–composed "Red Rubber Ball" by the Easton, Pennsylvania–based quintet The Cyrkle, which rose to the runner-up slot on the pop charts. He would go on to produce Simon and Garfunkel's *Bookends* and Leonard Cohen's debut, *Songs of Leonard Cohen*.

Working with artists whose careers had intersected with Dylan, Simon produced Al Kooper's experimental jazz-rock album with Blood, Sweat, and Tears, *Child Is Father to the Man*, in 1968 and Mike Bloomfield, Barry Goldberg, and Buddy Miles's jazz-blues-fusion group the Electric Flag's debut album the following year. At Kooper's suggestion, he resigned from Columbia and began to freelance as a producer.

Simon's path to The Band began when Ed Kleban, lyricist of *A Chorus Line*, introduced him to Peter Yarrow at the Monterey Pop Festival in 1967. Yarrow, who had heard the album that he had produced for Marshall McLuhan, invited him to work with him. Simon had little idea of what was to come. During his first visit to Woodstock, he recalled, "[Yarrow] stuck me and Howard Alk in this house with two movieolas (old editing machine) and reels and reels of film to make a movie [*You Are What You Eat*]."

Celebrating Alk's birthday and Halloween on October 31, 1967, Simon met the musicians who would become The Band. "There was this godawful sound coming from outside," he remembered, "and there were the guys from The Band—not Levon because he wasn't back on the scene yet—in funny costumes, playing instruments that they really couldn't play, serenading Howard for his birthday."

Simon had previously heard The Band's music on a tape they had recorded as a joke—*Even if it's a Pig—Part Two*. "It had Garth singing," he remembered. "It was really a send up, you know."

In addition to tracks by Paul Butterfield, the Electric Flag, and John Herald, the Simon-produced soundtrack of *You Are What You Eat* included four songs featuring Dylan and the ex-Hawks with Tiny Tim, a New York–born ukulele player, falsetto singer, music historian, and one-man house band at Steve Paul's Greenwich Village discotheque, The Scene. Dylan had invited the former Herbert Khaury to Woodstock. "[They] split hamburgers and French fries," said Tiny Tim biographer Justin Martell, "when they were both struggling in Greenwich Village in the early sixties."

Introduced to Grossman by Alk, Simon began working with artists under his management. He produced albums for Gordon Lightfoot (*Did She Mention My Name*) and Janis Joplin and Big Brother and the Holding Company (*Cheap Thrills*).

Simon slowly acclimated to The Band's music. " I was used to hearing songs pretty quickly," he said, "but Robbie made me hang around for a long time just to absorb the Woodstock vibe, which was a lot slower than the New York City vibe. I was up there for days before I heard anything. Then I went to the Big Pink basement, which was a tiny little room, maybe twelve feet by twelve feet. Garth had a little primitive reel-to-reel machine set up, and they played me some things they had done on the machine and some things live. I liked it, so I worked with them a little bit. I helped them to rearrange things like 'Tears of Rage' and 'Chest Fever.' Then Albert got some seed money from Capitol to do a session in the city."

In addition to his production expertise, Simon brought polished instrumental skill. "On the first album, I played piano on 'Caledonia Mission,'" he said, "and on the second album, I played electric piano on 'King Harvest (Has Surely Come).' On both of those albums, I played all of the baritone horn parts. 'Tears of Rage' was Garth on soprano sax and me on baritone horn. That became sort of the nucleus of The Band's horn sound. I also played tuba on 'Rag Mama Rag,' the first time I ever played tuba."

Working on *Music from Big Pink* and *The Band*, Simon approached overdubbing differently than most other rock producers. "We tried to get as many of the effects onto the tape as we could," he explained, "as opposed to adding them afterwards. [We thought that] if we made a commitment, and put the effects on the track, we would be stuck with that and everything else would conform to that. We would be painting a much fuller picture as we went along."

"We tried to get everything the first time through," said Helm. "We didn't know if lightning would strike twice in the same place. . . . It made the song more of a song, with everybody putting everything into it and singing and playing. It was more like making music than making tracks."

"Everybody played something that was meaningful and meshed," said Simon. "There were hardly any solos, and nothing was gratuitous. We recorded everything live on two tracks. The horns—Garth on soprano, me on baritone—went on the third track, and the fourth was saved for vocals and tambourine."

Manuel's lead vocals shone on his collaboration with Dylan ("Tears of Rage"), Dylan's "I Shall Be Released," Robertson's "Caledonia Mission," and three original tunes—"In a Station," "Lonesome Suzie," and "We Can Talk." "'In a Station' is about Overlook Mountain," Helm explained, "and the relative peace we were all feeling after those long years living on the road. 'Lonesome Suzie' was like a miniature portrait that Richard sang in his squeezed-out falsetto. It was a quiet song that told a story and was typical of Richard's general philosophy, which was to be kind to people. 'We Can Talk' is a funny song that really captured the way we spoke to one another, lots of outrageous rhymes and corny puns. Richard just got up one morning—or afternoon—sat down on the piano, and started playing this gospel music that became this song with its famous line, 'I'd rather be burned up in Canada, than freeze down in the South.'"

"Tears of Rage" combined a melody by Manuel with lyrics by Dylan. "I had a couple of musical movements that seemed to fit," the pianist remembered, "so I just elaborated a little. I wasn't sure what the lyrics meant, but I couldn't run upstairs and say, 'What's this mean, Bob?'"

In addition to recording three different versions with Dylan, The Band re-recorded "Tears of Rage" (sans Dylan) as the opening track of *Music from Big Pink*. At a time when the generation gap was at its widest, its parent–daughter theme and somber arrangement stood out. "[It] was just another way of rebelling against the rebellion," said Helm. "We were deliberately going against the grain. Few artists had ever opened an album with a slow song, so we had to. At the zenith of the psychedelic era with its flaming guitars and endless solos and elongated jams, we weren't about to make that kind of album."

Another song appearing on both *The Basement Tapes* and *Music from Big Pink*, "This Wheel's on Fire" by Dylan and Danko, would inspire the title of Helm's 1993 autobiography. "I was teaching myself to play piano," said Danko, "and some music I'd written on the piano the day before just seemed to fit with Bob's lyrics. I worked on the phrasing, and the melody, and then Bob and I wrote the chorus together."

"Garth got some distinctive sounds [on "This Wheel's on Fire"]," said Helm, "by running a telegraph key through a Roxochord toy organ. He just hit that key when he wanted that sound."

The groove-based "Chest Fever" was a reaction to the intellectual imagery of songs like "The Weight." "[I started thinking about] where we were going with all of these ideas and abstractions and all of the mythology," Robertson explained. "This music, for us, started as something that felt good and sounded good. . . . 'Chest Fever' doesn't make particularly any kind of sense in the lyrics, in the music, in the arrangement, in anything."

"'Chest Fever' had improvised lyrics that Robbie put together for the rehearsals," recalled Helm, "and [he] never got around to rewriting

[them]. The song came kinda late in the whole process and got recorded before it was finished."

An extended organ solo (dubbed "The Genetic Method" on *Rock of Ages*) introduced "Chest Fever" during live performances. "Garth put together an introduction from J. S. Bach's 'Toccata and Fugue in D Minor,'" said Helm, "with that Lowrey organ and a good solo in the middle."

"I Shall Be Released," the closing tune on *Music from Big Pink*, was, according to Helm, "a prisoner's lament that [Dylan] had sung on the basement tapes and Richard sings in his falsetto voice. Richard cut another version in his regular voice that was just as good. The drum sound was my playing the snares of an upside-down drum with my fingers. The windlike sound is Garth playing organ with one hand and manipulating the stops with the other."

Added at the last minute, "The Weight" provided *Music from Big Pink* with its most successful song. Charting at number sixty-three (US), thirty-five (Canada), and twenty-one (UK), *Rolling Stone* listed it at number forty-one on its list of the 500 greatest songs of all time. The Rock and Roll Hall of Fame declared it "one of the five hundred songs that shaped rock and roll." PBS called it "a masterpiece of Biblical allusions, enigmatic lines, and iconic characters." "It was one of the things that I had on the back burner," recalled Robertson. "In case we got stuck on something, I could always spring this one out. When we recorded it, and listened to it, we thought, 'Whoa, this works.' It was a song that we did not try any other way—we didn't try it slower or faster, different introduction, a shuffle instead of eighth notes, or any of those things. We just played it that way and it came so naturally. That was always a good sign."

Surrealistic films by Spanish-born (and Mexico-exiled) filmmaker Luis Buñuel, especially *Nazarin* (1959) and *Viridiana* (1961), provided inspiration. "[Buñuel] did so many films on the impossibility of sainthood," explained Robertson, "[with] people trying to be good and [finding that] it's impossible. Buñuel made films that had religious connotations to them, but it wasn't necessarily a religious meaning. In 'The Weight,' someone says, 'Listen, would you do me this favor—when you get there, will you say hello to somebody or will you give somebody this, or pick up one of these for me?' This is what it is all about—this guy goes [to Nazareth] and one thing leads to another and it's like, 'Holy shit, what's this turned into? I've only come here to say hello to somebody and I've got myself in this incredible predicament.'"

The opening line places the song's narrator/traveler in the Lehigh Valley, Pennsylvania–city of Nazareth, where guitar manufacturer C. F. Martin and Sons is located. "I wanted to take people on a journey," Robertson told *American Songwriter* in 2011, "to some place they hadn't been before. I stopped and looked into the sound hole of my guitar, and it being a

Martin, the first thing I saw was the word 'Nazareth.' It was one of those lucky accidents that just seemed absolutely perfect."

As the song unfolded, the narrator/traveler encountered a variety of unique characters based on real people. "Luke was Jimmy Ray Paulman," said Helm. "Young Anna Lee was Anna Lee Williams from Turkey Scratch. Crazy Chester was a guy we all knew from Fayetteville who came into town on Saturdays wearing a full set of cap guns on his hips and kinda walked around town to help keep the peace. He was like Hopalong Cassidy and he was a friend of The Hawks. Ronnie would always check with Crazy Chester to make sure there wasn't any trouble around town, and Chester would reassure him that everything was peaceable and not to worry, because he was on the case. Two big cap guns he wore, plus a toupee! There were also 'Carmen and the Devil,' 'Miss Moses,' and 'Fanny,' a name that just seemed to fit the picture (I believe she looked a lot like Caldonia). We recorded the song maybe four times. We weren't quite sure that it was going to be on the album, but people really liked it. Rick, Richard, and I switched off on the verses and we all sang the chorus—'Put the load right on me!'"

A woman in Orillia, Ontario, claiming to be Chester's granddaughter told a reporter that Danko had worked as a youngster on a tobacco farm owned by her grandfather, who had a dog named Jack and a horse named Fanny. "'The Weight' has been painting pictures for me for nearly twenty-five years now," said Peter Viney in 1994. "It's an intensely visual song, and my pictures aren't of anywhere in Pennsylvania. My Nazareth is a dusty western town sometime in the late nineteenth century—neighboring towns might be Jerusalem or Babylon . . . or Jericho. Carmen and the devil are strutting their stuff, in red silk dresses fringed with black cat fur, along a wooden sidewalk. Chester is the town character straight out of the CBS-TV series *Gunsmoke*, which was set in Dodge City in the 1880s. Carmen might be Miss Kitty, who owned the Long Branch Saloon—a tart with a heart. Old Luke is another town character whose rockin' chair ain't goin' nowhere as he puffs his pipe waiting on judgment Day. The Cannonball steams into the station, a great cow-catcher across the front—pure Americana."

Robertson took full credit for writing "The Weight," but Helm saw things differently. The rift would lead to the two musicians not speaking for more than three decades. "Everyone [in The Band] got performance royalties," explained Band biographer Barney Hoskyns in Jacob Hatley's biopic about Levon Helm, *Ain't in It for My Health*, "but only [Robertson] got additional publishing royalties as the primary songwriter of most of the songs. [Helm's] beef with Robertson might be, 'You took what I am and made songs out of that, and, then, you made all the money from those songs.'"

"I'm hesitant to villainize either one of them," said Larry Campbell, the New York–born multi-instrumentalist, producer, and musical director of Helm's post-2004 band, to *American Songwriter*, "because I don't have the facts. What I can tell you is, writing with Levon, my experience was he wasn't gonna do any labor where writing a song was concerned . . . when it came down to constructing the song, that was my job."

The cowriter, with Helm, of several songs, including "Growing Trade" from *Electric Dirt*, Campbell had a unique perspective of the conflict. "When I finished the rough draft [of "Growing Trade"]," he recalled, "we sat and discussed the subject matter, and I went back and completely rewrote the song. His input made it better, so I had to make him a cowriter. Is this what happened with him and Robbie? He seems to think so. He seems to think that his input was ignored in a lot of that stuff."

"'The Weight' is just like 'Life Is a Carnival,' or 'The W.S. Walcott Medicine Show' and 'Ophelia' and all the rest of 'em," claimed Helm. "It's a collaborative effort. Now you could say that Robertson was sixty percent responsible for the lyric, that Richard was twenty percent and maybe Rick got another twenty, and I got five or ten, then you talk about the music. You could give Garth chord credits, but the people who handle that stuff don't work for Garth, or Richard or me. They work for Robbie and Albert."

"There are two ways that a musician makes money from an album," said Delray Beach, Florida-based singer-songwriter, Rod MacDonald. "Everyone gets performing royalties, but only the songwriter gets songwriting royalties, as well. When a record label recoups its advance for recording the album, they take it out of the performing royalties. They don't touch the songwriting royalties."

"Robbie was fair, based on an old system," explained John Simon. "The old system of songwriting credits was very distinct—there were people who wrote songs and people who performed songs—and they were different people. Frank Sinatra, [who] on very few occasions wrote a song, was a singer. Sammy Cahn and Johnny Mercer were writers and not performers, like George and Ira Gershwin and Richard Rogers and Lorenz Hart. That's the system under which Robbie determined he would be songwriter of those songs. He wrote the lyrics, figured out the chords to the song, and dictated the melody and chords to the other players."

"I wrote songs before I ever met Levon," Robertson pointed out to Scott Spencer of *Rolling Stone*, "and I worked harder than anybody else. Somebody has to lead the charge; somebody has to draw the map. The guys were responsible for the arrangements, but that's what being a band is, that's your fucking job."

"I begged Levon to write songs or help me to write songs," he told Greg Kot of the *Chicago Tribune*. "I always encouraged everybody to write, [but] you can't make somebody do what they don't want to do, or can't do, and he's not a songwriter."

The influence of "The Weight" spread. Little Feat, the Allman Brothers Band, the Grateful Dead, New Riders of the Purple Sage, Spooky Tooth, John Denver, Old Crow Medicine Show, Al Kooper and Mike Bloomfield's Super Session, Bob Weir's Ratdog, Waylon Jennings, Dionne Warwick, Joe Cocker, Michelle Shocked, Joan Osborne, the Black Crowes, Old Crow Medicine Show, and Trampled by Turtles are only some to cover it. Diana Ross and the Supremes recorded it with The Temptations. Aretha Franklin's interpretation (with Duane Allman on guitar and King Curtis on saxophone) broke into pop's top twenty (reaching number three on the R&B charts). Jackie DeShannon released a version after initially resisting pressure from EMI-owned Liberty Records to record it. "I absolutely said, 'No way am I going to do it; it's The Band's record,'" recalled the Kentucky-born pop singer, "but the label kept calling me. Finally, I said, 'If you can get confirmation from The Band that they're not putting it out as a single, and I can do it with their permission, then, okay.' I recorded it, the record was going up the charts, and, all of a sudden, here comes The Band's single, then Aretha Franklin's version comes out. I was at a radio station, talking to the program director, and there were two other people promoting the same record outside the door."

The Band turned down an offer to provide its complete soundtrack, but Peter Fonda, Dennis Hopper, and Terry Southern used "The Weight" in a pivotal scene of their 1969 biker/counterculture movie *Easy Rider*. On the soundtrack album, a cover version by Los Angeles–based rockers The Smith replaced The Band's recording.

As part of the *Last Waltz Suite*, seven years later, The Band would join with the Staple Singers on an exceptionally soulful version of "The Weight." A few days after the "Last Waltz Concert," they would jointly record the studio version included on the soundtrack album. The popular gospel/R&B group (featuring guitarist/singer Roebuck "Pops" Staples and his daughters, Cleotha, Pervis, Yvonne, and Mavis) had been the first to cover the tune.

R&B singer, songwriter, and guitarist Curtis Mayfield inspired the guitar riffs that Robertson used at the start of "The Weight." "I got the introduction from [Mayfield's] attitude," he said. "That's all it is—an attitude. It's not necessarily what you're playing, but what mood you're playing."

Bruce Springsteen and the E Street Band and the Black Keys (with John Fogerty) performed "The Weight" during the final weeks of Helm's life. An all-star group, led by Elton John (who had recorded a tribute to Helm, "Levon," with lyrics by Bernie Taupin, in 1971), performed a rousing version during the Grammy Awards ceremonies in February 2013. "[It was] a gigantic group hug," said Dan Hyman of *Rolling Stone*. "[Elton John] played piano, while the other featured performers traded off on vocal duties. Zac Brown and Marcus Mumford [of Mumford and Sons] each chipped in with one verse apiece. . . . The two female performers stole the spotlight. [The Alabama Shakes' Brittany] Howard spiced up her verse with grizzly, rough-and-tumble charm and [Mavis] Staples, acting far younger than her seventy-three years, howled into the mic—long after the song's final note rang out."

A remixed CD version of *Music from Big Pink*, released in 2000, included seven previously unreleased tunes and alternate takes of "Lonesome Suzie" and "Tears of Rage." There were two cover tunes—"Key to the Highway" by Arkansas-born folk-blues performer Big Bill Broonzy and Charles Segar, and "If I Lose" by the Stanley Brothers. Robertson and Manuel's "Katie's Been Gone" was, according to Greil Marcus, "the kind of love song only Richard Manuel could pull off."

Three songs—"Long Distance Operator" by Dylan, "Yazoo Street Scandal" by Robertson, and "Orange Juice Blues (Blues for Breakfast)" by Manuel—had originally been recorded in the basement of Big Pink. Credited to Robertson and sung by Danko, "Ferdinand the Imposter" paid homage to Ferdinand Waldo Demara Jr., the Lawrence, Massachusetts–born subject of Robert Crichton's 1961 film *The Great Imposter* (adapted from his 1959 book of the same name), featuring Tony Curtis in the title role.

Although it sold only a quarter of a million copies, *Music from Big Pink* inspired musicians around the globe. "It gave us a buzz," said George Harrison. "We played it over and over again."

For Eric Clapton (then on tour with jam-intensive, blues-rock trio Cream), the masterful musicianship that he heard on a prerelease bootleg tape of *Music from Big Pink* was revelatory. "It stopped me in my tracks," he remembered in *Clapton: The Autobiography*, "and it also highlighted all the problems I thought [Cream] had. Here was a band that was really doing it right, incorporating influences from country music, blues, jazz, and rock, and writing great songs. I couldn't help but compare them to us (which was stupid and futile), but I was frantically looking for a yardstick, and here it was—the Woodstock sound—a kind of revolutionary revisionism, a radical return to popular music's storytelling roots, with songs of farmers and soldiers, quiet nights, and good women."

Inducting The Band into the Rock and Roll Hall of Fame in 1994, Eric Clapton confessed that *Music from Big Pink* "became my drug. At the end of a gig, [my band mates in Cream] Jack [Bruce] and Ginger [Baker] would go off and I would put the tape on and go into this other world. . . . [The members of The Band] were white, but they derived all they could from black music and combined it to make a beautiful hybrid. For me, it was serious and mature. It told stories and it had beautiful harmonies, fantastic singing, and beautiful musicianship."

Music from Big Pink made such an impact that Clapton traveled to Woodstock to meet The Band. "I went there to ask if I could join," he confessed in his induction speech, "but I didn't have the guts to say it."

Listening to Clapton's admission on television, Robertson (who missed the ceremonies) responded to *Rolling Stone*, "I had never heard that before. [Later, I asked Clapton,] 'Were you insinuating that you thought we needed two guitar players or coming to take my job?' He laughed, but he never answered me."

The Band's connection to Dylan caused many rock critics to take notice of *Music from Big Pink*. *Life* called it "bucketsful of clear, cool, country soul that washes the ears with a sound never heard before." Reviewing it for *Rolling Stone*, Al Kooper proclaimed it "white soul, not so much a white cat imitating a spade, but something else that reaches you on a non-Negro level, like church music or country music or Jewish music or Dylan."

Critical acclaim, however, was not universal. "That the Woodstock wonders had come up with something original," wrote *Village Voice* columnist Robert Christgau, "the way each voice captured what is essential about both soul and country inflection while imitating neither, for instance, was obvious the first time I heard the dub. But, I also knew that, even though it was theoretically everything rock should be, right down to that human roughness around the edges, I was in fact bored by the record and found most of it lugubrious. . . . I kept trying to dig the record but I always found myself liking the songs better when they were performed elsewhere. 'I Shall Be Released' is one of Dylan's best songs, but I would rather hear Bobby Darin sing it than Richard Manuel, and there are even versions of 'The Weight' that I prefer to The Band's, which is admittedly a joy."

The Band refused to tour in support of the album. "We had done a very long and hard tour with [Dylan]," Robertson told Susan Gordon of *Rolling Stone*. "Most of the weight was on him, but some of it was on us, too. We saw all that crazy success stuff going on, and it just put us back in our chairs for a couple of years. Actually, we had thought about it some: if we put out this record, and it does do really well, it might be nice not to jump onto the bandwagon, and say, 'It was us, it was us.' We thought we should go somewhere like Jamaica and watch it all happen from there, rather than jump right out and milk ourselves dry, because if things go well, we hope to be doing this for quite a while."

"Our policy was not to tour if we could help it," said Helm, who was recuperating from a motorcycle accident sustained shortly after completing the album, "[and] to keep making music using the methods and work habits that had kept us productive through the basement tapes and the Big Pink era. We didn't care about being stars. We just wanted to survive with our integrity."

Helm was not the only one healing. Manuel had sustained third degree burns when a barbecue grill he was lighting exploded, and Danko had been in an automobile accident and broken his neck. "People thought that we were up [in Woodstock] being mysterious," said Robertson. "We were actually waiting for [Danko] to be okay. He was in traction for months."

Like Dylan, the longer that The Band stayed out of the spotlight, the more public demand increased. "I was enjoying the idea of breaking the rules," Robertson recalled. "You just let this record mingle out there in the world and do whatever it's going to do on its own merit. I enjoyed that what all this did was it led up to this strange mystique for The Band."

"Just because we weren't available," remembered Danko, "the public and promoters really wanted us to play. At one point, it got ridiculous. [Our fee] went from two thousand dollars a night to fifty thousand dollars a night by the time we played our first shows."

Concert promoter Bill Graham traveled to Woodstock to plead with the reticent ensemble. "[Graham] comes up and he's all flustered and nervous," remembered Robertson, "huffing and puffing, and saying, 'I'm bringing you a message from the people.' He was convincing me of something that we are already convinced of, but we had not told anybody. He was preaching, saying, 'You've got to be out in the world. The people love you; you can't let them down, everything's at stake here.' He was making it a big drama. I said, 'What's really behind this, Bill? What should make us pack our suitcases?' He comes up to me, waving his hand, 'It's the people.' 'What people? We like it up here in the woods. We don't know any people.' He goes through the whole thing again, and I go, 'Oh, those people—okay, we'll do it.' He said, 'Great,' and hugged me. He didn't know about Rick and that we were just having a little fun."

"We played three nights for Bill Graham [at the Winterland Ballroom] on the West Coast," said Danko, "and two [at Graham's Fillmore East] on the East Coast [in May 1969]."

Flying into San Francisco for their debut shows the weekend of April 17–19, 1968, members of The Band felt uneasy. "I was nervous and worried about playing in public again," said Helm, "and it would be fair to say that we were all beside ourselves with concern about bringing out this music for the first time before an audience, and not just any audience: this was San Francisco! This was opening right at the top—no out-of-town preview or club date. It was Bill Graham Presents."

The nervousness added to flu-like symptoms for a bed-ridden Robertson. "I couldn't even rehearse," he remembered. "I was just too weak. The night we were supposed to play, everybody was going crazy."

As a final effort to get the guitarist to perform, Grossman and Graham summoned a hypnotist (obtained through the yellow pages). With the conjurer convincing him to get out of bed (and giving him verbal suggestions during the show), Robertson made it through the first night. "It was pretty rough," he said. "The second night, I started to feel a little bit better. By the third night, I was over this bug. It made for great coffee

[talk]—this hypnotist on the side of the stage giving me signals, but it worked."

Music from Big Pink may have established The Band as counterculture favorites, but its self-titled follow-up, or "the brown album," propelled them into the upper stratospheres of mainstream success. Released on September 22, 1969, it became one of the decade's iconic recordings. Peaking at number nine on the *Billboard* pop charts in 1969, it reached the tenth slot on *Billboard*'s top Internet chart when it was remixed and reissued in 2000. "Me and a bunch of guys from New Orleans would listen to that second album all the time," said Mac "Dr. John" Rebennack, "and it would just tickle us that Robbie was from Canada. The music sounded to me like a cross between Memphis and New Orleans, it was really in the pockets of those places without ever copying the original stuff. The way they presented it was so innocent; there was nothing slick about it."

Musically, *The Band* was very much in line with its predecessor. "It's like the first two records were the same project," said Helm. "We had songs that didn't get finished in time to go on the first record and we had ideas—we knew the titles of some of the songs that were going to be on the second one."

At the time of *The Band*'s release, radio programming split between two veins—AM and FM. Advertiser-driven AM aimed for the common denominator with slick, hook-laden pop hits, while FM, hampered by a less powerful signal, limited broadcast range, and the scarcity of car FM radios, was free to experiment. Tom "Big Daddy" Donohue (1928–1975), a South Bend, Indiana–born, top-forty DJ, nightclub owner, and coproducer of The Beatles' August 29, 1966, concert, at San Francisco's Candlestick Park (their final show), was one of the first to lose faith in AM's hit-minded approach. Making his feelings known in a scorching article, "AM Radio Is Dead and Its Rotting Corpse Is Stinking Up the Airwaves," published by *Rolling Stone* in 1967, Donohue backed up his claims when he took over a foreign-language station's programming and launched the first alternative free-form radio shows. Donohue, who went on to become co-owner of Autumn Records, a San Francisco–based label that scored hits with the Beau Brummels ("Laugh Laugh") and Bobby Freeman ("The Swim"), and where Sly Stone worked as staff producer, entered the Rock and Roll Hall of Fame, posthumously, as one of only three DJs in 1996.

The success of Donohue's station, KMPX, spawned similar stations throughout the United States—including WNEW-FM in New York and WBCN-FM in Boston. "There was so much great music on the radio," remembered Larry Campbell. "It was so fertile. FM radio was playing amazing things you would never hear anywhere else."

"Rock radio [became] my religion," wrote Stevie Van Zandt in his introduction to WNEW-FM disc jockey Richard Neer's *FM: The Rise and Fall of Rock Radio*, "my church, and these DJs my priests, rabbis, and gurus.... It was the Exodus of singles and the Revelations of albums, we listened and listened and listened and listened."

FM radio's antiformula programming inspired many musicians to re-imagine albums not as collections of unconnected tunes but as long-playing suites. Brian Wilson and the Beach Boys traded the hit-minded imagery of surfing and fast cars for songs about self-discovery on *Pet Sounds*—reluctantly adding "Sloop John B" at Capitol's insistence on a single. The Beatles framed the songs of *Sergeant Pepper's Lonely Hearts Club Band* into a revue hosted by the fictitious Billy Shears. On *Days of Future Passed*, the Moody Blues and the London Festival Orchestra musically traced the passing of a day from sunrise to nightfall.

As a theme for their second full-length outing, The Band turned to the American South. "[The album] felt like a passport back to America for people who had become so estranged from their own country that they felt like foreigners even when they were in it," said Greil Marcus. "It made people think, 'Yes, the Civil War is part of me. Yes, a time when people worked on farms and were destroyed by bad weather, when they were vulnerable to things, this is part of me."

"This record could have been called *America*," said Robertson. "It was thematically such a mirror, so many things that we knew from somewhere, some story, or somebody telling us something. Even if we were talking about a certain place, and something very American, I learned later on that it did have a universal quality to it."

"The music was good," recalled Helm, "and everybody's intention seemed to be so right on. Our goals seemed to be in line and everything seemed to be righteous."

Unlike his assessment of *Music from Big Pink*, Robert Christgau took a favorable view of *The Band*. "John Phillips [of the Mamas and the Papas] is more facile," he wrote, "John Sebastian [of the Lovin' Spoonful] more charming, Randy Newman more subtle, but Jaime Robbie Robertson (assuming he is the sole lyricist, probably an oversimplification) has become a more inventive writer than any of them, the best in America; this side of Dylan. Except for Dylan, he is the only American songwriter to write good fictional/dramatic songs ('Rockin' Chair,' 'The Night They Drove Old Dixie Down') and the only one to master the semi-literate tone, in which grammatical barbarisms and colloquial ellipses transcend affectation to enrich and qualify a song's meaning. Because the overdubbed music has a casual, almost unprofessional edge to it—as do the lyrics, the vocals, and the lead parts—that natural sound is unaffected. There is no distracting gloss to distort the added color, no studio effect."

Elliot Landy photographed the black-and-white close-up of The Band on the album's cover. "We were actually standing in the rain," remembered Robertson. "That's likely why we looked that way—not too cheerful."

Weary of working in a sterile recording studio, The Band had recorded the album in a temporary studio in the pool house of Sammy Davis Jr.'s Los Angeles home, just off Sunset Boulevard. "[Relocating to Southern California] had nothing to do with the culture," explained Robertson. "It had a lot to do with Woodstock having snow."

The Band was free to record at will. "It was the clubhouse technique of making music," said Robertson. "You [weren't] on the clock, and you could do whatever you wanted to do. There was nobody in a glass booth saying, 'What was that?' There was none of that."

By romanticizing the South, and humanizing its inhabitants, *The Band* defied how it had become perceived by many in the rest of the country. The civil rights era had spotlighted southern racism and injustice, while the assassinations of Medgar Evers in Mississippi and President John F. Kennedy in Texas, and such films as *In the Heat of the Night* and *Easy Rider*, further demonstrated southern intolerance.

"Across the Great Divide" kicked off *The Band* with optimism, urging listeners to "grab your hat and take the ride." Italian director Michelangelo Antonioni visited the studio as The Band worked on the song. "We had a film projector in the studio," said Helm, "so we could watch movies as part of this whole process. . . . [Antonioni] wanted us to consider doing the music for his first movie about America, *Zabriskie Point*. Signor Antonioni didn't speak much English, so it was funny when he heard Richard on the playback singing the beginning of the song—'Standin' by your window in vain, a pistol in your hand'—and Antonioni starts gesturing and shouting, 'pistoli,' in recognition."

"Rag Mama Rag," one of *The Band*'s two singles, reached the fifty-seventh position on *Billboard*'s pop charts. "We didn't understand its importance until after we'd recorded it," said Helm.

Recording the song initially as a straight-ahead rock tune (with Helm on drums), Robertson had been disappointed by the results. "It didn't feel like what I was hearing in my head," he remembered, "so Richard went to the drums, and Levon switched to the mandolin, John [Simon] huffed and puffed his way through a tuba line, and Rick took over my guitar riff on the fiddle, which gave the song it's 'rag' quality. Because this was in the tradition of ragtime music, Garth played an upright, ragtime piano. Somehow all the elements gelled, and you started to hear a real character in the music."

Helm was extremely excited when he heard the playback. "I thought 'Rag Mama Rag' was going to be a radio song," he said. "I didn't see it as number one with a bullet, but I thought that [it] had the elements that a song like 'Blue Suede Shoes' had. It swung and it was danceable."

"I never thought that it was going to be a hit single," countered Robertson, "or if it mattered. I thought it was a unique piece of music and I was proud of it as it was."

The most enduring song on *The Band*, and its second single, "The Night They Drove Old Dixie Down," outdid "Rag Mama Rag," breaking into pop's top twenty-five. Listed at number 245 on *Rolling Stone*'s list of the 500 greatest songs of all time, it was included in *Time*'s all-time one hundred. The Rock and Roll Hall of Fame named it one of the "five hundred songs that shaped rock and roll." "The only thing I can relate it to at all is *The Red Badge of Courage*," said Ralph Gleason. "It's a remarkable song. The rhythmic structure, [Helm's] voice, and the bass line with the drum accents, and the heavy close harmony of Levon, Richard, and Rick in the theme, make it seem impossible that this isn't some traditional material handed down from father to son straight from that winter of 1865 to today. It has that ring of truth and the whole aura of authenticity."

"It gets inside the sense of place and tradition that one finds in the South," claimed Robert Palmer, "with insights of rare acuity. It captures the emotional climax of that apocalyptic moment in southern history, the surrender, in a few exceptionally well-chosen words and a dignified, understated arrangement."

"It is hard for me to comprehend how any northerner," said Greil Marcus, "raised on a very different war than Virgil Caine's, could listen to this song without finding himself changed. You can't get out from under the singer's truth—not the whole truth, simply his truth—and the little autobiography closes the gap between us. The performance leaves behind a feeling that for all our oppositions, every American still shares this old event, because, to this day, none of us has escaped its impact. What we share is an ability to respond to a story like this one."

Inspiration for "The Night They Drove Old Dixie Down" sparked while Robertson was visiting Helm's parents. "At one point in the conversation," Robertson recalled, "his dad said, just kiddingly (but there was some sincerity, at the same time), 'You know, Robbie, one of these days the South is going to rise again.'"

Helm helped Robertson in his preparations for writing the song. "I remember taking [Robertson] to the library [in Woodstock]," he said, "so he could research the history and geography of that era for the lyrics and make General Robert E. Lee come out with all due respect."

The song became a vocal showcase for Helm. "I never sat down and said, 'Now, I'm going to write a song for Levon,'" Robertson told *Musician* magazine. "After I got a handle on the song, on what the song was about, then I thought, 'This would be a good song for Levon to sing, because a lot of the things in the songs I've heard him say in his own words.' I thought he could sing it with more sincerity than some Canadian, but I think it was a little embarrassing for Levon to hear that I wrote this song 'for' him, or 'at' him, or 'because' of him. It was a great thing to be able to do it for my friend, in a way, but it was accidental."

Set at the end of the Civil War, "The Night They Drove Old Dixie Down" told of Virgil Caine, a Confederate soldier who had served on the Danville supply train "until General Sherman's Union Calvary troops tore up the tracks." Back with his wife in Tennessee, he listens to bells ringing and people singing in celebration of the Union victory and realizes that his dreams are gone. As he remembers his brother who was "just eighteen, proud and brave, but a Yankee laid him in his grave," he considers the lost cause and sings, "You can't raise a Caine back up when he's in defeat," prompting comparisons to the biblical tale of Cain and Abel.

Robertson wrote the song's melody on piano. "My daughter, Alexandra, had just been born," he said, "and I had to be very quiet—'The baby is sleeping, don't make any noise'—I got used to working quietly, with little subtleties."

The tune's rhythms challenged Helm. "We found if we halved the beat," he explained, "we could lay the lyrics in a different place, and the pulse would be easier to move to, more danceable.... My problem was that I had to learn to sing and play this half-time meter at the same time. I'd grown up singing 'Short Fat Fanny' over a barroom din while playing at top speed."

Joan Baez had one of her biggest hits with her rendition of "The Night They Drove Old Dixie Down" in 1971, reaching number three on *Billboard*'s hot one hundred, and topping the easy-listening charts for five weeks. As she told *Rolling Stone*, Baez had learned the tune from The Band's album and (without printed lyrics) had made several unintentional errors. Robertson's words "till Stoneman's Cavalry came," referring to Union major general George Stoneman's sweep across the Blue Ridge Mountains into northwest North Carolina and southwest Virginia, was changed to the more generic "till so much cavalry came." Baez's version altered Robertson's reference to "May the tenth," which had been the date in 1865 when the Confederate capital city, Richmond, Virginia, had fallen to Sherman's troops, to "I took the train." Robertson's line "like my father before me, I will work the land" was changed to "like my father before me, I'm a working man," transforming the narrator of The Band recording from a farmer into a laborer. In another lyrical shift, Robertson's image of Virgil Caine watching General Robert E. Lee ride by was transferred to a Mississippi riverboat, the *Robert E. Lee*.

The Charlie Daniels Band, Big Country, Richie Havens, the Black Crowes, and the Jerry Garcia Band covered "The Night They Drove Old Dixie Down" with Robertson's original lyrics. Helm refused to sing it after *The Last Waltz*.

Three songs on *The Band* were collaborative efforts by Robertson and Manuel—"When You Awake," "Whispering Pines," and "Jawbone." "['When You Awake'] is a strange song," said Peter Viney, "in that it breaks up the full-blast Americana of the three preceding tracks and the following one. Listen to it again, and it hardly sounds like any kind of rock song at all. Like all their best tracks, you grab images as you relisten but you're hard put to connect these images together."

"It's a story about someone who passes something on to you," explained Robertson, "and you pass it on to someone else, but it's something you take to heart and carry with you your whole life."

Manuel's vocals on "Whispering Pines," according to Band biographer Barney Hoskyns, ranked among some "of the most beautiful he ever wrote, a song of intense loneliness set beside an ocean that seemed to symbolize the singer's endless sense of loss."

"Richard always had this very plaintive attitude in his voice," Robertson recalled, "and sometimes just in his sensitivity as a person. I tried to follow that, to go with it and find it musically. We both felt very good about this song."

A full-length version of "Whispering Pines," performed solo by Danko, was included on MTV's *Classic Albums — The Band*.

For "Jawbone," Manuel provided a soulful voice for a revengeful, self-analyzing, three-time-losing thief whose "name upon the post office wall put you on edge 'cause they wrote it too small." A late 1990s Band fanzine, edited by Manchester, England–based Lee Gabites, took its name from the tune.

"Jemima Surrender" and "The Unfaithful Servant" focused on familiar southern characters. During the former, by Helm and Robertson, the narrator attempts to seduce a potential lover, promising to "bring over my Fender and I'll play all night for you."

Although it originated with one of three daughters in the Old Testament's Book of Job, the name Jemima had become identified with the apron-wearing mammy shown on boxes of pancake mix since 1889. Like Uncle Ben's Rice and Cream of Wheat's Rastus, Jemima (in her apron and head kerchief) characterized postslavery hospitality on southern plantations. "[Manufacturers] used to use blacks to sell objects," David Pilgrim of the Jim Crow Museum of Racist Memorabilia at Ferris University, Michigan, told *Atlantic* magazine's Jennie Rothenberg. "If an object were black, like licorice or shoe polish, then it was very easy to use a very dark-skinned person to sell it, but it was also the case that, if you were trying to sell happiness or nostalgia, you might put a black Mammy or an Uncle Tom image on your product. You see these images on a lot of breakfast food labels, a lot of kitchen items."

Some listeners had problems with "Jemima Surrender." Psychology professor and author Naomi Weisstein told Rosalyn Baxandall and Linda Gordon in *Dear Sisters — Dispatches from the Women's Liberation Movement* how hearing the song on the radio in 1973 had inspired her to form the Chicago Women's Liberation Rock Band. "[When I heard it], I somersaulted off the sofa," she remembered, "leapt up into the air, and came down howling at the radio, 'Every fourteen-year-old girl in this city listens to rock!' How criminal to make the subjugation and suffering of women so sexy? We'll . . . we'll organize our own rock band."

"To write a song about this kind of thing is not really a very righteous thing to do," Robertson admitted to *Rolling Stone*, "because we're at the point now where there should be no differences between people. Everybody is now interested in being the same, so I was kind of playing a game in writing this song."

In the space of four minutes and seventeen seconds, Robertson's "The Unfaithful Servant" presented a story worthy of Faulkner or Hemingway. Danko sang lead, Robertson played acoustic guitar (switching to electric for *Rock of Ages*), and Manuel kept things anchored on piano. A horn section featuring Hudson (saxophone, trumpet), Danko (trombone), and John Simon (tuba) added spice. "If *The Band* as a 'concept album' can be said to take place in or around some imaginary country town," wrote Barney Hoskyns, "then ' The Unfaithful Servant' is definitely set in the 'mansion on the hill,' a Southern household of the kind Robbie read about in the plays of Tennessee Williams. . . . The overall effect was pure American Gothic."

"['The Unfaithful Servant'] was one of the few songs I've ever recorded in my life," said Danko, "where it was done the very first take. We recorded it, and then [we] did it thirty more times, forty more times. John Simon came in and said, 'Listen to this, Rick,' and I said, 'you're right.' That was the first take."

The hardest rocking song on *The Band*, "Look Out Cleveland," warned the people of Cleveland, Ohio, and Houston, Texas, that a storm "is coming through" with "thunder on the hill" and "chain lightnin', frightenin' as it may seem"—"the whole town is going to blow away." Jackie Greene and Albert Lee would cover it, while Phish would use it to open their June 12, 2011, show at the Blossom Music Center just outside of Cleveland. "When we were doing the album," explained Robertson, "there were all these riots and outbursts around the country, and it was kind of like [we were] living on the fault line of revolution."

"['Look Out Cleveland'] is unique in contemporary popular song," wrote Ralph Gleason, "so far removed from the obvious morbidity of some of the songs of past years as to be an adult to their child. (This music, of course, is mature, made by men who know who they are and what they want to do. Its appeal to the teenybopper Top 40 audience seems, on the evidence, to be limited.)"

The album's only tune without drums "Rockin' Chair" featured Helm on mandolin, Hudson on accordion, and Robertson on acoustic guitar. Sung by Manuel, Robertson's song provided a voice for a sailor ("pushin' age seventy three") who is ready to retire from the sea, and head "home again, down to Old Virginny" with "my very best friend, they call him Ragtime Willie." "Most people are knocked out by younger people," said

Robertson. "I'm knocked out by older people. Just look at their eyes. Hear them talk; they are not joking. They've seen things you'll never see."

Both sides of *The Band* closed with strong tunes. One of three tunes recorded at Hit Factory studios in New York, "Up On Cripple Creek" became a top twenty-five single in the United States (backed with "The Night They Drove Old Dixie Down") and reached the top ten in Canada—The Band's highest chart ranking. "It took 'Cripple Creek' a long time to seep into us," said Helm, who sang lead on the song. "It was like it just had to simmer with everybody for a while. We cut it two or three times, but nobody really liked it. It wasn't quite enough fun, but we fooled around with it, and finally one night we just got hold of it, doubled up a couple of chorus parts and harmony parts, and that was it."

According to Ralph Gleason, "Cripple Creek" tells "the story of a trucker and the gal he has stashed away in Lake Charles, Louisiana—'a drunkard's dream if I ever did see one.' It is a salty, sexy, earthy (rather than funky) ballad. . . . Levon's chuckle towards the end is surely the nastiest, dirtiest, evilest sexual snort in the history of the phonograph record, and again the rhythmic tension created between the interplay of the bass and drums and the line of the voice sets up a tremendously moving pulse."

"The song is about the narrator's memories of Bessie," said Peter Viney, "a love song in retrospect, a tale of a rush of blood, not a tale of a gold rush. The trucker is returning to his Big Mama, but his thoughts are on good times with Bessie. Maybe he'll never get back to Lake Charles."

"Little Bessie is an echo of [Danko's] song 'Bessie Smith' from *The Basement Tapes* [and included as an outtake on the remixed *Cahoots* in 2000]," said Helm. "People always wanted to know who she was, and I'd tell 'em, she was Caldonia's cousin."

"["Up on Cripple Creek"] is also, somehow, an extension of American mythology," explained Robertson, "this Americana going, 'We're not dealing with people at the top of the ladder, [but about the people in] that house out there in the middle of that field. What does this [person] think, with one light on upstairs, and that truck parked out there? That's who I'm curious about—the story of this person, as he drives these trucks across the whole country, and the characters that he drops in on on his travels—just following him, with a camera, is really what this song's all about."

The rhythmic funk of Hudson playing clavinet through a wah-wah pedal provided "Up on Cripple Creek" with its hook. Three years later, Stevie Wonder would adopt the technique for "Superstition." "It was very easy to do," said Hudson. "We tried it at home, not for that song, but it was good for that. It sounds like a bow harp with metal strings."

"It's the lead instrument," said Robertson. "The guitar doesn't come wailing up, the piano does little licks here and there." Hudson's "bow harp" clavinet sound recalled Cree singer-songwriter Buffy Sainte-Marie's 1964 mouthbow playing on "Cripple Creek," a traditional folk/bluegrass tune also recorded by Pete Seeger, Bill Monroe and the Bluegrass Boys, the Stanley Brothers, and Leo Kottke.

With his Arkansas twang, it was natural that Helm sing lead on "Up on Cripple Creek." "It's quite extraordinary how Levon could sing and play [drums] at the same time," said Robertson. "He didn't mix it up."

"People think it's harder [to play drums while you sing]," explained Helm, "but it's actually easier. You play along, and you leave holes—that's where you sing. You could punch your voice on the punch lines by adding the cymbals. You could cover a couple of patterns that might hit you in the middle of a tune. It felt better and made it more natural."

Coming immediately after the quiet sorrow of "The Unfaithful Servant," "King Harvest (Has Surely Come)," with Manuel and Helm alternating lead vocals on the verses and harmonizing with Danko on the chorus, completed the journey promised by "Across the Great Divide." The idealism at the beginning of the album had been replaced by the stark reality of a sharecropping farmer trying to endure the absence of rain ("Hey Rainmaker, can't you hear my call?"), the burning of his barn, and a period on skid row—his horse even went crazy. Recruited by a union organizer (perhaps from the Trade Union Unity League, which organized sharecroppers in the South between 1928 and 1935), he believes that a better day is on the horizon—despite his poverty ("just don't judge me by my shoes"). To add to his optimism, the summer has yielded to the promise of a new harvest. There is a yellow moon in the sky, corn is in the field, rice is blowing in the wind, there is a scent of magnolias in the air, and a carnival is coming to town.

An enthusiast of John Steinbeck's Dust Bowl migrant-worker novels, especially *Of Mice and Men* and *The Grapes of Wrath*, Robertson created what he called "just a kind of character study in a time period." "When the unions came in, they were a saving grace," he explained, "a way of fighting the big-money people, and they affected everybody from the people that worked in the big cities all the way around to the farm people. It is ironic because now so much of it is like gangsters, assassinations, power, greed, and insanity. I just thought it was incredible how it started and how it ended up.

"It's another piece I remember from my youth," he continued. "There are a lot of people that [have] the idea of, come autumn, come fall, that's when life begins. It's not the springtime, when we think it begins, but the fall, because [that's when] the harvest comes in.

"At that time of year, Woodstock was very impressive," he said. "Everything turned red and orange, and it made you think that this breeze was coming in; it was quite noticeable. It made me think how this was the culmination of the year for so many people. . . . Thematically, I kept coming back to that, and 'King Harvest' was the most focused of any of the material as far as coming right out and saying it."

"Some of the lyrics came out of a discussion we had one night about the times we'd seen and all had in common," said Helm. "It was an expression of feeling that came from five people. The group wanted to do one song that took in everything we could muster about life at that moment in time. It was the last thing we cut in California, and it was that magical feeling of 'King Harvest' that pulled us through. It was like, there, that's The Band."

"King Harvest (Has Surely Come)" climaxed *The Band* with jubilation. "The hymn-like quality of the voicing," wrote Ralph Gleason, "the use of counterpoint and contrapuntal rhythms by the singers, the weaving of the voices in and out into a pattern that grows each time you hear it, are the things that make the sound of this music so compelling. In 'King Harvest,' as in other songs, individual sections with contrasting timbres, moods, rhythms, and sounds are juxtaposed to make a totality that is so open it can cover whatever you feel."

"'King Harvest' is one [Band] tune that I really like," Helm told Robyn Flans of *Modern Drummer* in August 1984. I really like the drum pattern, and we left a corresponding hole for the backbeat. That was one track where I got my drums sounding the way I wanted them. There is enough wood in the sound. You could hear the stick, the bell of the cymbal, and so on."

"This was a new way of dealing with the guitar for me," said Robertson, "this very subtle playing, leaving out a lot of stuff, and just waiting until the last second, and then playing the thing in just the nick of time. It was an approach to playing [that was] so delicate, the opposite of the in-your-face guitar playing that I used to do. You have to hold your breath while playing these kinds of solos. You can't breathe or you'll throw yourself off."

Figure 4.1. Pete Seeger. © *Craig Harris.*

Figure 4.2.   Peter, Paul, and Mary. © *Craig Harris.*

Figure 4.3.   Al Kooper. © *Craig Harris.*

Figure 4.4. Joan Baez. © *Craig Harris.*

Figure 4.5. John Hammond, Jr. © *Craig Harris*.

Figure 4.6. Happy Traum (on right) and brother Artie Traum (on left), 1985. © *Craig Harris.*

Figure 4.7. Amy Helm. © *Craig Harris.*

Figure 4.8. Larry Campbell. © *Craig Harris*.

Figure 4.9. Levon Helm at the Philadelphia Folk Festival in 2010. © *Craig Harris.*

Figure 4.10. Richard Manuel. © *Craig Harris.*

Figure 4.11. Rick Danko and Garth Hudson. © *Craig Harris*.

Figure 4.12. Garth Hudson. © *Craig Harris.*

Figure 4.13. Byron Isaacs. © *Craig Harris.*

Figure 4.14. Jim Weider. © *Craig Harris.*

Figure 4.15. Teresa Williams. © *Craig Harris*.

Figure 4.16. Todd Rundgren. © *Craig Harris.*

FIVE
Rise and Descent

The Band's influence continued to grow. "They were people we were looking to for a great sound," said Happy Traum, who released his first album, with his brother, Artie, in 1970. "Some people have said that they were influenced by what we were doing, too. Artie and I were doing a certain kind of songwriting, especially Artie, and unique guitar arrangements. We came to it from a much more acoustic point of view, while The Band was coming from the country and blues-rock roadhouse tradition."

Playing acoustic guitar since his childhood, Artie Traum had absorbed what he could from artists like James Taylor, Bonnie Raitt, Muddy Waters, and Mississippi John Hurt, and broadened his scope with the improvisational music of John Coltrane, Miles Davis, Jim Hall, and the Modern Jazz Quartet. Making his recording debut at the age of eleven as a member of the True Endeavor Jug Band, with future Blues Project guitarist Danny Kalb, Sita Dimitroff, and Sam and Ann Charters, he went on to play guitar on Michigan-born blues vocalist Judy Roderick's *Woman Blue* (Vanguard) soon afterward. Cowriting three songs for Brian DePalma's first film, *Greetings*, starring Robert DeNiro (in his first major role), in 1968, he recorded the soundtrack with Bear, a group that he shared with Eric Kaz, Steve Soles, Darius Davenport, and ex-Lovin' Spoonful bassist Skip Boone. Traveling west, the younger Traum became active with the Berkeley, California, Folklore Center. He later helped to establish new-age guitar playing with a pair of masterful solo instrumental albums in the 1980s.

With its growing influx of musicians, Woodstock acquired a signature sound. "Artie was the instigator of things happening," said his older brother. "We hosted parties and get-togethers. He loved to stir the waters and get people together."

Uniting as the Woodstock Mountain Review, a superstar collection of artists collaborated on their first album, *Mud Acres*, in 1971. "Artie came up with the idea to do a record like we play at parties," said Traum. "I remember calling Ken Irwin of Rounder Records; they were just starting out. We went to a studio in Glens Falls, New York, got all these people—Maria Muldaur, Jim Rooney, Bill Keith, and John Herald—that we played with at parties and had a party for two days. We camped out, sleeping in sleeping bags on the floor of this funky studio. We picked songs, figured out who would do which lead, and who would do backup, and it just came out as it happened. It was such a scene."

Five years later, the Woodstock Mountain Revue renewed the project with the equally fun *Back to Mud Acres*. "We brought in John Sebastian, Paul Butterfield, Eric Andersen, Rory Block, and Paul Siebel," said Traum. "Folk and acoustic music are so open to hanging out and jamming. You don't need heavy rehearsals."

Reconnecting with Dylan in late 1971, Happy Traum helped to rerecord three *Basement Tapes* tunes ("Down in the Flood," "I Shall Be Released," and "You Ain't Goin' Nowhere") for the singer-songwriter's *Greatest Hits, Volume 2*. "[Dylan] had gone through the gigantic stardom when he became a household name," he reflected, "and he'd been through the international touring. He had completely slowed down his life. I think he had had a real scare. [After we became friends in Woodstock], we spent a lot of time just playing songs together. It was quite a different experience than when he was raw, young, and striving for fame and fortune. Now, he was on the other side of it and trying to find his way back to some kind of balance. He was doing acoustic-based music again.

"Other people had made hits of these songs," he continued, "and he wanted to put his own personal stamp on them. The Byrds had recorded 'You Ain't Goin' Nowhere' and The Band had done 'I Shall Be Released.' I don't think anyone had yet released 'Down in the Flood' [though it would be included on *The Basement Tapes*]. He said, 'Get a banjo, a guitar, and a bass, and come down to New York and we'll try these songs out. I took the bus to New York and we went into the studio. It was just him, a recording engineer, and me."

Another track recorded by Traum and Dylan, "Only a Hobo," waited more than three decades before being included on *The Bootleg Series Vol. 10—Another Self Portrait (1969–1971)* in 2013. "We never finished it," said Traum.

Both Traum brothers participated in Dylan-produced recording sessions for beat poet Allen Ginsberg (with John Hammond as executive producer). "Bob asked me to play bass," Happy remembered. "I was never a bass player, but if Bob asks you to bring a bass, you bring a bass. For me, it was trial and error. Allen was not exactly a precise musician, but we had some great musicians, like David Amram and John Sholle, who was a fabulous guitar player. There were some poets there. Gregory Corso was crazy the whole time, very disruptive and wanting attention. It was a lot of fun, a little chaotic. It took years for it to come out [on a four-CD boxset, *Holy Soul Jelly Roll*, in 1994]. I was horrified by some of the songs; the lyrics were pretty crude."

Happy Traum re-recorded "I Shall Be Released" for his 1975 solo album *Bright Morning Stars*. Manuel played piano and clavinet on the album's title track. "I loved his playing," Traum remembered. "He was very proactive. He came to the session, in this very little studio in Woodstock, and put everything that he had into it. He did not come with an attitude of doing me a big favor, play some notes on a piano, and leave. He really spent a lot of time and took it very seriously; we had a lot of fun."

The Band was still six weeks from its September 22, 1969, release when the quintet appeared at the Woodstock Music and Art Festival. Despite its name, the three-day festival was actually held fifty miles away, on an alfalfa farm owned by Max Yasgur in White Lake, a small unincorporated hamlet in the Sullivan County, New York, town of Bethel. The Woodstock-themed Museum at Bethel Woods and Bethel Woods Center for the Arts now occupy the site. "[The Woodstock Festival] was never planned for the actual little town of Woodstock," said festival coproducer Michael Lang. "It was first scheduled for Wallkill, New York, but we found that we didn't have the Wallkill site secured. This was after spending promotional dollars, putting up all the grading, and setting up the piping, everything except for the stage, which was the last thing to be put up. It was simply conservative politics; the Wallkill City Council at the Town meeting needed to approve the event." And they didn't.

"We started looking for towns with similar names," continued Lang. "We went to Woodmere; they didn't like the idea. We went to Woodburn and they did not like the idea. When we went to White Lake, we thought it was Wood Lake. The reason we did not change the name to Woodburn, Woodmere, or White Lake was that those names did not evoke the spirit we were looking for. I lived [in Woodstock], and I produced it, but beyond that, I had arguments with people on my staff [who wanted] to change it. 'What's it got to do with Woodstock?' It had everything to do with Woodstock, everything to do with the history of the town—from the Maverick Concerts to the Sound Outs [the free mini-festivals that had been held in Woodstock since 1967]—the fabric of what this town is about."

A Brooklyn-born UCLA dropout, Lang had moved to Miami, Florida, in the mid-1960s and opened a head shop in Coconut Grove. Turning to music, he coproduced the two-day (no camping) Miami Pop Festival at Gulfstream Park, Hallandale (thirty miles north of Miami), in May 1968. Relocating to Woodstock, he continued to dream of an even-bigger musical celebration. "The night the idea was born of Woodstock," remembered Artie Kornfeld, who resigned as Capitol Records' president to co-produce the festival with Lang, "Michael was with my wife, Linda, and me in our apartment. We had just finished playing bumper pool at two in the morning. It started out as a conversation about how I was only seeing Capitol-related groups and needed to go out and hear other things in the new music scene. I had stopped going to shows, but Michael was going to the Fillmore East and always hanging out. I guess it went down something like this: 'Wouldn't it be great if we had millions of dollars and could rent a little theater on Broadway to have a party and invite maybe one hundred of our friends? We could get Jimi Hendrix, the Rolling Stones, Creedence Clearwater, Sly Stone, The Beatles, and every other act that we would love to see perform. We won't charge anything and it will be one of the greatest parties of all time.' Michael thought we should take our mythical festival to Woodstock because he lived in Woodstock and it had become popular because it was an artist's colony."

Plans for the festival came together quickly. "Hector Morales was an old friend from the William Morris Agency," said Kornfeld, "and he also hung out with Michael as part of his inner circle. Somehow, he managed to get his friend Sly Stone to be the first act booked for the festival. After Sly said he'd play, all of his friends who were successful said they would do it. Then out of nowhere, Michael called and said, 'Artie, we've got Jimi Hendrix; he's agreed to play!' Bill Graham then came in with his package of West Coast acts, including the Jefferson Airplane and the Grateful Dead. Artists, managers, and agents were calling like crazy. We realized this could happen and that it was going to be big."

Producers envisioned Dylan headlining the Woodstock Festival, but the reclusive singer-songwriter had no desire to face such a large crowd, leaving two days before with his wife, Sara (who was expecting), and family aboard the Queen Elizabeth 2, heading to Europe. Forced to disembark when their eleven-year-old son, Jesse, became ill, the singer-songwriter and his wife flew to London, after he recuperated, twelve days later.

The Band's experience at the festival reinforced the wisdom of Dylan's decision. "It was a drag playing," remembered Robertson. "We got even less than a response from the audience. . . . We did about half a good set. The Band thought the whole idea of the festival was exciting because of what it stood for, but, when we flew in and saw the mass of people sitting on the hill, it was a frightful sight. It was like an army, a ripped army of mud people. We played between Ten Years After and Johnny Winter and came out like a bunch of preacher boys. It was very inappropriate for us.

"After three days of people being hammered by weather and music," he continued, "it was hard to get a take on the mood. We were playing the way we played in our living room, and that might have given the impression that we weren't up for it, but it could have been that we just couldn't get that same intimate feeling with a few hundred thousand people. As a musical experience for The Band, we were like orphans in the storm."

Along with other acts managed by Albert Grossman, including Janis Joplin and Blood, Sweat, and Tears, The Band's performance was missing from the Michael Wadleigh-directed film *Woodstock* and triple-album (and double-CD) soundtrack released by Atlantic Records. "Our tapes were the best of any of the groups," recalled Robertson, "but we didn't like the setup and the album sounded pretty shoddy."

The Band fared slightly better two weeks later when they appeared with Dylan at the Isle of Wight Festival in England on August 31. Appearing after high-energy sets by The Who and Grossman-managed Richie Havens, they managed to serve up a forty-five-minute set, British rock journalist Nik Cohn praised as "harmonies half-country, half-gospel, and the beat good rock."

Dylan's appearance, his first in three years, had been the most anticipated set of the weekend. Joining The Band onstage, porting a sparkling white suit, trimmed haircut, and fashionable beard, he proceeded to lead the way through an hour-long, seventeen-tune set that ranged from country-rockers like "She Belongs To Me," "I Threw It All Away," "Lay Lady Lay," "I'll Be Your Baby Tonight," I Pity the Poor Immigrant " (with Hudson on accordion), and "One Too Many Mornings," to hard-rocking treatments of "Quinn, the Eskimo," Highway 61 Revisited," and "Like a Rolling Stone." As an encore, they resurrected an Irish patriotic song, "Minstrel Boy," that Thomas Moore (1779–1852) had set to the melody of a traditional air, before segueing into a fiery rendition of the singer-songwriter's call for "everyone to get stoned" — "Rainy Day Women #12 and 35." Dylan performed four songs solo — "It Ain't Me Babe,' "To Ramona," "Mr. Tambourine Man," and traditional British folksong, "Wild Mountain Thyme." Available on various bootlegs for more than three decades, master tapes of the set were remastered and included on Dylan's *The Bootleg Series — Volume 10: Another Self Portrait* in 2013.

Among the audience of 150,000 to 200,000 people (including three Beatles, Yoko Ono, Eric Clapton, and members of the Rolling Stones), reviews of the performance were mixed. "I sat with John and Yoko for The Band and Dylan," remembered singer-songwriter Tom Paxton, "and [we] thought they were totally great."

Not everyone was so overwhelmed. "I was disappointed," Keith Richards told British music magazine, *NME*. "Dylan was beautiful, especially when he did songs by himself. He has a unique rhythm which only seems to come off when he's performing solo. The Band were too strict. It was like they were just playing the records on stage and at a fairly low volume, with very clear sound. I like some distortion, especially if something starts happening on stage."

Dylan and The Band would not share a stage again for a half decade. "Bob had an extra list of songs with about eight or ten different titles that we would've gone ahead and done had it seemed like the right thing to do," recalled Helm, "but it seemed like everyone was a bit tired; the festival was three days old by then."

Returning to Woodstock, as the town's only representative at the festival bearing its name encountered an unexpected reception. "I remember going to a bakery we had been going to for years," said Robertson. "This little old German woman ran the bakery and she was great at what she did. A couple of people came in after me and she took their orders. I was feeling that something [was up]. I went to the hardware store and they wouldn't sell me a pair of pliers. We had really insulted somebody. I thought, 'Oh, my God, they think it's our fault that Woodstock [had changed] from this little place that few people knew about to [being] the most famous small town in the world,' and they were holding it against us."

The ire of Woodstock's more conservative sector continued to plague The Band. When they sought permission to record their third album in front of a live audience at the Woodstock Playhouse, the town council turned them down. "We told them that we wanted to do it for the people of Woodstock," explained Robertson, "but they said, 'We hate that idea. It'll all be kids from [New York City] and New Jersey, and we'll be on the outside.'"

As *The Band* rose into Billboard's top five, the group had thrust further and further into the limelight. They appeared, along with Buck Owens, Pearl Bailey, and Rodney Dangerfield, on *The Ed Sullivan Show* on November 2, 1969. Two months later, *Time* spotlighted them in a cover story by Jay Cocks. "In the shifting, echoing cacophony of sound and sometimes fury that is the modern rock scene," wrote Cocks, "The Band has now emerged as the one group whose sheer fascination and musical skill may match the excellence—though not the international impact—of the Beatles."

Touring across North America, The Band became one of the continent's top acts. "We sold out Symphony Hall [in Boston]," said Helm, "and had 'em hanging from the balconies. We got ovations when we changed instruments between songs. We had a rabid audience for our shows at the Auditorium Theater in Chicago; they rushed the stage when we hit the encore, 'Don't Do It,' like an old-fashioned rockabilly show."

"We tried very hard to make the live performances like the records," said Robertson. "I've heard so many people's records that are great, then I've heard them in person and it's a big letdown. We thought it was a cop-out, to do the songs [with] a big long solo in the middle. If you are going to do a different version of a song, then do a different version. We tried very much to show that we could do it as good as we could on the records ... trying not to be disappointing in comparison."

Although they attempted to build on the enthusiasm of their shows, by the time they started working on their third album at the Woodstock

Playhouse, The Band had resigned to recording without an audience. The Band took a harder-hitting approach with *Stage Fright*. "After *The Band*, I thought this thing's being taken way to seriously," explained Robertson to Rob Bowman of *Goldmine* magazine in July 1991. "Let's have a little bit of goof here, do some touching things, some funny things, and do more of a good-time kind of record."

Helm was still fuming over songwriting credits, however, and darkness increasingly eclipsed the group's vision. "[The Band] was pretty much over [by the time we recorded *Stage Fright*]," he told John Hiatt in *Ain't in It for My Health*. "It was obvious that it was a screw job—the credits, money, were all screwed up. The Band was not together, but for three years. After that, it was The Band plays your favorites. We couldn't collaborate anymore."

America was experiencing a parallel diminishing of spirit. Six months before, violence (and a murder) at a daylong Rolling Stones–hosted concert at the Altamont Speedway in Northern California had shattered the jubilant spirit of the Woodstock Festival. The war in Vietnam had continued to rage on, while the antiwar movement had taken a hit when National Guardsmen shot and killed four students protesting on the campus of Kent State University in Ohio on May 4, 1970. Coupled with the assassinations of Martin Luther King Jr. and Robert Kennedy in 1968, and the premature deaths of Brian Jones, Janis Joplin, and Jimi Hendrix, the naivety of the summer of love was already a distant memory.

As Manuel and Robertson's "Just Another Whistle Stop" warned, there was an unstoppable train approaching, "bringin' souls from all around." A little more than a century before, the Hutchinson Family's song "Get off the Track" (about an oncoming train symbolizing emancipation) caused such a stir that researchers cite it as a cause of the Civil War.

There were some gentle moments on *Stage Fright*, including Manuel and Robertson's waltz-time "Sleeping," and "A La Glory," the lullaby that closed the first side, inspired by the birth of Robertson's first child, and masterfully sung by Helm. But paranoia, fear, and superstition flowed through much of the album. One song, "Daniel and the Sacred Harp," built on the myth of selling one's soul in exchange for a "famous harp." "I guess it's about greed in the context of Christian mythology," Robertson told Barney Hoskyns. "I was very into Sacred Harp shape-note singing, so I had that in the back of my mind."

The somber tone of *Stage Fright* reflected changes in the musicians' lives. Although the commercial success of their first two albums had propelled them to an economic level beyond their wildest dreams, some band members had been unprepared. "Ever make a million dollars fast?" Rick Danko once told a reporter. "I have—I've seen it kill people; it's a goddamned, crying shame what success can do to some people. Try having all the money and drugs you want."

"The Band was just fine until we became successful," Robertson agreed, "and then here came this strange phenomenon . . . like a disease. [Being a musician] was not a creative process for me anymore; I felt guilty of being one dimensional in my life. I wanted to be able to sit down, or play with the dog, or something. I was dying to be able, when someone asked, 'What are you doing?' to say, 'Nothing.'"

Stage Fright's title track, composed on piano by Robertson for Manuel to sing, became a vocal tour-de-force for Danko. "It needed [Danko's] warbly vulnerability," said Robertson, "[his] not being afraid to show fear."

The song's terrifying theme reflected the group's attitude toward being in the public eye. "There was something very private about [our music]," said Robertson. "The way we performed was not very flashy or showy. We just came for the business, so we could go on and play our hearts out. . . . It was more like classical music in performance than coming out and wearing cut-off leotards and buckskins. . . . It became so vulnerable and sensitive somehow, presenting this music in public."

The B-side of the "Time to Kill" single, Robertson's "The Shape I'm In," aimed a brotherly message at Manuel. "When I first met Richard," he explained, "he was seventeen [and already] a drunk. He had been drinking since he was very young. He was always an alcoholic and he decided to pursue it, you know, to the darkest degree that he could."

The song's narrator has lived hard—"out of nine lives, I spent seven." No matter what he does, he seems destined for failure. Recently released from jail after serving sixty days for "the crime of having no dough," he is "back on the street for the crime of having nowhere to go." Despite "two kids [who] might start a ruckus / you know they feel you trying to shuck us," self-preservation remained the key—"save your neck or save your brother / looks like it's one or the other." "How do you expect anybody to be so knowledgeable and so smart," asked Robertson, "[that they know] this fellow needs to go to a clinic and get into a program and that it's his one chance of getting through this alive. We don't know those things until it's too late."

Substance abuse increasingly infiltrated The Band. "It was the drug age," said Robertson. "There were a lot of crazy people around, and a lot of them were druggies. Everybody wanted to turn me on to something new. . . . Heroin was a problem. I never liked it, never understood it, and I was scared to death of it, but it came through, you know, like everything else came through."

With *Stage Fright* completed (and scheduled for release on August 17), The Band agreed to participate in the Transcontinental Pop Festival (or Festival Express). From June 27 until July 5, they would travel across Canada aboard a custom fourteen-car train (rented from the Canadian National Railway), with the Grateful Dead, Buddy Guy, Canadians Ian and Sylvia, and the New Riders of the Purple Sage, stopping off to play large-scale concerts. Janis Joplin would be there, with her new Full Tilt Boogie Band, featuring The Band's replacements in The Hawks—keyboardist Richard Bell and guitarist John Till (who had also played with Manuel in the Rockin' Revols). Partying and jamming as they traveled, they would, if all went well, recoup expenses through ticket sales. Instead of hundreds of thousands of people coming to a field-turned-temporary-concert-site, they would bring the music to the fans—and to more manageable, preexisting stadiums (with amenities including running water and bathrooms already installed). The idea seemed brilliant. "Woodstock was a feast for the audience," said Grossman employee Bob Shuster; "the train was a feast for the performers."

"You could float from car to car," recalled Bobby Weir, then with the Grateful Dead, "and get into any number of jams, some of which amounted to some heady stuff."

"You didn't ask what I was playing," said Buddy Guy. "You just looked at me and I looked at you. I nodded my head and vice-versa and you played."

The Festival Express represented the vision of Ken Walker, a then-twenty-three-years-old business administration graduate of what is now Ryerson University in Toronto. Walker had coproduced the Toronto Pop Festival (featuring the Velvet Underground, Alice Cooper, Steppenwolf, Johnny Winter, and Blood, Sweat, and Tears) in June 1969 and the Toronto Rock and Roll Revival (featuring Chuck Berry, Little Richard, Jerry Lee Lewis, The Doors, and John Lennon and Yoko Ono's Plastic Ono Band, with Eric Clapton) three months later.

After splitting from his former business partners, Walker had begun planning the musical train (with financial support from Thor Eaton and J. Lyn Craig of MacLean Hunter Publishing). "We have been flooded with requests from performers to be on the train," he told Melinda McCracken of Toronto's *Globe and Mail*. "There are just too many performers wanting to come along. They like the idea of the train. They normally travel by plane, so it's like a scenic tour for them."

In the aftermath of gatecrashers at Woodstock, and the violence at Altamont, city officials resisted the arrival of the Festival Express. The proposed first stop in Montreal, originally scheduled for June 20–21, was first changed to the 24th, and then cancelled after Lucien Saulnier, chairperson of the Montreal Executive Committee, claimed that, because the 24th was Saint-Jean-Baptiste Day, security would be compromised. The opening show changed to Robbie Robertson's hometown, Toronto, on June 27–28. City officials at the proposed final stop, Vancouver, also proved resistant, claiming that the intended venue was in the midst of installing artificial turf and unavailable. The traveling festival's final show, on July 4–5, moved to Calgary.

Conservative resistance was only one problem facing the tour. A left-wing activist group calling itself the Fourth of May Movement (in reference to the Kent State shootings a month before) leafleted Toronto claiming that the festival was capitalistic exploitation and that it should be a free event (tickets were priced at a modest $16 for both days, $14 in advance, and $10 for one day, $9 in advance). The Toronto press devoted much attention to their protest.

By the time that the Festival Express pulled into Toronto, tension was high. On Saturday morning, as the Canadian National Exhibition (CNE) Stadium filled with ticket buyers, approximately twenty-five hundred protestors crashed the gates, climbed barbed wire fences, and threw rocks and garbage cans at police, nine of whom were injured. "They wanted to have a riot," said Weir during a subsequent press conference. "They busted some cop's head. They busted it wide open. He's got a plate in his head now, and he may still be in critical condition. Is that worth sixteen fucking dollars—nearly killing a person?

"These people weren't looking for free music," he continued. "They were looking for trouble. They were looking for an excuse to bust cops' heads. They were pathologically anti-authoritarian. I know, I'm that way myself."

There were casualties on both sides. A medical staff that included four doctors (from different hospitals), ten senior nurses, and numerous volunteers treated not only 650 victims of bad LSD trips, but also ankles swollen by kicks from police horses, bruised arms and shoulders, and hands cut by barbed wire. Police arrested twenty-nine people. All but one had their sentences reduced to fines—a twenty-seventy-year-old from New York who was sentenced to thirty days in jail for grabbing the reins of a mounted officer's horse and spitting in the officer's face.

A compromise finally calmed things down—a free concert in Coronation Park. Starting out with a crowd of six thousand protesters, and joined by another six thousand after the stadium show ended at midnight, the Grateful Dead, Ian and Sylvia and Great Speckled Bird, and a variety of local groups, including the People's Revolutionary Band, performed on a flatbed truck until four in the morning. Another free concert on the second day of the festival drew a smaller crowd of approximately five hundred people.

On the day that it reported its coverage of the two-day festival, the Toronto *Globe and Mail* also acknowledged that gunshots had been fired at a rock festival in Iola, Wisconsin, after twenty-six people (reportedly members of motorcycle clubs) had begun fighting after a truck arrived with much-needed water.

Press coverage of the near riot in Toronto was fierce, drastically cutting into ticket sales for the remaining dates in Winnipeg and Calvary. The venture would lose more than three hundred and fifty thousand dollars. "I knew that we had lost a significant amount of money," said Walker, "and the bands knew it, but I said, 'Let's carry on and party.'"

For the remainder of the trip, the musicians took Walker up on his suggestion. Consuming all of the alcohol on the train, they passed a hat and raised eight hundred dollars. Walker ordered the train to stop in front of a small liquor store and bought out its entire inventory (including a humungous display bottle of Canadian Club).

The problems continued until the very end. At the final date, Calgary's mayor came backstage and demanded that the festival be free. Walker refused, emphasizing the point by punching the mayor in the face.

After the Festival Express concluded at Calgary's McMahon Stadium, Walker reassessed his career. "That was enough rock 'n' roll for me," he said. "I wasn't going to do it anymore. It was too much of a hassle for too small rewards. Everywhere I turned, I had a fight."

Fifty to seventy-five hours had been filmed aboard the train and during concerts, but the footage "disappeared" after cinematographers Peter Bizio (who would go on to win an Academy Award for *Mississippi Burning*) and Bob Fiore went unpaid. Each seized seven thousand feet of film as a lien against the seventy thousand dollars owed (for sound recording and legal fees).

More than three decades after the traveling train came to a stop, Grammy-winning director Bob Smeaton (*The Beatles Anthology*) and producer Gavin Poohman (the son of original producer Willem Poohman) reassembled footage that they found in Poohman's garage and in the Canadian National Film archives. Distributed by New York–based THINKfilms, *Festival Express* premiered during Toronto's International Film Festival in September 2003. Mixed by Eddie Kramer (producer/engineer for Jimi Hendrix, Led Zeppelin, and Santana), the film included three songs by The Band—"The Weight," "I Shall Be Released," and their set-closing cover of Little Richard's "Slippin' and Slidin'."

In a scene filmed aboard the train, Danko is seen leading a group that includes Jerry Garcia, John "Marmaduke" Dawson (of New Riders of the Purple Sage), and Janis Joplin (who would die three months later) in an extremely loose rendition of Huddie "Leadbelly" Ledbetter's "Ain't No More Cane (On the Brazos)," another song from *The Basement Tapes*. Video footage of "Long Black Veil" and "Rockin' Chair" from their Calgary performance was included on the DVD accompanying The Band's 2005 boxset *A Musical History*.

Edward Sharpe and the Magnetic Zeroes, Mumford and Sons, and Old Crow Medicine Show resurrected the spirit of the traveling festival with the Railroad Revival Tour, performing in six unique locations over six weeks in spring 2011.

As he withdrew following the death of Janis Joplin, The Band's relationship with Albert Grossman continued to deteriorate. Since moving to Woodstock, Grossman had shifted much of his focus to the empire that he was building in the small hamlet of Bearsville—complete with restaurants, a state-of-the-art analog recording studio, and a planned 250-seat theater (that would be completed by his widow). "I tried everything to get attention," remembered Odetta, one of his clients feeling neglected, "crying, screaming, and being logical, because he [built] his credibility on my success. I felt so betrayed by him that I could not hear the name Albert Grossman without the hairs on my back standing up."

"It all just got to be more than Albert could handle," The Band's former tour manager, Jonathan Taplin, told music journalist Paul Smart. "He began to let other people run things for him."

In the spring of 1970, Grossman had converted a barn into a pair of recording studios and launched the Bearsville Records label (distributed by Ampex until 1972 and by Warner Brothers afterward). In its fifteen years existence, the two studios would be used to record albums by 10cc, Foghat, Rory Block, Cheap Trick, Foreigner, New York Dolls, Bonnie Raitt, John Sebastian, Patti Smith, Spirit, They Might Be Giants, The Tubes, XTC, Muddy Waters, and Paul Butterfield's Better Days. The Rolling Stones rehearsed in one of the studios for a world tour in May 1978, with tapes bootlegged by Red Devil Records as the four-disc *The Complete Woodstock Tapes*. "[Bearsville is] our own studio," said Danko, "the first one we don't have to tear down after we're through."

"I had my own key to the studio," said Helm, "and drums set up that I never had to take down. I had this wonderful world built up in my head where The Band would just be making music all the time, and it would just be hand over fist with money and albums, and who's got time to count it?"

Bearsville's first four releases, in 1970, included jazz pianist and composer Gil Evans's eponymous seventh album. Robbie Robertson produced the debut album by Jesse Winchester, a gentle-voiced, Louisiana-born and Memphis-raised singer-songwriter who had taken refuge in Montreal (after receiving his draft notice). Like The Band's best work, Winchester's songs, including "Yankee Lady," "Biloxi," and "The Last Tennessee Waltz," yearned for the South. "I met Robbie in Ottawa in a basement of a church," said Winchester on BBC's *Old Grey Whistle Test*. "He was a friend of a friend. We made a demo tape and he brought it to Albert."

Recorded in Nashville (and released on Bearsville), Festival Express participants Ian and Sylvia Tyson's first album with their country-rock band, Great Speckled Bird, marked the production debut of Todd Rundgren, an Upper Darby, Pennsylvania–born technical/musical wizard for whom Grossman provided an outlet for creative expression.

After cutting his teeth with a Butterfield Blues Band–like group Woody's Truck Stop, Rundgren had joined a teenage psychedelic/garage band, Nazz, in 1967. Fueled by his self-penned pop songs, including "Hello, It's Me" (which he would re-record, at a slower pace, for his double-disc second solo album, *Something/Anything*, four years later),

Nazz toured through 1970, releasing three albums and inspiring The Yardbirds' song "The Nazz Are Blue. "To listen to The Nazz is to understand what rock and roll is all about," said music critic Jon Landau. "There is an exhilaration that rock has always sought to express."

Added to Grossman's roster when Nazz manager Michael Friedman joined Grossman's company, Rundgren released his debut solo outing, *Runt*, on Bearsville in June 1970. He would remain the label's most prolific artist—releasing nine solo albums and seven with progressive rock band Utopia before 1984. He would make his mark in production as well, overseeing albums by a lengthy list of artists including Badfinger, Grand Funk Railroad, Hall and Oates, Meat Loaf, Patti Smith, The Tubes, and the Psychedelic Furs and expanding to video production after the building of the multi-million-dollar Utopia Video Studios in 1979.

There is confusion concerning the mixing of *Stage Fright*. Rundgren, who engineered the recording sessions, and Glyn Johns, a British producer that The Band met at the Isle of Wight Festival, prepared mixes. On the original release, Johns was the only one credited. "[The Band] made an agreement with [Johns] to have him mix the album," Rundgren told *Relix* magazine in 2004, "but since I had recorded the whole album, they figured I should have a shot as well. They sent me, with the tapes, to London and put me in a studio [where I could] mix. I gave half the reels to Glyn and he mixed [those], while I was mixing the other half, and then we swapped reels and completed our mixes."

Rundgren presented both sets of mixes to The Band. "They weren't completely happy with either one," he recalled. "Glyn Johns was too busy to leave England, but [The Band and I] went back to Bearsville Studios and essentially went through a very long, torturous remix process. We would spend all day mixing a tune and then they would take the references back, and come back the next day with new ideas or start the mix all over again. It took a terrifically long time because you had to satisfy five. In the end, I have no idea which ones went on the original record or which ones might be on the reissue because in the end they made the decisions about which ones would go where."

Released three months after the conclusion of the Freedom Express journey, *Stage Fright* met with mixed critical reaction. "Memorable as most of these songs are," said Robert Christgau, "they never hook in—never give up the musical–verbal phrase that might encapsulate their every-which-way power, which perhaps means that they don't have much to say."

"How many times do we have to sit through this movie to see it," asked *Rolling Stone* critic John Burke.

Work on Grossman's studio was still in progress when The Band returned to Woodstock after a year of touring, but they wasted no time using it to record their next album—*Cahoots*. "Instead of sitting around home and turning on a two-track," said Helm, "we [could go] to the studio and turn on the sixteen-track."

Cahoots opened with "Life Is a Carnival," reminiscent of "W. S. Walcott Medicine Show" and credited to Robertson, Helm, and Danko. "It was one of the last of those real good Band songs that came out of that workshop setting we liked," said Helm. "Rick and I worked on that song's sprung rhythms for five days."

Hudson's accordion and Helm's mandolin accented the cosmopolitan feel of Dylan's "When I Paint My Masterpiece." Temporarily residing in Woodstock, Van Morrison shared slightly inebriated lead vocals with Manuel on "4% Pantomime" (the title referred to the difference between Johnny Walker black and red whiskeys). "Van and Richard were acting this whole thing out," Robertson told Peter Viney. "For a second, when I was watching it, it became soundless and it all became visuals—people's hands, veins, and people's necks. It was almost like this movement thing was going on and the music was carrying itself."

"You couldn't kill that kind of friendship and creativity," Helm told Andy Gill of *Mojo* magazine in November 2000. "[Whenever] you got [Manuel and Morrison] together, you [could] bet your ass it was gonna get good—'4% Pantomime' happened right in front of [our] fuckin' eyes, just like 'Don't Ya Tell Henry.'"

When it came to adding horns to "Life Is a Carnival," The Band reached out to New Orleans producer/arranger Allen Toussaint. The scion of a railroad-worker father and a piano-playing mother, Toussaint had bridged the piano playing of Professor Longhair and old-school R&B of Fats Domino and Dave Bartholomew with harder-edged funk and dance music and helped to craft a distinctive New Orleans style of R&B. He had recorded an album (as Al Tousan) for RCA in the late 1950s, but his greatest achievements would come out of the spotlight. As a staff producer for Minit Records and its Instant subsidiary in the early 1960s, and the co-owner (after 1965) of a production company with Marshall Sheorn, he would apply his magic to hits by Ernie K-Doe, Irma Thomas, Art and Aaron Neville, Chris Kenner, and Benny Spellman. As a songwriter, Toussaint was responsible for a treasure-trove of memorable tunes (some credited to his mother's name). Al Hirt ("Java") and Herb Alpert and the Tijuana Brass ("Whipped Cream") turned his early instrumentals into megahits, while Otis Redding covered his "Ruler of My Heart," originally recorded by Irma Thomas as "Pain in My Heart." Ernie K-Doe's "Mother-in-Law" topped the charts in 1961. Chris Kenner reached the charts with "I Like It Like That" and "Land of a Thousand Dances," while the Pointer Sisters scored a hit with "Yes We Can Can." Glen Campbell's recording of "Southern Nights" was a Grammy nominee for song of the year in 1977. The Rolling Stones and The Who covered Toussaint's "Fortune Teller," popularized by Benny Spellman. Robert

Plant and Alison Krauss included it on their 2005 collaboration, *Raising Sand*.

Toussaint worked on Paul McCartney and Wings' *Venus and Mars* in 1975 and collaborated with McCartney on a cover, "I Want to Walk You Home," included on a Fats Domino tribute album. He recorded an album and toured with Elvis Costello in 2006. The Rock and Roll Hall of Fame would induct him in 1998, the Louisiana Hall of Fame in 2009, and the Blues Hall of Fame in 2011.

Beginning in the mid-1960s, Toussaint worked with New Orleans–born R&B singer Lee Dorsey. Scoring a top-ten hit, "Ride Your Pony," in 1965, they followed with a trio of hits—"Get Out of My Life, Woman" (covered by the Butterfield Blues Band), "Holy Cow" (covered by The Band on *Moondog Matinee*), and the massive-selling "Working in a Coal Mine" (a staple of Danko's solo shows)—the following year.

Toussaint had just completed producing Dorsey's album *Yes, We Can* when The Band summoned him to arrange horns, a task he would later reprise for *Rock of Ages*. "He's just a master," Danko told me in 1991. "When he came up to Woodstock, he was running a fever. We put him in one of the cabins in the woods and asked him what he needed. He just needed some chicken soup, a tape recorder, headphones, and some [manuscript paper]. He wrote the arrangements off the top of his head; he didn't work with a piano."

Most of the songs on *Cahoots* failed to stir much excitement. "It was harder for me to find something different for every song," said Hudson. "We had more clarity, more highs, which meant more punch. I used a harder sound. The softer sound that made the earlier material a period piece didn't fit in with the overall dynamics in the *Cahoots* album."

"It was a frustrating, horrible feeling," said Robertson. "I just wasn't as inspired to write. . . . [There are tunes on the album] that I still enjoy, but it doesn't play comfortably for me; it nauseates me in places."

"Last of the Blacksmiths" and "Where Do We Go from Here" aimed for the rustic feel of The Band's first two albums, but, rather than romanticizing the South, the former asked, "How you gonna replace human hands?" and the latter mourned the passing of the railroad era, pondering, "How can you sleep when the whistle don't moan?" The hard-rocking "Smoke Signal" told about "young brothers in cahoots" trying to get by when their "neighborhood isn't there anymore."

Cahoots's lack of focus reflected the increasing disjointedness of The Band. "Everybody showed up [for recording sessions]," recalled Robertson, "but it wasn't like everybody was there. There was a feeling of pulling teeth. Everything was hard. It was painful trying to do some things. It was hard for me to write under those circumstances, hard for us to get together and make music."

Manuel's personal problems had begun infiltrating group dynamics. "Once [Manuel] dried up [as a songwriter]," said Jonathan Taplin, "Robbie had to write everything. He was up for it, but it put a lot more pressure on him."

"I did everything to get [Manuel] to write," said Robertson. "I begged him, I pleaded with him, I offered to become his partner in songwriting; there's no answer. My theory is that some people have one song in them, some have five, some have a hundred."

"It's tough when everybody's not pulling their weight," said Ronnie Hawkins, "when people aren't able to go onstage because they're falling down or puking into pianos."

Danko also struggled with personal demons. "I'm a cripple in disguise," he told *Rolling Stone*'s Mikal Gilmore in 1977. "Right after [*Music from Big Pink*], I had a car wreck and broke a lot of bones in my neck and back. On top of that, I took pills all my life for nerves."

Burdened by his band mates' travails, Robertson lost desire to tour. "It was like dragging this monster around the country," he said, "and, when you're in a group, you're very affected by it; it's no different than a family. If somebody is ill or an alcoholic, the whole family is affected. Everybody has to deal with it. It was a very difficult time. Everybody became separated and discouraged."

After another tenuous year of touring in Europe and the United States, it was time for The Band to take a break. Before their hiatus, however, they agreed to record their weeklong engagement (December 28–31, 1971) at New York's Academy of Music for a live album. Accompanied by a five-piece section, arranged by Toussaint with help from New Orleans' Mac "Dr. John" Rebennack, Bobby Charles (writer of "See You Later, Alligator" and "Walking to New Orleans"), and legendary pop/R&B songwriter Doc Pomus, the quintet revisited material from their first four albums with revived energy, adding a couple of well-played covers. There were four tunes from *Music from Big Pink*, five from *The Band*, three from *Stage Fright*, and one ("Life Is a Carnival") from *Cahoots*.

A Holland–Dozier–Holland tune popularized by Marvin Gaye and covered by the Rolling Stones and The Who, "Baby Don't Do It" opened the set, while a jubilant "(I Don't Want to Hang Up) My Rock and Roll Shoes," originally the B-side of R&B singer Chuck Willis's final single in 1958, concluded proceedings with optimism. A previously unreleased tune, "Get up Jake," written by Robertson, and reminiscent of The Band's early recordings, debuted.

The horn section represented some of jazz's best sidemen. Dayton, Ohio–born lead trumpet player Eugene Edward "Snooky" Young had played with big bands led by Jimmy Lunceford, Lionel Hampton, Count Basie, and Benny Carter. Alabama-born tuba, baritone saxophone, and euphonium player Howard Johnson had played with Ray Charles, Miles Davis, and Gil Evans, as well as being the cornerstone of Taj Mahal's early 1970s big band. He would later be a key member of Levon Helm's post-Band group in the 2000s. Chicago-born tenor and soprano saxophone and English horn player Joe Farrell had worked with Elvin Jones and Charles Mingus. At the time, he was in the midst of collaborating with Chick Corea, Airto Moreira, and Flora Purim on a new "crystal silence" approach to improvisation. Brooklyn-born trombone player Earl McIntyre would go on to record with Gil Evans, Charles Mingus, Miles Davis, McCoy Tyner, Lou Rawls, Stevie Wonder, Taj Mahal, Count Basie, and the Duke Ellington Orchestra. Newly arrived in New York when recruited by The Band, J. D. Parran, a multi-reeds player from St. Louis, went on to record with Stevie Wonder and John Lennon and teach jazz and African American studies at the Harlem School for the Arts and City College of New York. "With [Toussaint's arrangements], everybody played separately," said Robertson. "It was kind of like a Dixieland approach."

One of the highlights of The Band's concerts had been Hudson's improvised organ solo introduction to "Chest Fever." During the New Year's Eve show, the keyboardist summoned a montage of melodies (including "Auld Lang Syne") so distinctive that his solo became a musical experience on its own, credited on *Rock of Ages* as "The Genetic Method." "[Hudson] combined all his vast knowledge into one unbelievable solo shot," said Robertson. "I find Garth's organ playing a continual delight. He never blatantly quotes from his sources but rather builds improvisation or quotes, hinting at them, and ringing changes in your ears that haunt you. He has mastered the use of dissonance and the unexpected note in a line in something of the manner of Thelonious Monk. I break up laughing at what Garth does, and then am totally frustrated trying to sort out the rearrangement of music he presents in this kaleidoscopic manner—nursery rhymes, Celtic reels, late-night show organ music, old hymns, and ancient popular melodies."

Originally released as two vinyl discs, *Rock of Ages* expanded with an additional ten tracks when remixed for CD in 2001, adding "I Shall Be Released," "Up on Cripple Creek," "The Rumour," "Rockin' Chair," and "Time to Kill," and a Danko-crooned cover of the Stevie Wonder–penned Four Tops ballad "Loving You Is Sweeter Than Ever."

There were also four previously unavailable tracks recorded during The Band's New Year's Eve reunion with their former employer, Bob Dylan—"Crash on the Levee (Down in the Flood)," "When I Paint My Masterpiece," "Don't Ya Tell Henry," and "Like a Rolling Stone." "It was the final night," recalled Robertson. "There was a thrill in the air. We were excited about New Year's Eve and then Dylan joined us for the encore. When he came out, we thought we could wing it and wing it we did. We thought, 'We're not gonna fall off this wire.'"

"The crowd had already been with us for three hours," remembered Helm, "but they roared as Bob came on in an old corduroy jacket and strapped into a solid-body guitar. We ripped through a bunch of unrehearsed tunes that Bob called during group huddles onstage while the crowd shouted out hundreds of requests."

"[Dylan] wasn't doing any live performances," said Robertson to Bonnie Stiernberg of *Paste* magazine in 2013. "When I told him that we were gonna do this thing at the Academy of Music in New York and that we were gonna play these four nights and the last night was New Year's Eve, I said, 'Do you wanna come and spend New Year's Eve with us? We'll do an encore and then we'll hang out for New Year's Eve.' He said, 'That sounds good,' and because he hadn't been playing for quite a while, or very rarely doing anything, I didn't know whether he'd feel comfortable doing that, but he answered in a few seconds with, 'Yeah, that sounds good.' The only problem was in the way that it all worked out—we didn't rehearse with Bob—and I thought, 'Well, you know, we've played music so much together, we can wing it, we can handle it,' and that's what we did. And when I listen to these recordings now, we were so winging it." We didn't know what songs we were gonna do—we were figuring that out on the stage. It just enlightened a great moment."

Following the show, Helm spoke with Dylan in the dressing room. When the singer-songwriter told him that he had been considering touring with the Grateful Dead (an idea that would take another decade and a half to come to fruition), Helm suggested a reunion with The Band instead. Dylan told him that he would think about it.

Released on the third anniversary of the Woodstock Festival on August 15, 1971, *Rock of Ages* peaked at number six on *Billboard*'s top two hundred, with critics proclaiming it a masterpiece. "[*Rock of Ages*] immediately joins the ranks of such celebrated in-person recordings as Mingus at Monterey, Count Basie in Sweden, Duke Ellington's Seattle concert, Miles at the Blackhawk, and Ray Charles at Atlanta," said Ralph Gleason. "In other words, it is a classic."

"Rock of Ages addresses several different American archetypes," wrote C. Michael Bailey in the April 2012 issue of *All about Jazz*. "There is the subject of hard work, with promise ('King Harvest Will Surely Come') and avoidance ('Get up Jake'). There is toil and loss ('The Night They Drove Old Dixie Down') and fear ('Stage Fright'). Celebration and good times are represented in 'The W. S. Walcott Medicine Show,' 'Across the Great Divide,' and 'Life Is a Carnival.' [It even deals with] the Biblical, perhaps better than any other place in popular music—'The Weight,' 'Unfaithful Servant'—but these songs are just snapshots. The Band's play list is a document, a history, intelligently and sensitively rendered through music."

A four-CD/DVD collection, *Live at the Academy of Music, 1971*, released on September 17, 2013, included every song performed over the four nights, including fourteen previously unavailable tracks "uncut, unedited, and straight from the master tapes." The DVD featured two songs—

"King Harvest (Has Surely Come)" and "The W. S. Walcott Medicine Show"—filmed by Howard Alk and Murray Lerner.

Although they proved that their concerts could be as exciting as ever, the Academy of Music shows would put a cap to The Band's first era. It would be another year and half before the five musicians would again be onstage. "I was rebelling against the album/tour/album cycle," said Robertson, "and questioning whether that was the way to work."

"Some of us felt stronger about touring, others about recording," said Helm. "I preferred playing to just about anything."

Playing opportunities during their hiatus included an album by New Orleans' Bobby Charles, coproduced by Danko (with guest appearances by Hudson, Helm, Manuel, Dr. John, and Amos Garrett), and a cover of Paul Simon's song "Groundhog" on Peter Yarrow's *That's Enough for Me*, produced by Robertson, and featuring guest appearances by Helm, Hudson, and the songwriter.

For the most part, though, idle time dominated the lives of the musicians. Alcoholism increasingly plagued Manuel, while Helm and Danko continued to get into automobile accidents. "One element of danger surpassed the others until it was just frightening," said Robertson. "One thing equals another, whether it's drinking or drugging or driving as fast as you can or staying up for as long as you can."

Robertson had been working on an album-length suite, tentatively title *The Works*, inspired by the avant-garde music of Polish composer/conductor Krzysztof Penderecki. "It's very passionate music and depressing and weird," he said. "I can't remember what piece it was that influenced me, but it made me think of an idea that I started to work on at the time. I worked out this melody and then I found countermelodies for it, but I could not find any words for it, so I just kept working on it. . . . I would get fifteen minutes into it and be exhausted. I realized it was much more involved and advanced, that it took a whole other kind of writing and attention."

"There was nothing for The Band to do on it really," he added. "It didn't have anything to do with them and there was no demand for it. It was not something the record companies would be interested in, so I was doing it on my own, with an American Indian thing in mind. It was around the time or after the Wounded Knee episode—I was thinking about what happened to those people. They were going to make this movie about Wounded Knee—Marlon Brando was involved—and I was going to write it for that. It fell apart, so it was something that I didn't finish."

With Manuel no longer writing songs and Robertson's focus diverted to his unfinished project, The Band returned to the songs on which they had cut their musical teeth for their fifth album, *Moondog Matinee*. Tunes included Fats Domino's "I'm Ready," Chuck Berry's "The Promised Land," Sam Cooke's "A Change Is Gonna Come," Clarence "Frogman"

Henry's "Ain't Got a Home," and Allen Toussaint's "Holy Cow." Greil Marcus took the title of his 1975 study of American popular music, *Mystery Train*, from one of the album's most exciting tunes, a haunting rolling-blues song that had been recorded by Junior Parker, its composer, in 1953, and popularized by Elvis Presley a year later. "It was a nice way for all of us to get back together after a long sabbatical and play a little music," said Danko.

"That was all we could do at the time," Helm admitted to *Gritz* magazine in 2002. "We couldn't get along—we all knew that fairness was a bunch of shit. . . . We were getting screwed, we couldn't sit down [together] and play music, all that collaboration was over, and that type of song was all we could do."

Despite the friction between band members, The Band managed to give each song on *Moondog Matinee* a distinctive flavor. "It's the only album I've ever heard," said Robertson, "where I thought the interpretations came anywhere neared complementing the originals. To us, it was more than just a bunch of cover tunes. There was something of a strength-building factor involved in going after these songs."

Intended partly as a tribute to Allen Freed's rock-and-roll radio show, the title of *Moondog Matinee* also served as a reminder, according to Helm, of "the torrid afternoon shows we used to do in Toronto for the teenage-girl crowd ten years earlier, a much simpler time."

Many of the originators of rock and roll and R&B had faded into the past by the late 1960s, but resurgence sparked with a series of *Oldies but Goodies* concerts produced by Ron Delsener at Madison Square Garden. John Lennon and Yoko Ono and Bob Dylan were among attendees. Little Richard, Chuck Berry, Jerry Lee Lewis, and Ronnie Spector (of The Ronettes) revived their careers. Rick Nelson, frustrated that the crowd wanted to hear his hits and were inattentive when he tried playing new tunes, would write "The Garden Party."

John Lennon would release a Phil Spector–produced album of golden oldies (*Rock and Roll*) two years later, but *Moondog Matinee* was a disappointment to many of The Band's fans and critics. It barely broke into the top thirty and its only single, "Ain't Got a Home," backed with "Get up Jake," stalled at number seventy-three. "Unfortunately, people compared it to everything else we'd done," said Robertson.

Although they had agreed not to tour in support of *Moondog Matinee*, The Band consented to participating in the Summer Jam at the Watkins Glen Grand Prix Speedway in Watkins Glen, New York, on July 28, 1973. New York–based concert promoters Shelley Finkle and Jon Koplik had conceived the event after a Grateful Dead concert that they had booked in Hartford, Connecticut, in 1972 climaxed with a jam session with the Allman Brothers Band's Dickey Betts, Berry Oakley, and Jai Johanny Johanson joining the San Francisco–based band.

Neither Finkle nor Koplik had any idea that Watkins Glen would draw as many people as it did—six hundred thousand—at the time, the most people gathered for a concert, according to the *Guinness Book of World Records*, and far surpassing initial estimates of one hundred and fifty thousand. The intended one-day event became a three-day experience when gates opened two days early.

Four years after Woodstock, the Summer Jam radiated with a much different spirit. The Vietnam War had ended with the signing of a peace agreement seven months before, but coverage of the scandal that would lead to President Richard Nixon's resignation a year later had begun to dominate the daily newspaper. "Watkins Glen could easily have been an immensely powerful response to Nixon and the Watergate scandal," wrote Robert Santelli in *Aquarius Rising—The Rock Festival Years*, "but the youth of the nation had grown tired of being politically active. Many had tasted the partial delight of seeing some peace in Southeast Asia and felt it was enough. The word most commonly associated with the Watkins Glen festival, according to those reporters who covered the event, was 'party.'"

On the day before the concert, the crowd (which had grown to nearly half a million) witnessed mini-concert sound checks (requested by Robertson). The Band got things started with a set that began with "The Night They Drove Old Dixie Down" and ended with "The W. S. Walcott Medicine Show," with a pair of untitled instrumentals and covers of "Don't Do It" and Buddy Holly's "Raining in My Heart" in between.

The next day, after two lengthy sets by the Grateful Dead, The Band started their two-hour performance with covers of Chuck Berry's "Back to Memphis" and the Four Tops' "Loving You Is Sweeter Than Ever," segueing into solid versions of "The Shape I'm In," "The Weight," "Stage Fright," and "I Shall Be Released." After picking up the tempo with "Baby, Don't Do It," and a *Basement Tape* tune, "Endless Highway," a thunderstorm forced a break. As the rain began to lighten, Hudson returned to the stage and launched into his trademark organ improvisation. Just as the rain stopped and the sun came out, the rest of the group slipped onto the stage and launched into a version of "Chest Fever" that left all in astonishment. They kept the magic stirred with more crowd-rousing tunes—"The Night They Drove Old Dixie Down," "Across the Great Divide," "Life Is a Carnival," "Up on Cripple Creek," "This Wheel's on Fire," "The W. S. Walcott Medicine Show," and Bobby "Blue" Bland's "Share Your Love With Me." A well-deserved encore started with an especially turbo-charged take on Little Richard's "Slippin' and Slidin'" and concluded triumphantly with "Rag Mama Rag."

Members of The Band also regaled the audience after joining an hour-long concert-ending jam (following the Allman Brothers Band's three-hour set) that included Buddy Holly's "Not Fade Away," the Donovan-inspired "Mountain Jam," and Chuck Berry's "Johnny B. Goode."

Capitol released a CD, *Live at Watkins Glen*, in 1995, without The Band's participation, purporting to include ten tracks from their set, but liner notes to the 2001 remixed *Moondog Matinee* claimed that a cover of Chuck Berry's "The Promised Land" replaced the concert's opening tune "Going Back to Memphis." "Endless Highway" was later also revealed as an overdubbed post-*Cahoots* studio recording. *Live at Watkins Glen* was subsequently withdrawn.

Refusing to renew his contract with Columbia Records, Dylan relocated across the United States. After making an onscreen appearance (and providing the soundtrack) for the Sam Peckinpah–directed western *Pat Garrett and Billy the Kid*, costarring James Coburn and Kris Kristofferson, and filmed in Durango, Mexico, he had continued to Southern California, where he settled in a large estate on Pacific Coast Highway in Malibu. David Geffen, who had started Asylum Records in 1970, unrelentingly pursued him. "We heard that Geffen had offered Bob a lot of money and his own label," said Helm.

Geffen's interests in Dylan extended to The Band. "The word was that he wanted us to sign with his Asylum label," Helm recalled, "and we would do an album and tour with Bob."

Although Geffen invited him to dinner, Helm declined. "Then I heard he had flown off to Paris with Robbie and Joni Mitchell," he said. "Next thing we knew, Robbie had put his house on the market and moved his family to California."

"I'd always fantasized about living on the ocean," said Robertson. "I'd visited friends by the water and it had always moved me. I thought I'd try it for a while."

Arriving in the Golden State, Robertson felt like a fish that had found water. Moving into Carole King's former house, in Malibu, he made guest appearances on Joni Mitchell's song "Raised on Robbery" and Carly Simon and James Taylor's top-ten hit "Mockingbird." By October, the rest of The Band had joined him. "I'd been saying for a year that California was the logical next step," he said. "The music business had relocated to sunny Los Angeles and we needed to be there to survive."

"My original idea was to move to California for about three months," said Danko, who like Helm retained ownership of his Woodstock home. "Instead we came out and stayed eight years."

Originally conceived by tour promoter Bill Graham as maybe ten or twelve shows, Dylan and The Band's reunion expanded to twenty-one cities in forty days. Rehearsals at a Jewish boy's camp went smoothly. "We sat down and ran through an incredible number of tunes," said Robertson. "It was just instant. We would request tunes, and then Bob would ask to play certain tunes of ours."

Recorded between eight-hours-a-day tour rehearsals, *Planet Waves* included "On a Night Like This," "You Angel You," "Dirge," the possibly autobiographical "Wedding Song," and two versions of "Forever

Young." Side A closed with a country-rock version, while side B kicked off with a more rocking interpretation. Robertson later adopted the slow, delicate melody of "Hazel" for his lament for lost love, "It Makes No Difference."

Originally titled *Ceremonies of the Horsemen* (from a line in Dylan's "Love Minus Zero/No Limit") and scheduled for Christmastime release, the album's title changed to *Planet Waves* and the release date pushed to January 17, two weeks into the 1974 tour. Although it would become the first Dylan album to reach the top of the Billboard charts (based on advance orders of nearly six hundred thousand copies) and rise to number eighteen on the *Village Voice*'s Pazz and Jop Critics' Poll, it would sell a disappointing one hundred thousand copies (after initial orders). "In a time when all the most prestigious music, even what passes for funk, is coated with silicone grease," wrote Robert Christgau, "Dylan is telling us to take that grease and jam it. Sure, he's domestic, but his version of conjugal love is anything but smug, and this comes through in both the lyrics and the sound of the record itself. Blissful, sometimes, but sometimes it sounds like stray cat music—scrawny, cocky, and yowling up the stairs."

"It wasn't an appropriate Bob Dylan album," admitted Robertson, "and it wasn't super-unusual. All these songs were as simple as he's ever done, and people thought it wasn't a real effort."

Columbia Records responded to Dylan's temporary departure by releasing *Dylan*, a collection of outtakes from the *Self Portrait* and *New Morning* sessions that many critics agreed was the weakest in the singer-songwriter's catalogue. "Dylan didn't want the record to be released," said the *All Music Guide*'s Stephen Thomas Erlewine, "and it's easy to see why—the album is a collection of covers that are poorly performed on purpose."

The overwhelming demand for tickets had made Dylan and The Band's six-week tour one of the most financially successful of the decade. Musically, they more than stood up to the challenge. "The most significant thing about the '74 tour to me was proving that we weren't crazy," said Robertson. "It was not incredibly different from what we'd done with Bob before. It was just this kind of dynamics—it got loud and it got soft. We'd come way down when the singing came in, and when the solos started, we'd go screaming into the skies."

"It was like Frank and Jesse James getting back together again," said Danko, "and hitting a few banks."

Asylum released *Before the Flood*, a double-disc live album mostly recorded during Dylan and The Band's tour-ending shows on June 20, 1974. The *Village Voice* listed it in the fourth slot of their Pazz and Jop Critics' poll. "There is evidently an effort to match the material—nearly all from much earlier in [Dylan's] career—with a suitable style of delivery," wrote Tom Nolan in *Rolling Stone*, "a vocal stance which can express in a later year the brilliant and sometimes malevolent energy contained by these pieces when they were first created. Dylan's principal solution is to sing in aggressive, up-tempo fashion, borrowing voltage from the Band's rock backing to substitute for the hungry power both he and the Band have outgrown."

"The Band take part in transforming Dylan's classics," said Adam Thomas of *Sputnik Music*. "When relegated to a backing position they run with a loose, free-flowing, almost improvisational sound that brings the slight bluesiness in Dylan's original compositions to the forefront. . . . When given time to perform their own songs, The Band drops the barnstorming approach that they took while performing Dylan's material to become a tight and precise unit. This change in dynamic allows The Band's songs to compete with Dylan's for many of the top moments."

"The Rolling Stones are mechanical dolls by comparison," said Robert Christgau of The Band's performance on the album, "The Faces merely sloppy, the [Grateful] Dead positively quiet. The MC5 achieved something similar by ignoring musicianship altogether, but while The Band sounds undisciplined, threatening to destroy their headlong momentum by throwing out one foot or elbow too many, they never abandon their enormous technical ability. In this, they follow their boss."

Despite the critical acclaim, *Before the Flood* sold even less than *Planet Waves*. Peaking at number three on the charts, it would remain in the top ten for only ten weeks.

Unauthorized soundboard recordings of Dylan and The Band's Valentine's Day tour finale at Los Angeles' Forum circulated on *Paint the Daytime Black* (which combined most of the February 14 afternoon show and five tracks from the evening show) on the Q label, reissued (by TMOQ Japan) as *Saint Valentine's Day*. A four-CD set, *The Complete Before the Flood*, on Seymour Records included the full afternoon and late shows.

Down in the Flood, an unauthorized DVD documentary about Dylan and The Band's collaboration, was released in 2012. "[It covers] rich musical ground," said Michael Berick in *No Depression*, "and does so in a very informative, entertaining way. . . . The filmmakers do an excellent job coming up with a strong set of close associates and music experts to talk intelligently about the story."

Although they took most of the following months following the tour with Dylan off, members of The Band occasionally surfaced. Helm and Danko appeared on "Revolution Blues," one of the hardest hitting tunes on Toronto-born Neil Young's fifth solo album, *On the Beach*. In the song, narrated by a loner who lives "in a trailer at the edge of town" with "twenty-five rifles just to keep the population down," Young focuses on Laurel Canyon in the Hollywood Hills, "full of famous stars," singing, "I hate them worse than lepers and I'll kill them in the cars." Dedicating the tune to mass murderer Charlie Manson during a show in San Francisco in January 1983, Young touched on a still-sensitive nerve.

As the opening act on Crosby, Stills, Nash, and Young's summer of '74 world tour, The Band toured the United States and (joined by Joni Mitchell and Jesse Colin Young, former leader of pioneering folk-rock band The Youngbloods) Europe. The excitement of the headliners' performances still resonates on a three-CD/DVD box set released in August 2013. "We only multi-tracked eight or nine shows," Graham Nash told *Rolling Stone*, "but the spirit of [our] band [was incredible]—[we were] a fuckin' great band."

The Band had a tougher time. When they performed for seventy thousand people at London's Wembley Stadium, their intimate sound was "somehow so inappropriate—not dynamic enough, I guess," remembered Elvis Costello.

Returning to Malibu, The Band settled into Shangri-La, the recording studio that they had built in Helm's home near Zuma Beach. "It had been an expensive bordello in its previous incarnation," the drummer said, "so it came with a Naugahyde bar and a lot of mirrored walls, one of which I commandeered as my HQ. . . . We put in a good pool table, stocked the bar, and built a twenty-four-track recording studio in what had been the master suite."

"It felt like we were a street gang that had a place to go," said Robertson, who used the studio to produce *Beautiful Noise* for pop singer Neil Diamond and to "clean up" tracks that had been recorded in the basement of Big Pink to prepare them for release. "We'd go down to the studio," he remembered, "and shoot pool, play music, talk, and figure things out."

Manuel lived most of the year in a stable that had once housed TV's talking horse, Mr. Ed, and was converted into a small cottage behind the main house.

Returning to Woodstock, Helm reunited with Levon and the Hawks' former producer, Henry Glover, and launched RCO Productions. For its first project, they produced *The Muddy Waters Woodstock Album*, released on MCA/Chess. Hudson joined the sessions in February 1974. "I got a twelve-thousand-dollar advance from the record company," recalled Helm, "which helped to pay the plumbing bill for my barn."

Waters arrived in Woodstock with pianist Pinetop Perkins and guitarist Bob Margolin. "We produced a pretty good album for him," said Helm, "with [contributions by] artists like Dr. John and Paul Butterfield. . . . Most of The Band played on it as well."

The Band (minus Manuel) reunited with Dylan and Neil Young on March 3, 1975, to perform a benefit concert organized by Bill Graham for SNACK (Students Need Athletics, Culture, and Kicks). In addition to performing "Loving You Is Sweeter Than Ever" and "The Weight," they provided accompaniment for Young's "Are You Ready for the Country," "Ain't That a Lot of Love," and "Looking for a Love" and Dylan's "I Want You." A medley of Young's "Helpless" and Dylan's "Knockin' on

Heaven's Door" kicked the performance into overdrive, while a sing-along version of the Carter Family's "Will the Circle Be Unbroken" closed the short set.

For much of 1975, The Band worked on their sixth album (and their first studio recording in four years), *Northern Lights—Southern Cross*. "Of all of our albums, *Northern Lights—Southern Cross* took the longest," said Danko, who mostly played upright bass on its eight tracks, "because we had our own studio, everybody would just saunter in when they felt like it. It was hard to arrive in the same place at the same time."

With *Northern Lights—Southern Cross*, The Band proved capable of delivering an album as aurally strong as *Music from Big Pink* and *The Band*. The *Los Angeles Times'* Robert Hilburn called it "one of the most valuable and influential bodies of work in contemporary pop music." "We'd worked on this new music for months," said Helm, "on and off, and in the end we got eight extended songs, all credited to Robbie Robertson. I sang on half: 'Forbidden Fruit,' 'Ophelia,' 'Ring Your Bell,' and Robbie's tribute to the Cajuns, 'Acadian Driftwood,' which had that old three-voice Band mixture on the verses. Rick Danko did one of his best vocals on 'It Makes No Difference,' and Richard sang beautifully on 'Hobo Jungle' and 'Rags and Bones.'"

Unlimited accessibility to Shangri-La offered endless possibilities for Hudson, who overdubbed, according to Helm, "as many as half a dozen keyboard tracks onto a single song using the ARP, Roland, Mini Moog, and other synthesizers . . . giving the music an almost orchestral overlay."

Hudson's horns flavored much of the album. He dubbed a piccolo and bagpipe onto "Acadian Driftwood," blending with three-time national fiddle champion Byron Berline (Dillard and Clark, Flying Burrito Brothers, Country Gazette).

The opening track, "Forbidden Fruit," reminded listeners of The Band's best work. A modern-day parable with roots in the Old Testament, and set in New York's Times Square, it voiced the inner thoughts of a "high and lonesome" penniless drifter who's reflecting on his plight and reminding himself, "you've got one life that you'd better not waste."

Introduced as a bonus track on the 2001 remixed CD, "Twilight" offered a humanizing response to war, with the narrator (Danko) addressing a younger man (perhaps his son) who has gone off to "serve his country," while he's been left behind to "guard the home." Letters and "silly souvenirs from far away" are no substitute for the companionship that he misses as he grows older, and he realizes that "twilight is the loneliest time of the day."

"It Makes No Difference," sung by Danko, is one of pop music's saddest songs. Though he has tried all that he could to get over a failed romance, the song's protagonist cannot move on. The sun no longer shines, rain falls constantly, and "clouds never hung so low before."

Nostalgia for the past reflected in the album's first single, "Ophelia," backed with "Rags and Bones." In the former, the narrator (Helm) takes a cab to old stomping grounds and looks up an old friend. Discovering the windows boarded, despite mail by the door, he ponders, "Why would anybody leave so quickly?" Realizing that "the neighborhood just ain't the same," he questions, "Why do the best things always disappear?"

Sung by Manuel, "Rags and Bones" recalled the sounds that had fueled Robertson's passion for music as a youth. The singing of a "young Caruso on the fire escape" and the fiddling of a pencil-selling fiddler spark reminiscences of trolley cars, whistles blowing at noon, cat fights, watchdogs howling, fire engine sirens, an organ grinder and a monkey, and a "preacher on an orange crate with a Salvation Army band." Robertson's paternal great-grandfather appeared (during the chorus) as a ragman singing a "song of the street [that] keeps haunting my memory." "He was a scholar from Israel," Robertson told Harvey Kupernik of *Crawdaddy* in March 1976, "[but] when he got here, all he [had] studied was meaningless. He was capable of nothing but reading and intellectualizing. He became a ragman . . . [with] a horse and wagon and he would go up and down the lanes singing this song, 'Rags, Bones, and Old, Used Clothes.' I never saw him doing it, but the legacy carried on. When I was a kid, I would see a ragman and it [would be] a very frightening symbol to me. The chant would never leave my mind."

A timeless outlaw ballad, "Ring Your Bell" told of a "rebel with the Mounties on his trail" who advises his "renegade woman" companion to "run like hell, you can't hide from thunder," while requesting that she "love me like there's no tomorrow." As they pass time in "smoky bars and souped-up cars where we drowned all sorrow," they know that their running will soon be over as "bloodhounds comb the streets."

"Hobo Jungle" turns the focus to another side of life on the fringe. Cinematically zooming in on an encampment of drifters, where "nobody knows where they're goin', at the very same time, nobody's lost," the song suddenly shifts mood. The campfire is no longer burning and "an old man lays frozen on the cold, cold ground." The narrator attends the funeral, along with "drifters and rounded and distant friends," and empathizes with the old man's girlfriend, "long were they lovers, though they never could wed," never explaining why not.

A tour-de-force for Hudson's keyboards and synthesizer playing, with Robertson playing clavinet and both Helm and Manuel on drums, "Jupiter Hollow" offered a glimpse of "another world" with images of unicorns, dragons, and "an old soldier singin' a love song."

"Acadian Driftwood," like "Evangeline," recalled the eighteenth century plight of the people of Acadia, a former French colony that had once encompassed Nova Scotia, New Brunswick, Prince Edward Island, present-day Quebec, and parts of northern Maine. Expelled, by the British, at the start of the Seven Years' War (called the French and Indian War in the United States) between France and England, the Acadians dispersed throughout the American colonies, with many reuniting in the sympathetic French colony of Louisiana. Sung with Emmylou Harris during *The Last Waltz,* "Evangeline" took its title from one of the characters in the song—"Evangeline from the Maritimes." "The ones who went to Louisiana became the Cajuns," explained Robertson in his liner notes for The Band's *Anthology, Volume Two,* "and the ones who stayed became Canada's outcasts."

Released in November 1975, *Northern Lights—Southern Cross* came out at a time when popular music was undergoing metamorphosis. Since the Woodstock Festival, advertisers had increasingly embraced the youthful counterculture as a marketing target. After barely getting by with record label ads, magazines like *Rolling Stone* became financially solvent by selling advertising space to heavy-spending tobacco, alcohol, clothing, and automobile corporations.

Added to government-applied pressure to curtail "left-wing" programming, the potential for commercial success prompted many FM radio stations to replace free-form programming with playlists nearly as formulaic as that on the AM dial. "The FCC was not happy with progressive radio," said Richard Neer, who hosted his first show for New York's WNEW-FM in 1971. "Richard Nixon was constantly vilified and its strident antiwar political bent chafed the administration. As we now know, the president didn't hesitate to punish his enemies with whatever means were at his disposal."

"By the early '70s, I started to get a little disillusioned with where radio was headed," Larry Campbell told David Schultz of Jamband.com in April 2012. "Somehow, the formula had been discovered and tinkered with and everything was back in its box again. There was depth to groups like Cream, the San Francisco bands like Moby Grape and Jefferson Airplane, and even Zeppelin that seemed to be missing from the bands of the Seventies."

Some radio stations, hoping to tap the spirit of the "Woodstock generation," adapted a soft-rock format that promised an alternative to the heavy metal and acid rock dominating the airwaves. With its bland approximation of roots music, however, the format quickly lost listeners and many stations switched to a more profitable mix of innocuous pop and electronic dance music. Lost in the shuffle, *Northern Lights—Southern Cross* barely broke into Billboard's top twenty-five.

Members of The Band continued to sit in on recording sessions at Shangri-La. Hudson guested on Poco's *Head Over Heels* (as Al Hudson), while Helm appeared on Graham Nash and David Crosby's *Wind on the Water.* The entire group participated in the recording of Eric Clapton's 1976 album *No Reason to Cry.* Danko and Manuel cowrote the opening track, "Beautiful Thing," while Danko shared lead vocals on "All Our Past Times," which he cowrote with Clapton. The song would inspire the title of the bass player's final solo album, *Times Like These*, released posthumously in August 2000. Dylan also appeared on Clapton's album, singing a duet on his previously unreleased song "Seven Days," which featured a blistering solo by Robertson.

As producer of *Hirth from Earth*, the first of two albums by East Los Angeles–born singer-songwriter Hirth Martinez, Robertson became involved in one of his strangest projects. "I totally related to him," Robertson told Harvey Kupernik. "His music fused melodies with eccentric chord changes and mixed time signatures, and he sang of UFOs as well as loneliness and self-doubt."

Robertson reached further from the roots-oriented music of The Band as producer of Brooklyn-born pop music icon Neil Diamond's *Beautiful Noise* (and later the two-disc concert recording *Love at the Greek*). "We're working around a story," Diamond told a reporter, "telling a tale musically about a certain period of time, and using the events and music of that period. The time is just about the early '60s—The Beatles, Kennedy, some of the social stuff that was going down—seen through the eyes of the songwriter."

Robertson was constantly busy. When Ronnie Hawkins paid his former guitarist a visit, he found him "takin' care of business. He was doin' movie scores, the phone was ringin', and Warren Beatty was comin' over for dinner. He'd become a white-collar worker, a big boss . . . what we used to call a tah-coon."

The guitarist denied that his extracurricular activities interfered with his involvement with The Band. "There's never a conflict between my Band role and my projects," he told Kupernik. "It's not that kind of relationship anyway. We've watched each other grow up and go from teenage kids to grown men. . . . There [have] been obvious changes and responsibilities, but it's never in control, and it will never be in control, I hope, because it would make things very boring. It changes all the time. That is what enables us to work together—it is never the same old story. We are five individuals who make music together. That's the way we've always seen ourselves."

As their first tour in two years, scheduled for the summer of 1976, approached, few members of The Band looked forward to being back on the road. "I like to tour, but there's a real danger of burning yourself out," said Helm, who was building a two-hundred-and-fifty-thousand-dollar recording studio at his home in Woodstock. "A lot of people have criticized us for not touring enough and taking too much time between albums, but that's the way we are. . . . It's great to play in just about the best band around, but it's no life-and-death struggle like so many people wanna make it out to be."

Kicked off with a celebrity-attended show at Stanford University in Palo Alto on June 27, the tour started well. Syndicated radio show *King Biscuit Flower Hour* taped The Band's seventy-two minute July 17 show at the Carter Barron Amphitheater in Washington, DC, for national broadcast.

Things began to unravel about two-thirds into the tour. "Robbie's son was born around then," said Helm, "making it harder for him to get on that plane and go to the show. We had a couple of bumpy rides on that tour, and it didn't take too much air turbulence to make us remember our prayers."

"The touring got harder and harder by the day," remembered Robertson. "It was particularly hard on Richard, whose health was not great (he had been in a boating accident, but had resumed touring after spending three days in bed, massaged constantly by Tibetan healers). . . . We weren't able to go out and give it our best shot, working with our full force."

At their first concert following Manuel's accident, at the Palladium Theater (which had taken over the former site of the Academy of Music) on September 18, a horn section and fiddler Larry Packer supplemented The Band. During the encore, Paul Butterfield added his harmonica to "Life Is a Carnival" and "The W. S. Walcott Medicine Show."

Not long afterward, Robertson's attorneys notified Helm that the guitarist planned to "kill The Band and go out with a bang." "He wanted everyone we'd played with along the way—from Ronnie Hawkins to Bob Dylan—to perform (at our last concert)," the drummer recalled, "but without bringing their own musicians. We would be the backup group for our guests. They were already lining up people from all phases of our career: Hawk, Muddy Waters, Paul Butterfield, Van Morrison, Neil Young, Ringo [Starr], Eric Clapton, Allen Toussaint, the *Rock of Ages* horn section. It was [going to] be the concert of the century, maybe the show to end the whole so-called rock era. That's what they told me, anyway."

Although he tried convincing him to reconsider, Helm realized that Robertson's decision was irreversible. "He was sick of it all," recalled the drummer. "He said he wanted to keep on recording and making music with us, but he didn't want to go on the road anymore. 'We're not learning anything, man,' he told me. 'It's not doing anything for us, and in fact it feels dangerous to me. . . . Every time I get on the plane I'm thinking about this stuff. The whole thing isn't healthy anymore.'

"I don't completely understand what your motives are to destroy this group," Helm remembered telling Robertson, "but I do know it's a crying shame to take this band from productivity to retirement because you're superstitious, or for the sake of a final payday. I know you got all your lawyers and accountants and whatever on your side—if you ask me, they could all use a stake driven through their hearts for all the good they did us—but this whole thing is dead wrong."

Preparations for *The Last Waltz* came together quickly. Hearing of The Band's plans, Bill Graham booked the Wonderland Ballroom in San Francisco (where they had played their first show) for Thanksgiving Day, November 25, and started making plans for the once-in-a-lifetime event.

"I wanted to make it an all-in-one concert and Thanksgiving dinner," said Graham, "one price, and I didn't want to announce who the guests were. I told Robbie, 'Trust me that our reputation in San Francisco is good enough that when we say "The Band and Friends" and a seven-course meal for twenty-five dollars they know they'll get something."

With the release of their ninth album, a ten-song best-of collection, The Band needed only one more album to complete their contract with Capitol. Meanwhile, Robertson and film director Martin Scorsese had (unknown to the rest of The Band) formed "Last Waltz Productions" and signed (with Warner Brothers) to produce a movie and soundtrack of *The Last Waltz*.

As they rehearsed for *The Last Waltz*, The Band started work on what would be their final studio album—*Islands*. A loose collection of tunes, it would be their most forgettable release. "Even true believers admit that this sounds like a listless farewell to old habits," said Robert Christgau, "recording as a group for Capitol, for instance. The best song ["Christmas Must Be Tonight"] is about the baby Jesus and almost made me gag first time I heard it; the second best ["The Saga of Pepote Rouge"] is about a traveling evangelist and strikes a familiar note; and the third best [Manuel's vocal tour-de-force "Georgia on My Mind"] is a remake that sounds like it."

"The whole experience was long and grueling," recalled Robertson. "I was wearing too many hats on both business and artistic levels, and it wore me out."

As supporters of Georgia Governor Jimmy Carter's bid for president, The Band performed "Georgia on My Mind" on the October 30 broadcast of *Saturday Night Live*, three days before the election. Carter would go on to beat incumbent president Gerald Ford with slightly more than fifty percent of the votes. "We'd been out to [Carter's] place in Plains, Georgia," explained Manuel, "riding out in a three motorcycle escort, in front of the limousine, smoking a joint in the back seat. [First Lady Rosalind Carter] served us early breakfast, scrambled eggs."

Preparations for *The Last Waltz* remained fierce. "I was against the idea," said Helm. "I figured that with all the guest artists coming in, we already had to learn more than twenty new songs—chord changes and dynamics—that we'd never played before in our lives, and new artists were being added to the show all the time."

The guest list became the source of intense argument. Helm pushed for Muddy Waters and questioned the addition of Neil Diamond.

Conflicts continued after Robertson hired Martin Scorsese to film *The Last Waltz*. The New York–born son of Sicilian immigrants, Scorsese had been a product of New York University, where he earned a bachelor's degree in English in 1964 and a Masters of Fine Arts in film two years later. An assistant director and supervising editor of the documentary film *Woodstock*, he had operated a camera during the filming of the Altamont segment of the Rolling Stones' "Gimme Shelter."

One of several innovative filmmakers, including Francis Ford Coppola, Brian DePalma, George Lucas, and Steven Spielberg, who would go on to dominate popular cinema, Scorsese's breakthrough had come via his involvement with New York–born actor, director, and producer Robert DeNiro. Working together, they immediately broke new ground with *Mean Streets* in 1974 and *Taxi Driver* two years later. Scorsese continued his ascent in 1977 with *Alice Doesn't Live Here Anymore*, for which Ellen Burstyn won a best actress Academy Award.

Scorsese was in the midst of putting the final touches on *New York, New York*, his third film with DeNiro (and costarring Liza Minnelli), when Robertson contacted him. "You know, *The Last Waltz* saved me at the time," Scorsese told Mark Jacobson of *New York* magazine. "I wasn't in it the way Robbie was. It wasn't my last show, but it could have been. I didn't have any self-confidence at the time. I'd finished *New York, New York*, a big experiment, maybe not such a good one. . . . Nothing excited me—no work. I was going to give up, go to Italy, and make films about the lives of the saints, but here was the Band and Robbie. For me, the music creates the images. The Band had this great creativity I was so desperate for. I had to stay close to that energy, that passion."

From the start, Robertson and Scorsese aimed for more than the standard concert film. "I came up with the idea of shooting in 35 mm," said Scorsese, "with full synch sound and seven cameras. The Band was paying for the raw stock (one hundred and fifty thousand dollars), while the cameramen and I would get a percentage if the picture was ever made, and in the meantime, we'd enjoy the show."

The Last Waltz was indeed an event. A preconcert Thanksgiving feast, costing forty two thousand dollars, included two thousand pounds of candied yams, eight hundred pounds of mincemeat and pumpkin pies, six thousand rolls, four hundred gallons of apple juice, ninety gallons of gravy, and cranberry sauce. The stuffing consisted of five hundred pounds each of onions and celery, seventy bunches of parsley, and sixteen quarts of herbs sautéed in one hundred pounds of butter. In addition to two hundred and twenty turkeys, there was four hundred pounds of fresh salmon flown in from Alaska. After dinner, guests danced to a thirty-eight-piece orchestra, led by three teams of professional dancers.

The concert began with a full two-hour set by The Band. "[We began] with 'Up on Cripple Creek,'" remembered Helm, "and [went] through 'The Shape I'm In,' 'It Makes No Difference' (with Garth soloing on that curved soprano), 'Life Is a Carnival,' 'This Wheel's on Fire.'"

Joined by a five-piece horn section, The Band continued with "The W. S. Walcott Medicine Show," "Georgia on My Mind," "Ophelia," "King Harvest (Has Surely Come)," "The Night They Drove Old Dixie Down," "Stage Fright" and "Rag Mama Rag."

Without taking a break, The Band began introducing special guests. "We brought out Ronnie Hawkins first," said Helm, "as a tribute to our original chief and mentor, the man who taught as all we knew, or at least some of it."

Hawkins brought things back to the days of The Hawks with a rousing version of Bo Diddley's "Who Do You Love," with Robertson reprising the solo he had played on Hawkins's 1963 single.

Continuing with a nod toward New Orleans, Dr. John sang "Such a Night" and Bobby Charles offered "Down South in New Orleans." Moving to the blues, Paul Butterfield led The Band through "Mystery Train" and, joined by Muddy Waters, Pinetop Perkins, and Bob Margolin, plowed through a shaky Caldonia" and a sizzling, stop-them-in-their-tracks "Mannish Boy." "We realized that because of some fuckup, all but one camera had been turned off," said Helm. "We almost missed [Waters's] entire segment."

Eric Clapton next performed "All Our Past Times," the song he had cowritten with Danko and recorded with The Band at Shangri-La, and Bobby "Blue" Bland's "Further on Up the Road," a staple of Ronnie Hawkins and the Hawks' shows. Expatriated Canadians Neil Young ("Helpless" and "Four Strong Winds") and Joni Mitchell ("Coyote," "Shadows and Light," and "Furry Sings the Blues") followed. Neil Diamond continued with "Dry Your Eyes," written with Robertson.

Van Morrison joined The Band for two songs. Opening with "Tura-Lura-Lural," a ballad that American songwriter James Royce had based on an Irish lullaby, in 1916, and Bing Crosby had popularized in the 1944 film *Going My Way*. He kept the flame burning with his up-tempo 1970 FM hit "Caravan." "I don't usually come out in situations like this," the Northern Ireland-born vocalist would tell a reporter. "I didn't want the promotion, but it was the right situation because of something karmic."

Returning to the stage, Neil Young and Joni Mitchell added their harmonies as The Band closed the concert's lengthy first half with "Acadian Driftwood."

Following a forty-minute break during which attendees listened to San Francisco poets, including Michael McClure, Diane Di Prima, and Lawrence Ferlinghetti, Garth Hudson started the second half with a solo that Robert Palmer remembered as a montage of "organs, synths, and prerecorded tapes of Tibetan monks and a cow mooing for effects that were truly otherworldly."

Joining Hudson onstage and triumphantly transitioning into "Chest Fever," The Band followed with the trio of tunes that made up *The Last Waltz Suite*. After an instrumental title track similar to "Third Man Theme" on *Moondog Matinee*, the suite segued into Robertson's "Evangeline," featuring Helm on mandolin, Manuel on drums, Hudson on accordion, and Robertson on acoustic guitar. Danko played fiddle and shared lead vocals with Helm. "The Weight" followed. Sessions for the three songs at MGM Studios in Hollywood would be filmed and replace concert footage in *The Last Waltz*. "Those were done literally like a feature film," said Scorsese. "It took three days to shoot 'The Weight' (with the Staple Singers), two for 'Evangeline' (with Emmylou Harris), and one for 'The Last Waltz.'"

There was really only one way for *The Last Waltz* concert to end. Although he had been resistant, believing that his appearance in *The Last Waltz* would compete with his in-progress film *Renaldo and Clara*, Dylan's participation was essential to his former backup group's celebration. "[Dylan] walked out in a big white hat that seemed to glow under the spotlight," remembered Helm, "black leather jacket, polka-dot shirt. He plugged right in, said hello, and stormed into 'Baby, Let Me Follow You Down.'"

Originally recorded as "Don't Tear My Clothes" in 1935 by the State Street Boys (who included Big Bill Broonzy and Indianola, Mississippi–born harmonica player William McKinley "Jazz" Gillum), "Baby Let Me Follow You Down" had continued to spread under various titles. Eric Von Schmidt's version (which Dylan credited as his source) had been based on Blind Boy Fuller's 1938 rendition, titled "Mama Let Me Lay It on You," while Dylan credited Reverend Gary Davis for three-quarters of the words that he sang. "Bob's guitar was tuned way up," recalled Helm, "so I just took it fast. Things certainly got lively. Bob shouted out the lyrics . . . and danced around the stage. In the audience: pandemonium."

Dylan and the former Hawks slowed things down with a pair of tunes from *Planet Waves*—"Hazel" and "Forever Young"—separated by a steamy revision of "I Don't Believe You (She Acts Like We Never Have Met)" from 1963's *Another Side of Bob Dylan*. After a reprise of "Baby Let Me Follow You Down," the set concluded with a version of "I Shall Be Released," featuring Manuel and Dylan sharing vocals, with Ringo Starr playing Manuel's drums and Ron Wood playing guitar.

Once the stage cleared, Starr and Helm looked at one another. "[We] figured it was time to play a little music," remembered Helm, "so [we] started up. Dr. John came out, then Stephen Stills and Carl Radle (Eric Clapton's bassist), then Neil Young, Garth, and Rick Danko. Bill Graham dragged Eric Clapton out and strapped him into his guitar for the jam, and Ronnie Wood came out. We jammed for maybe thirty minutes, judging by the tapes. Finally, The Band came out and we did our last song, 'Don't Do It.'"

"I didn't think I played as a well as I did," Hudson told the *Globe and Mail*'s Jason Schneider in July 2002. "Some of the solos are better than I thought they were. When you are really participating in the music, you become hardened. Maybe part of that is because you know you can't change certain things."

After a postconcert party and a week at the MGM Studios, The Band returned to Shangri-La to complete *Islands*. As the first of the five musicians to sign a solo record deal (with Arista), Rick Danko was simultaneously working on his self-titled debut album. Released shortly after the Helm-led RCO All Stars' debut in 1977, its ten songs would be completely written by Danko, either alone or with lyricists Bobby Charles or Emmett Grogan, the Brooklyn-born founder of the Diggers, a radical community group that supplied free food, housing, and medical aid to runaways in San Francisco's Haight-Ashbury. "I love playing with The Band," Danko told *Rolling Stone*. "I'm sure they would never abandon me and I would never want to abandon them, but it's a very collective thing, and I'm only one-fifth of it. I plan to write my own music for my solo situation, but I really want Robbie to be my writer in The Band, because he is very special; he's got some songs for this next album that are killers. We keep that whole thing in a safe place right now. Nobody wants to hear anybody yell or scream, least of all me."

Everyone in The Band contributed to Danko's album. Helm sang on "Once Upon a Time," Manuel played electric piano on "Shake It," Robertson played lead guitar on "Java Blues," and Hudson played accordion on "New Mexico." Guests included Ronnie Wood, Gerry Beckley (America), Eric Clapton, and Blondie Chapman, a South Africa–born ex-guitarist for the Beach Boys who would go on to play with Danko's solo projects and the reunited Band.

According to Robertson, The Band initially viewed the break following *The Last Waltz* as temporary. "The idea was that everybody was going to take a step back," he said, "gather themselves, refocus, and we were going to come back and do some great, creative work together. Everyone went off and did individual projects, to shuffle the deck, and nobody came back. At some point, you have to read the writing on the wall, whether the passion is gone or the direction is gone. I don't know; it is what it is."

"We obviously didn't break up," said Manuel in November 1984, "we just haven't released an album since *The Last Waltz*. If you go to see *The Last Waltz* again, and pay attention, you will see that Robbie is the only one that says that he has had it with the road, quote, 'It's a God-damned hell of a way to make a living.'"

"We never broke up," agreed Hudson. "Each member just ended up doing their own recordings for a while. Rick did an album with Clive Davis, and Levon had the RCO All Stars. I met (Fender Telecaster guitarist) Thumbs Carllile many times in the valley in LA, and I worked with Jo-El Sonnier, a great [Cajun] singer and [accordion] player from Bogalusa, Louisiana. He's a guy who can go to any country and represent his music with dignity and finesse—even though he speaks in a broken language."

Hudson also added his distinctive keyboards playing to the early 1980s music of Santa Cruz, California–based rock band The Call. "They knew [The Band's] songs," Hudson told Nick DeRiso of *Something Else*

Reviews in October 2012, "and they had apparently performed them. In fact, they once asked me about the bridge of one song we did on *Cahoots* that I had forgotten and that they couldn't quite figure out. They wanted me to play on their demo.... I wound up doing five songs on their first album, *The Call*, and five more on their second album, *Modern Romans*. I played on their third album, *Scene beyond Dreams*, and I played various other pieces with them. We played in the Veterans' Hall in Santa Cruz for a flood relief fund, and we were playing [a] tune that I didn't recognize at first. We got into it, and I began learning it as we went along; it turned out to be 'Knockin' Lost John' from *Islands*."

On The Call's fourth and most commercially successful album, *Reconciled*, Robertson took Hudson's place, playing guitar on "This Morning."

Helm briefly played with a Southern California–based band with guitarists David Lindley and Jesse Ed Davis, and guested on transplanted Greenwich Village folksinger David Blue's 1976 album *Cupid's Arrow*. With Henry Glover serving as "band master," he formed the RCO All Stars with keyboardist Booker T. Jones, guitarist Steve Cropper, and bassist Donald "Duck" Dunn (of Stax Records' house band Booker T and the MGs), ex-Hawk guitarist Fred Carter Jr., Paul Butterfield, and Dr. John, and a horn section of Howard Johnson, Tom Malone, Lou Marini, and Alan Rubin. With such a stellar lineup, they seemed headed for superstardom when they debuted on a March 19, 1977, telecast of *Saturday Night Live*. "I felt strength in numbers," Helm told *Musician* magazine's Joshua Baer. "It's just a hell of a lot more fun to cut up anything with your friends, no matter how good or bad you do it by yourself."

Of two-dozen tracks recorded at Shangri-La and at Helm's Woodstock studio, ten made it to the RCO All-Stars' first (and only studio) album. Songwriting credits were shared among Jones ("You Got Me"), Glover ("Blues So Bad" and "Rain Down Tears," written with Rudolph Toombs), Carter ("A Mood I Was In"), and Dr. John ("Washer Woman," and "The Tie That Binds," written with Bobby Charles). Dr. John collaborated with Helm in rewriting a traditional tune, "That's My Home." Reworkings of Chuck Berry's "Havana Moon," Earl King's "Sing, Sing, Sing," and "Milk Cow Boogie," based on a blues tune written and first recorded by Kokomo Arnold in 1934 and covered by a lengthy list that included Robert Johnson and Elvis Presley, rounded out the album.

The first post-Band album by any of its members, the RCO All Stars' debut sold less than a quarter of a million copies and stalled at number 142 on the *Billboard* charts. Even an extravagant barbecue/listening session for bused-in music journalists at Helm's Woodstock home failed to generate much excitement. In April 2006, the Levon Helm Studios label released the thirteen-track *Live at the Palladium, NYC*, recorded during the RCO All Stars' New Year's Eve show at the former site of the Academy of Music on December 31, 1977. "The main reason that the All Stars didn't go faster and further and longer," Helm told *Musician* magazine, "was too many chiefs and not enough Indians, too many schedules, and too much outside advice."

Adopting the superstar concept a dozen years later, Ringo Starr would include Helm and Danko in the first edition of his All-Starr Band, along with Billy Preston, Dr. John, Joe Walsh, Nils Lofgren, Clarence Clemens, and Jim Keltner.

The Last Waltz premiered in New York on April 26, 1978, to critical acclaim. Some critics called it the greatest concert film of all time. "The exciting part of [the premiere]," Hudson remembered, "was the red-carpet procession, with all the photographers and cameramen. I arrived with Purna Das and members of [an East Indian ensemble] the Bengali Bauls he had been working with, two of whom appeared on the cover of Dylan's *John Wesley Harding*. They were dressed in Bengali colors, so, as far as I could see, I had the most colorful entourage. . . . The only thing that I can say about the film is that it was the best promotion/publicity I could have hoped for; I could say that more eloquently, but that's it."

For Helm, the Scorsese-directed and Robertson/Taplin-produced, film only intensified his anger. "[It] was mostly Robertson showing off and acting like he was the king," complained the drummer. "For two hours, the camera focused almost exclusively on him—long and loving close-ups of his heavily made-up face and expensive haircut."

"[Robertson] had something to prove," he continued. "He wanted to show that he was the leader of The Band. Let me ask you this: how many shots of Richard Manuel are in that movie? If I would have had all the lawyers and attorneys working for me, then I would have been the star of that movie, but I'll tell you what, I would have had some shots of [Manuel] in it. Man, you should have seen what got pushed out of the movie to make room for Robbie taking the credit for all the things he never done."

Helm remained bitter about *The Last Waltz*. "We don't get any royalties," he told Dallas, Texas–based journalist Robert Wilonsky in 2002. "I don't want Muddy Waters' family to think that I'm getting a fucking nickel out of *The Last Waltz*, because I know they've been fucked from the very beginning, and I want them to know that I have too."

SIX
Resurrection

In the aftermath of *The Last Waltz*, Helm continued to struggle as a solo artist, though there were moments on his early albums worth remembering. The first of two self-titled albums, *Levon Helm*, was produced by Donald "Duck" Dunn in 1977, and recorded at Cherokee Studios in Hollywood and the Muscle Shoals Studios in Alabama. Consisting of cover tunes, it included renditions of Allen Toussaint's "Play Something Sweet," the Cate Brothers' "Standing on a Mountain Top," and the Al Green/Mabon "Teenie" Hodges–composed and Talking Heads–popularized "Take Me to the River."

Country roots increasingly resurfaced in Helm's post-Band music. In 1979, he starred in the singing title role on British singer-songwriter Paul Kennerley's concept album *The Legend of Jesse James* (produced/engineered by Glyn Johns), joining a cast that also included Johnny Cash, Emmylou Harris, and Charlie Daniels.

Helm's return to his rural roots continued with his film debut as country music songstress Loretta Lynn's father, Ted Webb, in *Coal Miner's Daughter*. "The part was such an honorable one," he said. "This man had labored in the mines for his family, and growing up in the cotton fields, I knew what it was to work for the company store."

A session for the soundtrack of *Coal Miner's Daughter* proved so satisfying that an additional twenty tunes were recorded, including Patsy Cline's "Walking after Midnight," "I Fell to Pieces," the Willie Nelson–penned "Crazy," and Harlan Howard's "Watermelon Picking Time in Georgia." "They wanted me to cut a version of Bill Monroe's 'Blue Moon of Kentucky,'" recalled Helm, "and I had to swallow hard on that one and ask the producer how he'd like to follow the Blue Grass Boys and Elvis Presley. I went into Bradley's Barn in Nashville (where *Ronnie Hawkins Sings the Songs of Hank Williams* had been recorded), with the

Cate Brothers and Fred Carter Jr. (and additional Nashville session players), and after we did 'Blue Moon of Kentucky,' we figured why not put a little hay in the barn." Ten tracks from the session were included on Helm's third post-Band album, *American Son*.

Movies continued to command Helm's attention. His portrayal of General Chuck Yeager's friend Major Jack Ridley in *The Right Stuff*, Philip Whelan's film adaptation of Tom Wolfe's book about the test pilots of the high-speed aeronautical research at Edwards Air Force base (twenty-two miles northeast of Lancaster, California) and the astronauts of the United States' first manned space flights, drew critical acclaim. Although *Coal Miner's Daughter* and *The Right Stuff* represented the peak of his movie career, Helm continued to act. He played opposite Jane Fonda in an ABC movie called *Dollmaker* in 1984; appeared in a dope smuggler movie, *The Best Revenge*, filmed in southern Spain by a Canadian outfit; and had a role in *Smooth Talk* with Laura Dern and Treat Williams. "The ensemble aspects [of making a film] make it a lot like playing music," he explained, "and I try to look at it in a musical kind of way. When I worked with Sissy Spacek or Tommy Lee Jones in a scene, I would go about it as though they were singing lead and I was singing the harmony part. I tried to back them up and guard their gun sack, musically. I associated the director for the producer, the prop manager for the road manager, and so forth."

Cinema also provided an outlet for Robbie Robertson. Residing in Martin Scorsese's house in the eastern Santa Monica Mountains while they edited *The Last Waltz*, he developed both a friendship and a working relationship with the director. "Scorsese's as good as it gets," Robertson told Edward Kiersh in *Where Are You Now, Bo Diddley: The Artists Who Made Us Rock and Where They Are Now*. "He's my best friend; it's hard to get excited about working with anyone else. His movies are about passion, obsession, and people who just rip through life with their guts. . . . He's a little stick of dynamite, and he's sometimes hard to deal with, but he's so vivid, so intense, and alive. . . . He takes chances going against what's fashionable, and that's what I want to do. Hollywood is a rough game. Maybe that makes him a tough guy, delving into the underside of life (whores, gang members, drug dealers), but who should I like—Disney characters, little guys in space suits."

Temporarily separating from his wife, Robertson moved into Scorsese's house. "I brought these huge stereo speakers into the living room," he recalled, "and on the other side of the house, he turned a bedroom into a screening room. The screen was a whole bedroom wall. He showed me movies that he had done, wonderful things like *Mean Streets* and *Taxi Driver*, and we talked about what he was going to be working on next, *Raging Bull*. I played lots of music for him."

The experience was equally enlightening for the director. In an interview with Mark Jacobson of *New York* magazine, Scorsese recalled, "The

Last Waltz saved me at the time. I was not into it the way that Robbie was. It wasn't my last show, but it could have been. I didn't have any self-confidence at the time. I had finished *New York, New York*, a big experiment, maybe not such a good one. I was thirty-two or thirty-three, going on sixteen, seventeen, or one hundred and seventeen. Nothing excited me—no work. I was going to give up, go to Italy, and make films about the lives of the saints, but here was the Band and Robbie. For me, the music creates the images. The Band had this great creativity that I was so desperate to get. I had to stay close to that energy, that passion."

Scorsese provided Robertson with not only a creative partner but also a comrade in arms. "It was a crazy period," said Robertson. "Marty and I were the 'misunderstood artists.' Our wives threw us out. We just got lost in the storm. [When] you are a tamed house pet, and [you get] thrown out in the woods for a while, soon you are not tame anymore. All of a sudden, you're like a wild dog. We just ran amok."

Continuing their recklessness during the promotional tour for *The Last Waltz*, their partying came to a sudden stop after Scorsese experienced an asthma attack that was so severe that he needed hospitalization. For Robertson, it was a wake-up call. "It was either change [my] lifestyle or die," he said. "I remember seeing him in the hospital and thinking, 'Boy, this is definitely the end of an era, right here.'"

Deluged by offers to appear onscreen, Robertson (who had moved out of Scorsese's house and returned to his family) agreed to produce and star, alongside Gary Busey and Jodie Foster, in *Carny*, the Robert Kaylor–directed adaptation of Thomas Baum's tale of a modern-day carnival. "It just came down to what story I wanted," he told *Musician* magazine, "and I liked that story. It was personal for me, because, when I was young, before I went off on my rock 'n' roll adventure, I worked in a carnival. I left that experience and it just stayed with me. . . . In all of the images, pictures, and stories that you tell, there's no way of avoiding the traveling carnival; it's a conglomeration of freaks, hustlers, illusions, and lies. There is such a parallel to rock 'n' roll music. It never really changed much for the carnival, only that the carnival turned into local fairs and cattle shows and became clean-cut. The origin of the traveling carnival was this thing that everybody wanted to get rid of; they wished it would just evaporate.

"I was thinking about using the writer for some other project I was working on," he continued, "[and] I read the script by accident. It had been around for about five years. I read it, and [then] I talked with the writer. I told him that I cared about the subject matter, but I said, 'You're not going to get this project off the ground, nobody's going to make this movie.' We sat down and rewrote it, went to the studios, saw three people and three people said yes."

Working with Alex North (whose orchestral scores had been heard in *Spartacus, Viva Zapata,* and *Who's Afraid of Virginia Woolf*), Robertson recorded a soundtrack for *Carny* (with Dr. John and Randall Bramlett) that included original instrumentals ("Pagan Knight," "Freak's Lament," and "The Garden of Earthly Delights) and a cover of Fats Domino's "The Fat Man," with additional lyrics by Robertson.

Despite its potential, *Carny* was a flop. Shortly after its premiere on June 13, 1980, Lorimar Films went out of business. "The movie wasn't really released," Robertson told Joshua Baer. "The company only spent one hundred and forty-six thousand dollars to release it throughout the whole country."

Although he would make brief appearances in other films, including Sean Penn's *The Crossing Guard* in 1995, most of Robertson's experiences with movies would come behind the scenes. When Martin Scorsese encountered problems with the soundtrack of *Raging Bull*, his biopic about middleweight champion boxer Jake LaMotta, he called his old friend. "[Scorsese] had no clue [about what he wanted for the soundtrack]," recalled Robertson, "and he wanted to know if I had any ideas."

As they spoke, Scorsese became convinced that the former Band guitarist/songwriter was the only one who could provide him with what he needed and persuaded him to sign on as a consultant. Robertson's score included an original instrumental ("Webster Hall"), a piano transcription of Mack Gordon and Harry Warren's love song "At Last" from the 1941 musical film *Orchestral Wives*, and a variety of other 1930s and '40s pop and big-band recordings. "Once again there was a revolution going on," recalled Robertson. "This wasn't the same music that people had used in film. I learned some things from it. The big thing for me is the growing process. I was thinking, 'I've been making records and doing tours and writing songs.' I just wanted off the train for a while. I wanted to go to a different destination for a bit. I didn't feel a need to write songs all the time."

Robertson continued to work with Scorsese as music director of *The King of Comedy*, starring Robert DeNiro and Jerry Lewis, in 1983. The soundtrack incorporated previously recorded releases (or outtakes) by Ric Ocasek (The Cars), The Pretenders, Talking Heads, and Rickie Lee Jones, and new recordings by B. B. King ("T'ain't Nobody's Business"), Van Morrison ("Wonderful Remark"), and Ray Charles ("Come Rain or Come Shine"). The death (from meningitis) of Scorsese's assistant, "Cowboy" Dan Johnson, inspired Robertson's first post-Band song, "Between Trains," which he would record with Garth Hudson on synthesizer and Richard Manuel on background vocals. Hudson and Manuel would again reunite with their former band mate when they guested on "Southern Accents," a Dave Stewart and Robbie Robertson–produced song on Tom Petty and the Heartbreakers' *Best of Everything*.

Robertson would go on to assemble a score for Scorsese's 1986 movie *The Color of Money* that spanned from the jazz of Gil Evans to the Chicago blues of Willie Dixon. Cowritten with Eric Clapton for the film, "It's in the Way That You Use It" was subsequently also used as the opening track of Clapton's album *August*. Robertson persuaded Robert Palmer to sing Little Willie John's "My Baby's in Love with Another Guy" for the film.

The following year, Robertson served as creative consultant of the Taylor Hackford–directed *Chuck Berry: Hail Rock and Roll*. Extras on the four-DVD set released in 2006 include a thirty-minute segment during which Robertson and Berry explore Berry's scrapbook and collaborate on a series of poetic recitations with Berry's orating accompanied by Robertson on acoustic guitar.

As the executive album producer of the Bronwen Hughes–directed *Forces of Nature* in 1999, Robertson oversaw the recording of updated 1960s and '70s hits. U2 revived the Robert Knight–popularized "Everlasting Love," while Chris Tart resurrected Stephen Stills's "Love the One You're With." [British alt-rockers] Swervedriver redid The Who's "Magic Bus."

Taking over as music supervisor for *Gangs of New York*, Scorsese's historical film set in the mid-nineteenth century, after the original orchestrated score by Elmer Bernstein was scrapped, Robertson sculpted an eclectic blend of pop, folk, and neoclassical tracks.

For Jay Russell's 2004 homage to Baltimore fire fighters, *Ladder 49*, Robertson recorded an original hymn, "Shine Your Light," and a symphonic piece, "Reflection/Adagio," orchestrated by alt-rocker Beck's father, David Campbell. He repeated the music supervisor assignment for the 2010 gothic thriller *Shutter Island*, using modern classical music to set the film's ominous tone.

Additional projects kept Robertson busy. As an A&R executive for Geffen Records in 1986, he produced the debut album by aspiring singer-songwriter Gary Gersh. Though it failed to sell more than a few thousand copies, Gersh would go on to a very successful career behind the scenes, serving a presidency at Capitol Records, signing Nirvana and Sonic Youth to Geffen, and managing artists like Hebrew reggae-rocker Matisyahu.

Robertson may have found satisfaction out of the spotlight, but his former band mates were not producers or soundtrack compilers but working musicians. Helm had accidentally shot himself in the leg, severing the tibia nerve, while preparing to portray a United States Marshall in Willie Nelson's 1980 film *Red Headed Stranger*, and doctors had told him that he wouldn't be able to play the drums for a couple of years (if at all), but he was not ready to give up playing music. With accompaniment provided by the Cate Brothers and his nephew, Terry Cagle, on drums, he toured in 1981. Although they initially played songs by The Band, they continued to evolve. "Eventually, we were only doing 'The Weight,'" recalled Helm, "which our customers basically demanded to hear, and 'Evangeline,' familiar from the movie. I was more comfortable doing the

American blues numbers I'd grown up with—Sonny Boy, Muddy—and old rock-and-roll songs like 'Short Fat Fanny.'"

Helm continued to pursue an R&B sound for the second of his two self-titled solo albums in 1982 (followed by a tour with the Muscle Shoals All-Stars, featuring Mike Chapman on bass, Milton Sledge on drums, Randall Bramlett on saxophone, and the Amazing Rhythm Aces' singer-songwriter Russell Smith and keyboardist James Hooker), but post-Band success remained illusive. "I never could quite get a project to flip over just right in a commercial sort of way," he said.

Danko had already taken steps toward a post-Band career, recording his debut solo album while the group was still together and touring with Chicago blues harmonica player Paul Butterfield. "For me to sing three or four songs," he explained, "do some background vocals, and not go on tour, well, that's not enough to keep my mind occupied."

Briefly returning to Woodstock in 1982 with plans to sell his house and settle permanently on the West Coast, Danko ran into Helm at a local hardware store. The meeting was so inspiring (and Woodstock had so recovered from its postfestival frenzy) that the bass player took his house off the market, and he and his former band mate agreed to reunite as a duo in early 1983 to perform intimate, acoustic, "living room" shows in small clubs and colleges. "This is completely new to me," said Helm. "Rick's already done shows on his own, but I've never looked at it any way other than as a drummer for a high-powered band. I've come all the way back to the basics, but it's really all the same. The main thing that juices me up is to get over there the night of the job, and the man running the joint knows I'm coming and he invites me in, and helps me set up, and I play, and he pays me. That's the only way I've ever wanted it."

The highlight of the duo's tour came, on February 16, 1983, with Bob Dylan's appearance partway through their show at the Lone Star Café in New York. "When we got word that Bob was hanging around the bar," remembered Helm, "Rick called him up to the stage. He took off his hat, and was handed a guitar, and amid the pandemonium of the packed house, we played a rather liquid 'Your Cheatin' Heart' before launching into a funny medley of '[Willie and the] Hand Jive,' and 'Ain't No More Cane On the Brazos.'"

Manuel had continued to follow a self-destructive path. "When he vacated his Malibu beach house, in 1976," claimed *Toronto Life* reporter Martin Levy in March 1996, "they found two thousand empty Grand Marnier bottles. He had to take placidyl to sleep. Naked, he looked as if his liver was bulging out of his abdomen. He was so saturated with alcohol that even his skin seemed to sag on his bones."

By 1978, though, Manuel had, according to Helm, "stopped drinking, entered a detox program, and been dry for several years." As he began to recover, the pianist missed playing with his former band mates. After contributing to Robertson's *Raging Bull* soundtrack and playing some shows in Los Angeles with a power-pop band, The Pencils, he replaced Helm in some duo shows with Danko.

Manuel's increased activity spurred talk of a Band reunion. Only Robertson remained resistant. "I really couldn't honestly do it," he said. "After *The Last Waltz*, people were saying, 'A year from now, they'll show up for this big comeback,' and I thought, 'No, not at all.' I had dreamed up the idea when The Band was suffering some real wear and tear; and I talked about it so enthusiastically, I think it just carried everyone along. Maybe they didn't want to hurt my feelings, I don't know, but everybody just had to follow their path and the light, and it led them back to playing on the road, but, at the same time, I didn't think it would be good for me to recycle."

With all but their former guitarist/songwriter aboard, The Band resurrected as a larger group augmented by Earl Cate (guitar), Ernie Cate (keyboards), Ron Eoff (bass), Helm's nephew Terry Cagle (drums), and Woodstock-born Jim Weider (guitar). Weider had lived in Nashville in the 1970s, playing country music with Johnny Paycheck and blues with James Talley, and doing session work. Returning to Woodstock in the early 1980s, he had worked with pop singer Robbie Dupree. "Weider has damn sure earned his seat with the band," insisted Helm in December 1998. "He's had to listen to 'Where's Robbie?' more than anyone. That was so long ago, it ought to be put to rest; The Band ain't Robbie Robertson."

"People say they may blemish what The Band has done as a group," said Robertson, "even that it's sacrilegious. I don't think people should write about it that way. I mean, we are not talking about Matthew, Mark, Luke, and John here. [They are] just some [musicians] in a rock 'n' roll band who miss [playing music]. I hope they have a real good time and don't stay up too late."

The resurrection of The Band paralleled growth in the popularity of roots music. A new breed of singer-songwriter, including Bill Morrissey and Patti Larkin in Boston and *Fast Folk Musical Magazine* regulars Jack Hardy, Suzanne Vega, Shawn Colvin, Cliff Eberhardt, Rod MacDonald, and Christine Lavin in New York, was expanding the possibilities of acoustic-based songwriting. In Nashville, modern-minded instrumentalists such as Bela Fleck, Jerry Douglas, and Sam Bush had brought a fresh sensibility to bluegrass and country music, and former Woodstock Mountains Revue member Jim Rooney produced pace-setting albums for Nanci Griffith, Iris Dement, Hal Ketchum, and John Prine.

After a series of shows in Canada, the reorganized Band made its United States debut in San Jose, California, on July 21, 1983. An appearance at the New York Folk Festival was followed by a tour of Japan and a cross-country tour of the United States (including some shows as openers for the Grateful Dead). "We could see that feelings ran high out in the audience," remembered Helm. "People sang along with these songs like they were old friends, and I think it was Richard who said to me after one show, 'Levon, do you realize we have become these songs?'"

Despite the absence of their former guitarist, The Band continued to build on the spirit of their music. "Levon is our biggest ally," drummer Randy Ciarlante told Ron Balley of the *Tucson Weekly* in June 1996. "He's built The Band back again. When it comes to the music, Garth Hudson is the leader. Rick and Levon are the leaders when it comes to the vocals, and when it comes to making them sound good, [Richard Bell, Jim Weider, and I] are the leaders. It is quite a gumbo; the more we play the stronger we get."

"I think we're on the right path," Weider told Walter Tunis of the *Lexington Herald-Leader*. "We're getting closer and closer to where we need to be. The Band's sound has changed and developed. It rocks a bit harder now than it did years ago, but in a good way. . . . Progress is being made."

Resuming their schedule with shows on the West Coast in March 1984, The Band continued on to the East Coast by April, followed by a mini-tour of Florida in May and Canada in June. Returning to the United States, they toured as opening act for Crosby, Stills, and Nash in August and made their first appearance in northwest Arkansas since 1963 during a Labor Day memorial concert (on the tenth anniversary of concert promoter Dayton Stratton's death).

With the completion of the tour, Helm assembled an aggregate of musicians, including former Woodstock Mountain Revue members Larry Packer, Artie Traum, and Cyndi Cashdollar and ex-Hawks keyboardist Stan Szelest, in early 1985, and they toured East Coast clubs.

Frustrated by the long periods between tours, Manuel had begun to envision life apart from The Band. He continued to perform duo shows with Rick Danko and joined the bass player on a tour celebrating the twentieth anniversary of The Byrds' formation, with a group led by former Byrds Gene Clark and Michael Clarke. "I sobered up," Manuel told Ruth Albert Spencer in November 1984, "and realized what we threw away. We benched it, and, in just this last year and a half, I have seen millions of dollars go by. Doors open, but we did not take advantage of it. I'm irked to the point of just saying, 'Fellas, this is it, I'm going on with my own career.' I have been planning how to catapult this whole thing with myself into a position where I can remain occupied all the time, and have some work at all times, because the down time drives me crazy. I get nuts when I'm not working, when there's nothing to look forward to, when there's no work."

The absence of new material disturbed Manuel. "I'm tired of dwelling in the past," he said. "We're well established in the history books and I don't want to continue doing what we've done for the last year and a half, because we've done it to the point where we're dragging ourselves down unless we come up with new product."

Although they continued to perform for arena-sized crowds (as Crosby, Stills, and Nash's opening act) during the summer of 1985, The Band had been forced to scale things down. Dismissing Cates and Eoff partway through the tour, they had retained Weider on guitar and returned to their original five-piece alignment. "It was heartbreaking to see the boys go," said Helm, "but there was nothing that I could do."

Manuel seemed to be making great strides. Accompanied by Danko (acoustic guitar/vocals), Jim Weider (electric guitar), and longtime Danko cohort Steven "Sredni" Vollmer (harmonica), he had performed a series of shows, in an intimate Saugerties, New York, club, that were documented on a posthumous live album *Whispering Pines, Live at the Getaway, January 1985*. A bonus track on a 2005 Canadian reissue, "Mitzi's Blues" added Levon Helm on drums and Garth Hudson on piano.

Returning to his birthplace, Stratford, Ontario, in early November 1985, Manuel reunited with guitarist John Till and bassist Ken Kalmusky as his pre-Hawks band, the Rockin' Revols opened a benefit concert (for Stratford's Shakespeare festival) headlined by The Band. "It's a return to my roots," he said, "and I'm bringing my partners of twenty-five years with me."

The reunion may have been Manuel's last hurrah. By the time that The Band came together again to tour in February 1986, alcoholism had regained its control. "That disease comes back like a sledgehammer," said Robertson. "It drove him crazy. People were telling him, 'I'm so disappointed in you,' and all this stuff, but he was the poor guy left at the end of the pack, saying, 'Wait for me. I can't help myself.'"

There is no one who truly understands what was going through the pianist's mind, but the pressure must have been considerable. After performing with The Band at the Cheek-to-Cheek Lounge in Winter Haven, Florida, on March 4, 1986, he thanked Hudson for "twenty-five years of incredible music" and headed to the Quality Inn, where he and the rest of the group were staying. Stopping off at Helm's room, he visited with the drummer until two or two-thirty in the morning. "[Manuel] was not depressed," Helm later told police. "He was not mad. He sat on the edge of my bed and talked about songs and people."

Saying goodnight, he continued on to the room that he shared with his second wife, Arlie, and reportedly consumed a bottle of Grand Marnier and snorted a few lines of cocaine. It would be the last time that anyone would see him alive. "I don't know what got crosswise in his mind," Helm told police, "between leaving the foot of my bed and going into his own bathroom."

Sometime around noon, Arlie Manuel had woken and gone for breakfast. When she returned, she discovered her husband's lifeless body. "[When I had gotten up], I thought Richard might be eating on the tour bus," she remembered. "I didn't even go into the bathroom, which I always do. When I came back, I went to the bathroom and [saw that]

Richard was hanging from the shower curtain rod. I began to scream. I ran out to get Rick. He didn't believe me and sent his wife, Elizabeth. She saw what had happened and finally Rick and Levon took him down. It was horrible. I called 911 and kept screaming, kept pounding [on his chest]."

"[Manuel's suicide] was one of the biggest, most sophisticated mistakes," Danko told me in 1992. "I'm sure that there was no way that he planned that one. He might have been reaching out for some kind of attention from his lady, I don't know. It was terrible—no way in a million years would you expect something like that to happen.

"He was a very special friend," the bass player continued, "very sensitive, obviously. He stopped drinking for many years, but on that particular night, he was drinking again. It was in this place that was so packed that it was overcrowded. I remember seeing him pick up somebody's drink [and drinking it]."

A little more than a month before, on January 25, Albert Grossman had suffered a fatal heart attack while flying to London, England. At the memorial service in Woodstock in late March, Manuel, accompanied by Hudson's accordion, performed an especially moving rendition of "I Shall Be Released." "Albert's death really got to Richard," said Helm. "It may have even seemed like abandonment, because Albert was looking after Richard's affairs, and I don't think that Richard knew who to turn to anymore when things got bad."

"I was madly in love with Richard," Eric Clapton confessed to Timothy White in 1989, "because we were going through a lot of the same difficulties—screwing around with drugs and drink—going pretty crazy down deep."

"[Manuel] was an extremely creative person," said Robertson, "and he was almost a victim of his creative ability. It controlled him, somehow, which made him really good at what he did, but sometimes, you didn't know if the horse was pulling the cart, or how it was really working."

When The Band's three Canadian members received a special Juno Award in 1989, Manuel's daughter, Paula, accepted for her father. "It just tore the place apart," recalled Robertson. "It was so touching and so beautiful."

Although they honored their bookings, with Blondie Chaplin playing piano, guitar, and drums, Manuel's death profoundly affected The Band. After the tour ended, Helm recalled, "we decided to let things drift for a few years until the right opportunities presented themselves. I hunkered down in Woodstock with [my wife] Sandy, enjoying life and occasionally taking to the road with the Cate Brothers. . . . I played some shows with drummer Max Weinberg of [Bruce Springsteen's] E Street Band. Garth did a Band gig, in Spain, with the Cate Brothers because I didn't feel like going (we always figured it was still The Band if Garth showed up)."

The death of Danko's nineteen-year-old son, on March 3, 1989, hit the bassist extremely hard. A student at the State University of New York in Albany, Eli Damian Danko had been at a party the night before and had reportedly consumed a massive quantity of alcohol. According to the report filed by the Albany County Coroner, he had choked on his own vomit and been found dead in his dormitory room. "He had an asthma attack," Danko told me, "which was something he had had problems with before."

Music continued to provide relief, with Danko joining Helm in the summer of 1989 as charter members of Ringo Starr's All-Starr Band. "Some reviewers said it was one of the best shows they'd ever seen," recalled Helm. "The old Beatle fans were very emotional toward Ringo, and when Rick and I would do a few Band songs, the amphitheaters and sheds that we'd sold out would simply explode."

Although they occasionally reunited as The Band, Helm, Hudson (who had joined Dr. John as members of British songstress Marianne Faithfull's band in late 1989), and Danko were unable to recapture their previous glory. The Band's renewed hope, spurred by the arrival of drummer Randy Ciarlante and ex-Hawks pianist Stan Szelest in late 1990, crashed with Szelest's death from a fatal heart attack shortly after the New Year.

The tenure of Szelest's replacement, William Everett "Billy" Preston lasted less than three weeks. Playing his first show with The Band on August 3 at a benefit concert for the Woodstock Youth Center, the one-time prodigy who had gone from playing keyboards for Ray Charles and Little Richard to recording with The Beatles and the Rolling Stones was charged with possession of cocaine, being under the influence of a controlled substance, and showing pornographic materials to an underage boy, and placed under arrest. . . . Richard Bell, the ex-Hawk who had played with Janis Joplin's Full Tilt Boogie Band, replaced the jailed keyboardist.

Helm experienced a setback when a fire caused by faulty stove wiring destroyed the barn where he lived. "The damn fire took nearly everything we had," he remembered, "although a concrete storage vault containing my archives and other important material survived intact.

"I had just built the studio," he continued, "[but we] lost the building, or most of it. The night the building burned down, damned if Dr. Henry Glover did not die that night. . . . What a day. When it rains, it pours. He sure did right by us. We did the Muddy Waters Woodstock record, and Butterfield did some great stuff. Henry did some string things with Butterfield that I don't think people have gotten to hear yet, where Butterfield's playing and singing with strings behind his voice and his harp. It's great stuff. He helped me do the RCO All Star thing, and he did the horn arrangements for Van Morrison on *The Last Waltz*. With Henry Glover being around, music would happen all the time—something good was always happening."

After playing on John Simon's solo album (*Out on the Street*) in 1992, the reformed Band continued to work on their first album in sixteen years. Without Robertson's input, however, new material proved evasive. Although they signed with Columbia in 1991, they were unable to complete the album before the label bought out their contract. Rhino Records subsidiary Pyramid Records released songs intended for the album as *Jericho* in 1993. "With [so] many revolutions of the world come and gone," Danko told Larry McMahon of the *Daily Beacon* in June 1994, "it doesn't seem so sinful for old-timers to try and make some music. The Band will make Band music, but I don't think this album sounds like we're lingering in the past."

Harkening back to their formative years with covers of Muddy Waters's "Stuff You Gotta Watch," Willie Dixon's "The Same Thing," and The Delmore Brothers/Henry Glover's "Blues Stay Away from Me," the former Hawks turned to Bob Dylan ("Blind Willie McTell"), Bruce Springsteen ("Atlantic City"), and Artie Traum ("Amazon [River of Dreams]") for newer songs. Original tunes included the opening track, "Remedy," by Colin Linden and Jim Weider; "The Caves of Jericho" by Bell, Helm, Danko, and John Simon; and "Move to Japan" by Helm, Simon, Szelest, Weider, and Joe Flood.

Jericho presented the reunited Band at its most ambitious. Among the sixteen guest musicians employed were blues pianist Champion Jack Dupree (on "Blind Willie McTell") and bluegrass/jazz fiddler Vassar Clements (on "The Walls of Jericho" and "Stuff You Gotta Watch"). "Individual mastery has been subsumed by a carefully crafted production," said Richard C. Walls in his review for *Rolling Stone*; "what was once a singular quilt work of homey instruments is now a predictably plush carpet, very early '90s in its seamless meshing."

Manuel's spirit permeated throughout the album. "Too Soon Gone" by Woodstock-based Jules Shear and Szelest paid homage to his memory (as well as that of Paul Butterfield, who had died of an "accidental drug overdose" on May 4, 1987), while "Country Boy" became the final song to feature his distinctive piano playing and soulful singing. "An effective sentimentality is achieved," said Walls of Manuel's performance of the song. "His wry, whiskey-voice drawl gives the self-effacing lyrics an edge of good-natured melancholy."

When pop music's greatest musicians joined at Madison Square Garden to celebrate Bob Dylan's thirtieth anniversary as a recording artist, it was natural that The Band be included. Introduced by Eric Clapton, Helm (mandolin), Danko (guitar), and Hudson (accordion), joined by Weider, Bell, and Ciarlante, performed an acoustic version of "When I Paint My Masterpiece." Robertson failed to appear. "Backstage was like a reunion of our entire career," said Helm, "including John Hammond Jr.,

Neil Young, Eric Clapton, Ron Wood, Johnny Cash and family, Tom Petty, Roger McGuinn, and many more than I can remember. We met a new generation of stars, like Shawn Colvin, Mary Chapin Carpenter, and the guys in Pearl Jam."

The Band released its second album since reorganizing, *High on the Hog*, in February 1996. Coproduced by Hudson and Aaron "Professor Louie" Hurwitz, leader of The Crowmatix (a Woodstock-based band that would back Helm during solo shows in 1996 and 1997), the album relied heavily on cover tunes by Bruce Channel ("Stand Up"), Johnnie Johnson ("Back to Memphis"), J. J. Cale ("Crazy Mama"), and Blondie Chapman ("Where I Should Always Be"). In addition to reviving "Forever Young" from *Planet Waves*, they introduced one of Dylan's lesser-known tunes, "I Must Love You Too Much," cowritten with Helena Springs. Ciarlante, Weider, Helm, and Danko collaborated with Rob Leon and Champion Jack Dupree on the album-closing track, "Ramble Jungle." "I definitely think, in the future, [there is] going to be more [songwriting]," said Randy Ciarlante to John Feins of the National Academy of Songwriters in January 1999. "The Band is going to write eighty-five or ninety percent of the next record. . . . Rick will tell you, if you talk to him, he feels confident in his songwriting. He is really proficient, you know—it just takes [him] a long time to [write a song]. You've got to sit in that room, sit in that pink house."

A third album by the reformed Band, *Jubilation*, followed in September 1998. Recorded in Helm's Woodstock studio, it included only three cover tunes—Paul Jost's "Book Faded Brown," John Hiatt's "Bound by Love," and Allen Toussaint's "You See Me." The Band wrote songs with Kevin Doherty ("Don't Wait") and Bobby Charles ("Last Train to Memphis"). Danko and Helm cowrote "High Cotton" with Tom Pacheco, a Massachusetts-born and Greenwich Village–based singer-songwriter on whose album, *Woodstock Winter*, The Band had appeared. Danko and Pacheco also collaborated on the gunfighter ballad "If I Should Fail." Helm paid tribute to The Hawks' bandleader with "White Cadillac (Ode to Ronnie Hawkins)," written with Ciarlante and Weider, while Hudson contributed the album's closing instrumental, "French Girls." "We made this record more or less for ourselves," said Danko, "as opposed to making it for some company, with some kind of deadline. We were able to take our time and just produce it at our speed. It's just a nice way to work. The community, that rural feeling, the way we live our lives, is what I was trying to express. "

"*Jubilation* has a remarkably appealing sense of urgency that's pure and true," wrote John Metzger of *The Music Box*. "The music rings freely with passion, conviction, and confidence that should not only win back many of their old fans, but harvest a few new ones."

"We went back to the way we cut *Music from Big Pink*," explained Helm to Scott Jordan of Louisiana music magazine *Offbeat*, "which was to get in the building together in the studio, and record the song, then tear it up and rewrite it and do it again, and do that until it was right. Then, we had some friends come in and help us do some songs—Bobby Charles, John Hiatt, and Eric Clapton. We cowrote things with each other. We started in January and worked until pretty close to the end of the summer. We were doing it as a tribute—it was the thirtieth anniversary of *Music from Big Pink*—and seeing if we could come up with some songs that would last."

Hudson and Ciarlante, however, were the only Band members, along with Hurwitz and The Crowmatix's Maria Spinosa, to appear on all eleven of the album's tracks; Helm and Danko were each missing from a tune. Bell appeared on three songs. " We made this record for ourselves," Danko reminded CBS Radio's Paul James. "It was made for the art of the music. It had nothing to do with taking the money and running."

Between tours with The Band, Danko had continued to pursue a variety of musical projects. He had toured as a duo with Helm and Manuel, and had continued to play shows with Paul Butterfield. "The last show that [Butterfield and I] did was in Pittsburgh in 1987," Danko told me. "I made a deal with him—no drugging, no drinking, before the show. Then afterwards, we had a couple shots of tequila. He was in good shape. I have learned to give the position [of entertainer] a lot of respect. It is easier not to be drunk or high. It is more natural and the evening goes by quicker. I'm getting too old; I can't bounce back like I used to."

In the early 1990s, Danko joined with singer-songwriter Eric Andersen and Norway's Jonas Fjeld to tour mostly small clubs and record a pair of studio albums—Danko/Andersen/Fjeld in 1991 and *Ridin' on the Blinds* three years later. A third album, *One More Shot*, recorded live, came out in 2002. "I sang with [Danko] at the Wetlands in New York in 1990," Andersen told me two years later. "I did some rockabilly songs and Rick couldn't believe it. He had always thought that I was a folksinger, and that I did not have it in me to sing rockabilly, but the first things that we heard—Dylan, me, and probably Phil Ochs—was Buddy Holly and Little Richard. [After the show], we went back to my apartment and talked about songwriting."

Although Danko and Andersen discussed teaming up, the partnership seemed destined to become one more unfulfilled late-night scheme. "I had forgotten all about it," said Andersen, "but my daughter, Sarah, said, 'Call Rick when you get back from Europe.' When I called, he invited me up to his house in Woodstock, and we started to work."

An intended three days of songwriting turned out to be a monthlong collaboration. "[Andersen] was up to my place," recalled Danko, "and he was saying, 'Rick, you've got a couple of cars inside the garage and a couple of cars outside. You have a front yard and a backyard, what am I doing wrong?' Just as a joke, I said, 'Maybe, you're being too greedy and selfish.' He looked at me. The weekend ended up being a month."

"Rick said, 'I have an appetite, but it isn't so huge,'" added Andersen. "He said, 'If it gets too huge, you've got to feed it. I don't have to feed such a huge appetite.'"

The partnership solidified after Fjeld came to the United States to play guitar and sing on three new songs augmenting Andersen's long-lost album *Stages*. "The three of us got on stage and played together," recalled Danko. "It was magical, something that money could not buy."

"We sang a song," added Andersen, "and the harmonies exploded the molecules in the air. People went crazy, and we did too. We realized that we had a beautiful thing to give to the world."

The trio agreed to tour together in Norway and Switzerland in February 1991. "It was an incredible energy," remembered Danko. "Those people were so energized and well read. It was another level of togetherness. We played at the Montreux Jazz Festival when our record was at number four. We were supposed to play a party [at the festival] for four hundred people. They sold twenty-five hundred tickets and had to move to a larger venue that held three thousand people. An extra thousand people showed up and couldn't get in. We left the doors and windows open."

Despite several attempts at rehabilitation, Danko never truly kicked his addictions. Touring with Andersen and Fjeld in 1996, he was arrested in Chiba, Japan, after receiving a package (allegedly sent by his wife) with 1.25 grams of heroin divided into small packages and hidden inside magazines, and received a two-and-a-half-year suspended sentence. To raise money for his defense, he released a live album, *In Concert*, recorded at the Orpheum Theater in Boston, with the reunited Band's drummer, Randy Ciarlante, pianist Aaron "Professor Louie" Hurwitz, and harmonica player Sredni Vollmer. "It was one of those dumb, foolish mistakes," Danko told Greg Alexander of the *Woodstock Journal* about his arrest. "You're going to have to wait until I write the book; that chapter in the book, you know, but it's behind me now, and I'm glad that it is. It was unfortunate [that] it took that time to go through the process, but I'm better for it and it gave me some time to reflect. It was a pretty good sabbatical for me. I got to lose some weight, read some books, write some songs. I used the time to my advantage as opposed to sitting and sucking my thumb."

The bass player released a second live album, *Live at Breeze Hill*, on May 23, 1998. The opening track, "Sip the Wine," which updated a version on Danko's 1977 solo album, was a studio recording, but the remainder documented a club performance by the Rick Danko Band (which included Hudson, Weider, Ciarlante, and Hurwitz) and a three-piece horn section. "This guy threw a party," Danko told Woodstock radio station WDST during his final interview, on December 7, 1999, three days before his death, "and he wanted me to put together a great horn section. When I found out that he was serving rack of lamb from Australia, and he was serving lobster sandwiches, and nobody was getting married, and he [was giving] me a twenty thousand dollar budget, I was like, 'Wow, let's record this.' I think we did a pretty good job."

In preparation for a second solo studio album, Danko had recorded the Grateful Dead's "Ripple" and a new rendition of "All Our Past Times," which he had cowritten with Eric Clapton in the 1970s and played at *The Last Waltz*. They would be combined with tracks from a variety of sources (live and in the studio) and included on the posthumously released *Times Like These*.

Danko's hard living wore his heart out. Going to bed on December 10, 1999, the day after his fifty-sixth birthday, he experienced a heart attack and died in his sleep. "The only good thing about his dying," said Helm, "was that Rick got to die in his own bed. Nobody got to say the drugs did him in, or the bottle done him in, or if he just wouldn't have played with that gun, dammit. You know what I mean—old Rick died at home."

"Not to hear that voice again," said Robertson, "or to hear him play, or feel his spirit, that's a big loss."

"I miss him every day," said Helm. "Rick's death left a big hole in our lives. He was our neighbor, brother, and partner, and we miss him every day."

Helm blamed Robertson, and his business associates, for Danko's death. "If Rick's money wasn't in their pockets," he claimed, "I don't think Rick would have died because Rick worked himself to death; he wasn't that old and he wasn't that sick. He just worked himself to death and the reason Rick had to work all the time was because he'd been [cheated] out of his money."

SEVEN

Extending Community

Levon Helm's woes began when his voice became hoarse after performing at the Helena Blues Festival in October 1996. Doctors diagnosed him with lung cancer (after smoking three packs of cigarettes a day). Two years of intensive radioactive treatment at Memorial Sloan-Kittering Cancer Center in New York removed the tumor but rendered him unable to speak beyond a whisper. Helm's daughter, Amy, played an essential role in her father's recovery. "When I got my diagnosis," he told *Rolling Stone* in 1997, "it scared the hell out of me, but thank God for my baby. I didn't want her to see me scared, so I acted like I wasn't.

"Amy's love and devotion in this period probably saved my life," he continued. "She basically took over the case. She started driving me to Manhattan every week for radiation therapy: real intense sessions that gradually burned the cancer right out of there.... She made me realize how lucky I was to have my own flesh and blood to sit through this with me. When I lost faith, she reminded me that I was a dead son of a pup if I didn't go through with this. Amy, bless her heart, was able to stand in the foxhole with me, and I'm still here to tell you the story because of her."

"[My father] walked through a lot of real dark times when he first got sick," remembered Amy. "There was nobody around, no scene, no Midnight Ramble. He was really walking through bankruptcy and illness."

A mother of two, Amy Helm was born in Rhinebeck, New York (about twenty miles from Woodstock), on December 3, 1970. She had lived with her parents (Helm and Libby Titus) in Woodstock and Los Angeles until their split, and had continued to spend weekends with her father and weekdays with her mother. Although she earned a degree in psychology from the University of Wisconsin, music retained its hold. "I got depressed when I wasn't playing," she told Brian Turk of Listen Up Denver. "I realized even if it doesn't pay the bills, I had to do it."

Music remained the guiding force for her father as well. If he couldn't sing, he could still play drums. Forming an R&B band, the Barn Burners, he began performing weekly at Woodstock nightspot the Joyous Lake. "I've got more musical energy than I've had in my whole life," he told Scott Spencer of *Rolling Stone* in April 2000. "I'm back to my true calling, which is being a drummer, and I'm playing the blues, man—the real Delta blues."

Amy Helm sang (and played unamplified keyboards) with the Barn Burners at their weekly shows. "It was a chance to practice," she said. "I worked on singing and being onstage. My dad was showing me how to serve that singular vision—the music. He took me under his wing and taught me how to strive for that. I think all of us want to be more confident and present in our art."

Seeking an additional outlet for his music, and hoping to raise money to pay mounting medical bills, Levon Helm began presenting Midnight Ramble shows at his spacious recording studio/home, the Barn. "You can't afford to pay your bills and buy your medicine," he told Karen Schoemer of *New York* magazine. "You've got to give up one or the other. I got behind on my mortgage and the only way that I could hang onto the place was to declare bankruptcy. I didn't know if I was going to hang onto the place, but I thought, 'I'm going to go out with a bang. I'm going to have as many Rambles as I can, and have as many people as I can get to come here and see the place."

Helm had no reason to worry about financial ruin. As word of his plight spread, top-notch musicians flocked to the Barn to perform at the biweekly Midnight Rambles. Those lucky enough to score one of two hundred tickets witnessed unforgettable performances by Elvis Costello, Emmylou Harris, Dr. John, John Sebastian, Billy Bob Thornton, the Muddy Waters Band, Steve Jordan, Hot Tuna, Kris Kristofferson, the Black Crowes, Nitty Gritty Dirt Band, Norah Jones, the Bacon Brothers, Robbie Dupree, My Morning Jacket, Steve Earle, Sam Bush, Allen Toussaint, and others. "[The Midnight Ramble] was a way [for Helm] to make money without having to go anywhere," said Larry Campbell.

"The show is far from cheap (prices were just raised to two hundred dollars per ticket), or convenient (Woodstock is a two-hour drive from New York City)," pointed out Andy Greene of *Rolling Stone*, "but, in a day when tickets to a boomer band costs upwards to four hundred dollars, the intimate show is a relative bargain."

"It started as a modern version of the old-fashioned rent party," said Helm, "but the musicians that have taken part in it have really raised it to another level. We have people coming in from all over the place to celebrate with us, and that includes the players, too."

The Midnight Ramble linked Helm with his earliest memories. As a youngster, he loved the performances of the African American medicine and minstrel shows, including F. S. Walcott's Rabbit's Foot Minstrels, who traveled the South from 1900 to 1960, bringing top-notch black entertainers, including Ma Rainey, Bessie Smith, Big Joe Williams, Brownie McGhee, Rufus Thomas, and Louis Jordan (whose father conducted the troupe's band), to audiences of all races. Helm's memories had inspired the Robertson-penned "The W. S. Walcott Medicine Show" and "Life Is a Carnival." "When folks ask me where rock and roll came from," said Helm, "I always think of our southern medicine shows and that wild Midnight Ramble. Chuck Berry's duck walk, Elvis Presley's rockabilly gyrations, Little Richard's dancing on the piano, Jerry Lee Lewis's antics, and Ronnie Hawkins's camel walk could have come right off F. S. Walcott's stage.

"In those kinda shows—with horns and a full rhythm section," he continued, "the drums always looked like the best seat in the house. The sound of cymbals and the snare drum popping in there just sounded like Saturday night and good times."

As a teenager, Helm looked especially forward to the Midnight Rambles that followed the family-oriented medicine show. For an additional fee, audiences could remain in their seats and experience what he recalled as "a hootchy-kootchy show." "The comedians would do some of their raunchier material," he said, "and people'd be holding their sides. The band would get into its louder rhumba-style things, and the dancers would come out in outfits that would be right in style today but were bare and outrageous back then."

Chuck Berry's former pianist Johnnie Johnson helped to christen Helm's Midnight Ramble in January 2004. "It was mainly for friends and people who found out about it through word of mouth," remembered Amy Helm. "We sold a few tickets over the phone and people came. It was a little hectic, but good fun. It became a magnet for the right people."

"Little" Sammy Davis (1928–) handled lead vocals during the Levon Helm Band's shows. A Winona, Mississippi–born blues harmonica player, Davis had accompanied Earl Hooker, Pinetop Perkins, Muddy Waters, and Jimmy Reed in the 1950s before marrying and relocating to Poughkeepsie, New York. Though he had retired from music after his wife's death in 1970, he experienced a major revival two decades later after being "discovered" playing harmonica in a barbershop. Named "comeback musician of the year" by *Living Blues* magazine after releasing his first full-length album, *I Ain't Lyin'*, in 1996, he followed with a second album, *Ten Years and Forty Days*, in 2000.

A trio of CD/DVD sets, *The Midnight Ramble Sessions, Volumes I–III*, document the excitement of the Barn concerts. The first volume spotlighted Davis's singing, while the second volume featured Helm's first vocals in more than a decade. The third volume, released in November 2011, included guest appearances by Allen Toussaint and the Black Crowes' Chris Robinson. "The Midnight Ramble was a place where musicians [were] free enough to try out new things," said Amy Helm, "and not have to be self-conscious or feel like they were putting on 'a show.' Part of [my father's] dream was that it would be a place where musicians could woodshed new material—a safe place to experiment and create, but with an audience."

As soon as he learned of his departure from Dylan's band in February 2004, Helm phoned multi-instrumentalist/producer Larry Campbell. "He said, 'Let's make some music together,'" remembered Campbell, "and I thought, 'Well, what else would you rather do with your life?' It never ceases to amaze me how satisfying it is to play music with him. If you want something to sound real, just have Levon sing it, or play it, and all the fat [trims] away; you get to the basic beauty of the music.

"[Helm] can shift seamlessly between genres in American roots music," continued Campbell, "which is what The Band did. They took all these genres, threw them in a pot, and came out with a unique sound in which you can hear those elements in everything they do. At a Ramble, you're not going to hear a blues concert, a country concert, or a rock show—you're going to hear all those things and nothing will seem out of place, and the root of all of that is the blues. Even when we do a Ralph Stanley tune or a Cajun tune, you still feel a blues base to it. We don't do a Ralph Stanley tune bluegrass style; it has this other sexy thing underneath."

Playing guitar from the age of nine and self-taught as a musician, Campbell launched his career with a bluegrass/country/rock band, Cottonmouth, in 1971. "My father and my mother had this incredibly eclectic record collection," he told music writer Blair Jackson, "and they played it all the time while I was growing up. A lot of the stuff in there was Hank Williams, Jimmie Rodgers, the Sons of the Pioneers, Elton Britt [a Rodgers-style yodeler]—obscure and not so-obscure country music."

Rock and roll had an early impact. "The first year [that I played the guitar], it was The Beatles," he recalled, "that's all I was interested in. I was also copping stuff off the radio, like Sam the Sham, but the biggest discovery I made was copping the changes for the Lovin' Spoonful's 'Summer in the City.' I had never heard that progression anywhere else. I really struggled with it, but I finally got it and thought, 'Oh, man, I am so cool.'"

Country and roots music increasingly drew Campbell's focus. "I started remembering how much I dug all that Hank Williams and Jimmie Rodgers stuff," he said, "and became enthralled with how simple it was to play. Then I started listening closely to the electric guitar [on Hank Williams's recordings] and [saw] that the rhythm playing that he did, and some of the solos, were not difficult to cop. That stuff has always hit me on an emotional level that nothing else does."

Campbell's interests in country music continued to expand. "I saw [Jerry] Garcia with a pedal steel at the bandshell in Central Park," he said, "and that blew me away. I started hearing the Flying Burrito Brothers and listening to what The Byrds were doing. I became enamored with all things country and bluegrass. It really got under my skin. I had to learn the fiddle, I had to learn mandolin, I had to learn banjo, and I had to learn pedal steel, but I didn't want to start learning these instruments and do it halfway.... There are very gifted people who can put in a little time on an instrument and make it sound wonderful. That's not me. For me, it's all about hours and hours of work."

Spending most of the 1970s playing with country music cover bands in Mississippi and Southern California, Campbell immersed himself in New York's music scene upon his return at the end of the decade. "The Urban Cowboy thing was such a huge fashion trend," he recalled. "It opened up a lot of people to hearing country music—the good stuff, too—and that became a great opportunity for me. Clubs all around New York suddenly wanted country music—even though some of them didn't really know what that meant. Any band that was put together with good knowledge of, and healthy respect for, country music was going to work."

The Lone Star Café, at the corner of Fifth Avenue and 13th Street in Manhattan, provided Campbell with a home base. "It was just a magical place," he remembered. "I first went in there to play with Kinky Friedman—he had a regular Sunday night gig—and through that I ended up working with Doug Sahm [Sir Douglas Quintet], Buddy Miller, Willie Nelson—all sorts of great people."

The Lone Star Café also provided a semiregular stop for Levon Helm and his band. "I don't have to swallow my pride to play the Lone Star Cafe," he said. "From my side of it, it's been the same since the early part of my life. I'm still learning and trying to transform musical sounds for people. When people start throwing beer bottles, I'll quit, but not until then."

A member of the Woodstock Mountain Revue in the 1970s, Campbell played with singer-songwriter Buddy Miller's early 1980s band (which became the Shawn Colvin Band after Miller's departure). He recorded with Happy Traum, Steve Forbert, Rob Stoner, Willie Nile, and the superbanjo trio of Tony Trischka, Bill Keith, and Bela Fleck; toured with Cyndi Lauper, k.d. lang, and Roseanne Cash; and played in orchestras for musical productions *Alaska: The Musical*, *Big River*, and *Rhythm Ranch*. He spent 1991 and 1992 with *The Will Rogers Follies* at the Palace Theater on Broadway.

Joining Dylan's Never Ending tour in March 1997, Campbell would become the singer-songwriter's right-hand man. He had been in the audience when Dylan and The Band appeared at the Woody Guthrie tribute concert at Carnegie Hall in 1968. "I loved every minute of [the concert]," he remembered. "Then, at the end, here comes this ragged rock 'n' roll band and Bob Dylan. My jaw hit the floor; it was mind-blowing. That was the first time The Band came into my sights. They seemed to me a big extension of that acoustic guitar. It wasn't about flashy playing. It wasn't about hot licks. It wasn't about anything but making that song, propelling that song. [Dylan's] band, with Charlie Sexton, Tony Garnier, George Reconcile, and David Kemper before him, and me, had that element to it, too. Everyone was sensitive to the song."

In addition to working with Dylan until February 2004, Campbell continued to be involved with a multitude of outside projects. He played on albums by Richard Shindell, Rory Block, Dar Williams, Kenny Kosek, Cheryl Wheeler, Lucy Kaplansky, B. B. King, Judy Collins, the Black Crowes, and Paul Simon and performed as a duo with his vocalist wife, Teresa Williams. "We met in 1986," he said. "She had a gig at the Bottom Line [in New York] and hired me to play guitar, but on the day of the rehearsal I cut my finger and couldn't play the guitar. I ended up playing pedal steel and John Leventhal played the guitar."

The producer of Jewish cowboy/songwriter/humorist Kinky Friedman's self-titled debut album in 1974 and Friedman's *Live from the Lone Star* eight years later, Campbell continued to lend his insight to other artists' recordings, producing albums by Lucy Kaplansky, Richard Shindell, Marie Knight, Catherine Russell, Tara Nevins, Garland Jeffreys, Jorma Kaukonen, and Hot Tuna. As producer/arranger of the gospel singing Dixie Hummingbirds' seventy-fifth anniversary album, *Diamond Jubilation*, in 2003, he worked with Helm and Hudson, who guested on the recording. "Garth and Levon with the Dixie Hummingbirds," said Campbell, "what a great idea."

Helm later covered "When I Go Away," one of Campbell's original songs on the Dixie Hummingbirds album, and included it on *Electric Dirt*.

Although she continued to perform with her father, Amy Helm set a more personal pace as a founding member of Ollabelle. Taking the name of Appalachian folksinger Ola Belle Reed, the gospel-folk group had coalesced during weekly gospel music sessions (Sunday School for Sinners) in a small Lower East Side bar, 9C (at the corner of East Ninth Street and Avenue C), in New York. "We're sort of allergic to dishonesty," said bassist/songwriter Byron Isaacs, who would go on to anchor Levon and Amy Helm's band, the Handsome Strangers. "If something doesn't sound honest to us, then it's back to the drawing board. We're always looking for that absolute, undeniable honesty in the approach. Now you can take a song pretty far out, if you want, just as long as that honesty of intention is still rooted somewhere. Pushing those boundaries, actually, is part of what makes this music so much fun."

Releasing their self-title debut album, produced by *O Brother, Where Art Thou* soundtrack producer T-Bone Burnett (with Levon Helm playing drums on two tracks), in 2004, Ollabelle appeared on the threshold of success. Alison Krauss invited them to open shows, Jake Guralnick, son of music writer Peter Guralnick, took over their management.

Assuming production duties for Ollabelle's sophomore release, *Riverside Battle Songs*, Campbell entwined further into the Helm legacy. "There was a little bar in [Greenwich] Village called the Bouche Bar," he remembered. "Teresa and I would go down there [after Ollabelle recording sessions] and play. Amy heard us and started singing with Teresa. That was a beautiful combination, and when Amy and I started working on Levon's record [*Dirt Farmer*], she spared me the potential act of nepotism and brought Teresa into [her father's band]—Amy, Teresa, and Levon sounded so good together."

Working with Dr. Dennis Kraus, director of the Speech, Hearing, and Rehabilitation Center at the Memorial Sloan-Kittering Cancer Center, Helm slowly regained his Arkansas twang. Before long, he was singing again. "I would try and double Amy's vocal, or Little Sammy's vocal, and sing some background parts," he said, "and I sang in my head all the time. Someone told me that even though you're not physically singing, just to do it in your head affects those parts of you that do the singing. I kept doing that."

"It's different," said Campbell of the drummer's voice. "You hear the damage that's been done, but it's got all the honesty and fire that's always been there—none of that is missing—it might even be enhanced by the grittiness in his voice now."

"I've always worried about singing in the middle of the note," said Helm, "and trying to get it as pitch-perfect as possible. I can hear a lot better than I can sing, so it's a hell of a challenge to get it to please my ear. I realized that there were nights when I'd been overly hard on myself. Now, if I hit a bad note, I don't fall out with myself a bit."

"When you have everything taken away," Helm told Peter Aaron in 2008, "you're just so glad to get it back, which is what I've been fortunate enough to do. It just makes playing so much more joyful. Every opportunity to play just means so much more than the last one."

Helm's daughter provided the spark leading to *Dirt Farmer*, his first solo album in a quarter of a century. "I really wanted the record to be a platform for [my father's] vocals and history," she told Stephen Deusner, "and for his history to really shine—to keep it as simple as possible and acoustic."

"The original idea was for [Amy] to do a duet record with Levon," explained Campbell, who had alternated performances with Helm's band between 2005 and 2007 with tours with Phil Lesh's band. "Amy asked if I would coproduce it with her. It started with songs that Levon grew up with and became something larger."

"Larry [and I] shared the same vision," said Amy Helm, "and we began to take it one day at a time with recording. We would do a handful of songs one day, and then a week would go by, and we'd get together for a couple of days and try some other song. My father kept bringing songs into the fold that rounded out the album and allowed the vision to complete itself."

"It couldn't have gone better," added Campbell. "It's probably the coolest thing that's happened to me in my career, because it's Levon, who sings all the kinds of music I love with complete authority. Having an opportunity to do a record that gets back to the roots of where he came from, and the roots of his influence in The Band, and having Amy and Teresa involved [along with pianist/accordionist Brian Mitchell and pump organ player Glen Patscha], and Byron Isaacs, it was an amazing experience all around."

Dirt Farmer reconnected Helm with the kinds of songs that he remembered from his childhood. "Songs like 'The Girl I Left Behind, 'Blind Girl,' and 'Little Birds' are the first songs that I ever learned," he told the *Wall Street Journal*. "My mom and my older sister were good singers and my dad played guitar and sang for Saturday-night dances out in the country. We all came from that generation, you know. If you wanted to hear music back then, you had to sing it for yourself and play for each other."

Period-sounding tunes by Steve Earle ("The Mountain"), Buddy and Julie Miller ("Wide River to Cross"), Chicago bluesman J. B. Lenoir ("Feelin' Good"), and the Carter Family ("Single Girl, Married Girl") balanced with traditional folksongs "Poor Old Dirt Farmer" and "The Girl I Left Behind." Two songs, "A Train Robbery" and "Got Me a Woman," were by *The Legend of Jesse James* singer-songwriter Paul Kennerly. Byron Isaacs contributed the funky lament "Calvary." An updated rendition of "Little Birds," the traditional tune that The Band had performed at their debut concert nearly four decades before, was also included.

Released on October 30, 2007, *Dirt Farmer* scored a Grammy award as the year's best traditional folk album. *New York* magazine proclaimed that it "seizes the southern pastoralism that always lurked in The Band's music and blows it up full size, in all its gritty, rollicking, joyous, melancholic, and even absurd wonder."

"To say it is [Helm's] best solo album is understating the case," asserted singer, songwriter, and music critic Peter Stone Brown. "It virtually wipes out his previous solo albums as well as those by the reformed Band. It's the first album I've heard in ages that made me reach for the CD booklet to see who was playing what. Helm's voice is not what it once was. After throat surgery and twenty-eight radiation treatments, how could it be? It doesn't matter. The heart and soul, the all-important ingredients in making music magical, are there in abundance."

"The territory [*Dirt Farmer*] inhabits is the one Bruce Springsteen sought in *Nebraska, The Ghost of Tom Joad,* and *The Seeger Sessions,*" pointed out Peter Viney, "the territory Dylan's explored in detail for the last fifteen years. The difference is that, while Springsteen and Dylan embrace, and perform in, a traditional style, Levon Helm is simply the authentic article."

On the night that he received a Grammy for *Dirt Farmer*, and The Band received a Lifetime Achievement Award, Helm was not in attendance. In a scene in *Ain't in It for My Health*, he discussed his absence with his wife, Sandy. "I would go if they could tell me what good it would do Rick or Richard," he explained. "They never wanted to do a god-damned thing for them when they were around. I have my doubts about how sincere it is, anyway. Of course, I'm not that sincere about it myself, bastards."

Unlike other groups who had received lifetime achievement honors in the past, there was no chance that The Band would celebrate the occasion with their music. "Rick Danko and Richard Manuel aren't with us anymore," Robertson told Jane Stevenson of *Sun Media*. "There's no way to re-enact, or put something together, without it being, in our minds, just a little bit of an uneasy feeling to their memory. It's not bittersweet but a sadness that definitely runs through your heart; it's unexplainable. You can't beat your head against the wall, but it's something that when you think about it, you're baffled that you're still here and they're not. It gets to you regardless of how much time has gone by; I'm sure it's the same thing with Ringo, thinking about George or John, you never get over it."

Helm remained active. His rendition of Arthur Alexander's 1962 R&B hit "You'd Better Move On," produced by Campbell, was included on the first multi-artist edition of *The Imus Ranch Record* in September 2008. The album, which also included tracks by Patty Loveless, Lucinda Williams, Raul Malo (The Mavericks), Randy Travis, Willie Nelson, Dwight Yoakam, John Hiatt, Vince Gill, and Little Richard, benefited radio talk show host Don Imus and his wife's nonprofit working cattle ranch in Ribera, New Mexico (fifty miles from Santa Fe), where youngsters with cancer came to build self-esteem. For the second volume, which also included songs by the Blind Boys of Alabama, Sam Moore, and Kinky Friedman, in 2010, Helm contributed a cover of Bob Dylan's "It Takes a Lot to Laugh, It Takes a Train to Cry."

Recorded in the Barn studio, with Campbell producing, *Electric Dirt* projected a broader scope. Opening with a cover of the Jerry Garcia/Robert Hunter–penned "Tennessee Jed," the album continued with a re-brewing of the influences that had enriched The Band's best recordings. Gospel tunes by the Staples Singers ("Move along Train"), Ollabelle ("Heaven's Pearls"), and Campbell ("When I Go Away") balanced with Muddy Waters's "You Can't Lose What You Never Had" and "Stuff You Gotta Watch" (recorded by The Band for *Jubilation*) and Carter Stanley's "White Dove." A New Orleans influence was reflected in Helm's cover of "Kingfish," Randy Newman's ode to Louisiana's outspoken fortieth governor, Huey P. Long (1893–1935). Helm and Campbell collaborated on "Growing Trade," about a farmer forced to grow marijuana in order to pay his bills.

Critical acclaim was overwhelming. According to the *Los Angeles Times*, *Electric Dirt* (which scored the first-ever Grammy Award for best Americana album) showed that Helm's voice had "lost almost all traces of the cancer-treatment damage that was periodically evident on *Dirt Farmer*, returning him to what approaches the full glory of his prime."

"Helm's voice is nearly as supple as it was during his days with The Band," agreed *All Music Guide*'s Mark Deming, "and even when it shows signs of wear and tear, his sense of phrasing and his ability to bring the characters in these songs to life are as good as they've ever been."

"When he was young, [Helm] sounded like a wise old man," said *New Yorker* critic Ben Greenman. "Now, he sounds like an oracle."

A live album, *Ramble at the Ryman*, recorded in Nashville's historic Ryman Auditorium (former home of the Grand Ol' Opry) in May 2011, with guest appearances by Buddy Miller, John Hiatt, Sheryl Crow, Sam Bush, and Billy Bob Thornton, earned Helm his third consecutive Grammy Award—his second in a row for the year's best Americana album.

The drummer's cancer had not been completely eradicated, though. After performing a series of memorable shows, including appearances at the Newport Folk Festival and the Philadelphia Folk Festival during the summer of 2011, he became ill by the following spring. His wife, Sandy, and daughter, Amy, addressed his friends and longtime fans in a message posted on his official website on April 17, 2012. "Levon is in the final stages of his battle with cancer," they announced. "Please send your prayers and love to him as he makes his way through this part of his journey."

A few weeks before, Robertson had paid a visit to his old friend in the hospital. Together for the first time in thirty-six years, he believed that Helm's anger had begun to dissipate. In a statement posted on his Facebook page, the former Band guitarist wrote, "I was shocked and so saddened to hear that my old band mate, Levon, was in the final stages of his battle with cancer. It hit me really hard because I thought he had beaten throat cancer and had no idea that he was this ill."

As he visited with his ailing former band mate, Robertson later said he "thought of the incredible and beautiful times we had together. Levon is one of the most extraordinarily talented people I have ever known and very much like an older brother to me."

Succumbing to his ailments on April 26, 2012, Helm left behind many touched by his music. A public wake at the Barn drew more than two thousand mourners. The next day, the drummer was buried, near Danko's gravesite, in the Woodstock Cemetery. "The last few years, he was a changed person than when I knew him when he was with The Band," said Happy Traum. "He had found a way to get the respect, adulation, and some financial compensation (though it wasn't as much as he needed) and, at the same time, play the music that he truly loved. He found a band of people that he loved to play with. The icing on the cake was playing with his enormously talented daughter. All of that made him a genuinely happy guy. It showed when you talked to him. He was positive. He could complain and be acerbic about certain topics, and he was still bitter from the old days. He never wanted *The Last Waltz* to happen and he never forgave Robbie for giving up The Band. At the same time, having gone through the new incarnation of The Band, which was actually pretty darn good, with Jim Weider playing guitar, it was only in his last eight or nine years that he found this new musical life. It was a great way to go out—in a blaze of glory. People adored him. When we drove through Woodstock after his funeral service, they lined the streets watching the hearse go by. You could see the respect people here in town had for him. That was very uplifting."

"He was my bosom buddy friend to the end," wrote Bob Dylan on his official website, "one of the last true great spirits of my or any generation. This is just so sad to think about; I can still remember the first day I met him and the last day that I saw him. We go back pretty far and [we] had been through some trials together. I'm going to miss him and I'm sure a whole lot of others will too."

A memorial concert, *Love for Levon*, at the Izod Center in East Rutherford, New Jersey, on October 3, 2012, featuring such guests as Roger Waters, My Morning Jacket, Gregg Allman, John Mayer, Mavis Staples, David Bromberg, John Hiatt, Jorma Kaukonen, Robert Randolph, Joe Walsh, John Prine, Lucinda Williams, and Dylan's son Jakob, was released on CD/DVD the following March. "It was a great night," executive producer Keith Wortman told *Billboard*. "Levon was so well loved and so highly regarded, especially by his fellow musicians, we could have filled up three, four, or five shows with completely different lineups."

Since the drummer's death, a Keep It Goin' movement (inspired by words he uttered on his final day) has worked to preserve the Midnight Rambles. Two offshoots of the Levon Helm Band—the Dirt Farmer Band, featuring Larry Campbell, Amy Helm, Teresa Williams, Byron Isaacs, and Justin Guip, and the Midnight Ramble Band, which adds Jim Weider (guitar), Brian Mitchell (keyboards, accordion), Erik Lawrence (saxophone/flute), Howard Johnson (tuba), Steven Bernstein and Clark Gayton (trombones), and Jay Collins (saxophone)—continue to make appearances. In June 2013, Amy Helm announced the launching of a weekly Friday-night Midnight Ramble. "People want to be a part of something," she told *Rolling Stone*. "[The Midnight Ramble is] a party, that's part of its magic. We're honoring [my father], and hopefully doing what he would want us to do, by building opportunities for music to be made and people to have a good time."

In addition to playing with the Dirt Farmers and Midnight Ramble Band, the drummer's daughter has been touring with her own group, Amy Helm and the Handsome Strangers, featuring Byron Isaacs (who cowrote half of the songs on her yet-to-be-released debut album) and

Justin Guip, along with lead guitarist Dan Littleton. "I feel a really deep responsibility to continue [my father's] legacy," she told Chris Parker of the *Colorado Springs Independent* in July 2013. "I never thought about delineating my own sound from his, because I guess it just didn't translate that way to me. It felt like he was my teacher and I was learning a broad range of music—and just to stay true to the song, and sing what is you, and what you can deliver honestly."

Helm's debut album is due for a late 2013 release. "It's got some blues stuff," she said, "and my dad plays drums on four songs. I worked on [it] off and on for about three and a half years when I was touring with my dad. It just feels like the right time to put this collection of songs out. I feel I have something to say that's honest."

The peak of Amy Helm's shows continues to come when she resurrects songs, including "It Makes No Difference" and "Long Black Veil," associated with her father. "I really love the music of The Band," she told Stephen Deusner, "and I really admire my dad's music, of course. I think he's a badass. I would do anything to be able to sing like that. I put him right up there with Mavis Staples or Dolly Parton or any of my other heroes. If I could sing like him, or Richard [Manuel], or Rick [Danko], I'd be really psyched. You put on one of the songs that they sang and you get sort of inspired to try harder and aim for something in yourself that has the same level of soul. I count myself a big fan."

The recipient of a Lifetime Achievement Award (for his instrumental work) at the 2013 Americana Awards ceremony, Larry Campbell remains busy. He produced David Bromberg's album *Only Slightly Mad* at Helm's Barn studio. "I originally intended it to be all Chicago-style blues," said Bromberg in the album's liner notes, "but to my surprise, Larry said he'd like to produce a CD like the ones I recorded on Columbia, Fantasy, and Rounder; that is, a CD with all the genres of music that I like to perform—everything but the kitchen sink. Larry is about the only person that I can think of who had a deep understanding of all these genres."

The musical secret weapon of The Band, Garth Hudson remains its most prolific member. Norah Jones, Neko Case, Los Lobos, the Gipsy Kings, Leonard Cohen, Van Morrison, Roger Waters, Cyndi Lauper, John Sebastian, Geoff Muldaur, Tom Rush, Livingston Taylor, Emmylou Harris, Champion Jack Dupree, David Bromberg, the Indigo Girls, Sinead O'Connor, Keith Richards, Donovan, Wilco, and the Dixie Hummingbirds are some of the many artists who have welcomed his keyboards, accordion, and saxophone playing. Together with Dr. John, he joined British songstress Marianne Faithfull's band in 1989.

The following April, Faithfull's management staged a special concert, billed as "Garth Hudson and Friends," at St. Ann's Church in Brooklyn, New York. Members of the New York Choral Society accompanied the keyboardist's wife, Maud, on two songs, "Old Folks" and Cowboy Angel." "Maud has a beautiful voice," wrote the *Woodstock Times'* Twinker Twina, "and her phrasing is graceful and thoughtful."

A decade and a half Hudson's junior, Maud, wheelchair bound since an automobile accident, has sung with her husband since they met in early 1974, shortly after *The Last Waltz* concert. "I was recording with Hirth Martinez in Hollywood," she told Ross W. Muir of the *Midland Free Press*. "Robbie Robertson was producing it and Garth was playing on it. Hirth and his wife said I should stay for dinner with Garth, and [afterward] I couldn't get him out of my mind. I fell in love with him before I even knew that he played [with The Band]."

Since marrying Hudson in January 1979, the Los Angeles–raised vocalist has overseen his career as publicist and manager. Although they have struggled financially (declaring bankruptcy numerous times), they have remained committed to their musical ambitions.

Hudson's first solo album, *The Sea to the North*, released on September 11, 2001, featured a pair of instrumentals—"Little Island," performed solo, and "Third Order," with Levon Helm and Dan Brubeck on drums, along with Purna Das and Bauls of Bengal. Maud Hudson sang six songs. Professor Louis and the Crowmatix played on "The Saga of Cyrus and Mulgrew" and a cover of the Grateful Dead's "Dark Star." The Call's drummer, Stan Musick, and guitarist Michael Been appeared on "The Breakers." "During the recording process, I envisioned it [as] being two guys in a canoe in the year 1740," explained Hudson in the album's liner notes, "or a Paris fashion show, or an ice skating routine, or mountain climbing, or driving a vehicle, or being part of that special moment. I hope *The Sea to the North* makes you feel good and takes you somewhere you've never been before—somewhere you will want to return to often."

"[*The Sea to the North*] transcends all barriers, all frontiers," proclaimed Peter Viney. "This is genius. You can file it under jazz, classical, rock, new age. Better still—file it under all of them. More people might buy it that way, and this deserves to reach the widest audience. The very greatest keyboard player of the twentieth century has entered the twenty-first century with a truly original, near-perfect album."

Hudson continued to participate in a variety of projects. He played jazz and blues tunes during a solo performance in Toronto, and he recorded two albums (*Georgia Peach* and *The Whole Enchilada*) and toured France, Holland, and Zurich with pedal steel player "Sneaky" Pete Kleinow's country-rock band, Burrito Deluxe. "I like to go on stage with whoever is playing good," he said, "and stay with that musical language. I don't include any bebop licks in my country projects."

Accompanied by his wife, Hudson returned to London, Ontario (where he had been raised and educated), to help christen the city's new library and Wolf Performance Hall on September 8, 2002. Their duo performance, which included renditions of The Band's "It Makes No Difference," "The Weight," and "Blind Willie McTell" and Hudson's collaboration with Eric Andersen, "Beyond the Breakers," was recorded and released as *Live at the Wolf*.

In 2010, Hudson produced the two-volume *Garth Hudson Presents: A Canadian Celebration of The Band*, accompanying Canadian artists including Neil Young, Bruce Cockburn, Blue Rodeo, Great Big Sea, and the Cowboy Junkies on tunes from his past. The keyboardist also reconnected with The Band's legacy during performances with Jim Weider's ProJECT PERCoLAToR. "The Band [was] very structured," said Weider, "but we'll do 'The Weight,' and, in the middle of it, go into a reggae jam section that double-times, and let Garth take off. He does all kinds of wild sounds. There are sections where somebody will take the lead and take you on a trip—Garth will take you on a journey. We feel real lucky to have him; it fits like a glove."

Applying a modern pop sensibility, on his solo recordings, Robertson failed to reach many enthusiasts of The Band. Although his self-titled debut solo album received a Juno Award (Canada's equivalent to the Grammy) as the best album of the year in 1987, with Robertson and Daniel Lanois sharing producer of the year honors, it barely broke into *Billboard*'s top forty. Some blamed the guitarist's limited range as a singer. "It doesn't take long to realize why Robertson took only two lead vocals during his tenure with The Band," said *All Music Guide*'s Mark Deming. "His dry, reedy voice isn't bad, but it lacks the force and authority to communicate the big themes."

Born in Gatineau, Quebec's oldest village, Hull, in 1951, Daniel Lanois (who moved to Hamilton, Ontario, after his parents' separation in 1963) descends from a long line of musicians. "My grandfather and dad were violoneux," he told Olivia Mather of UCLA's campus newspaper, *The Echo*, "which is a French term for fiddler. On my mom's side, we had singers. They sang traditional French Canadian folk songs, not unlike the Cajun communities—'we've worked hard all week, it's the weekend, let's have some fun'—a self-entertainment society. The violins would come out, and there'd be some tap dancing, and singing these old folk songs. . . . You actually got a chance to hear something real, rather than somebody playing you records of something real. . . . It's the difference between reality and study."

Starting out with a crude studio in the laundry room of their mother's house, Lanois and his brother, Robert, advanced quickly. Soon after purchasing a four-track recorder in 1970, they moved to the larger Grant Avenue Studios, where Lanois would produce albums for folksinger Jackie Washington, children's performer Raffi, and Canadian New Wave band Martha and the Muffins.

Introduced to ex–Roxy Music keyboardist/composer Brian Eno in the early 1980s, Lanois coproduced Eno's heavily textural solo albums *Ambient 4/On Land* (1982), *Apollo: Atmospheres and Soundtracks* (1983), and *Thursday Afternoon* (1985), and his collaborations with Canadian guitarist

Michael Brook (Hybrid) and Los Angeles–born avant-garde poet Harold Budd, *The Pearl*.

As coproducer, Lanois worked with Eno on *The Unforgettable Fire*, the fourth studio album by Irish rock band U2. He also began working with Peter Gabriel, coproducing the British progressive rock singer-songwriter's soundtrack for the Alan Parker–directed film *Birdy*.

Lanois, who would go on to produce albums for Bob Dylan (*Oh Mercy*, *Time Out of Mind*), the Neville Brothers (*Yellow Moon*), and Emmylou Harris (*Wrecking Ball*), as well as recording on his own, was in the midst of producing U2's Grammy-winning *Joshua Tree* and Gabriel's commercial breakthrough *So* when he began work with Robertson.

Robertson's album included his only solo hit in the United Kingdom, "Somewhere Down This Crazy River"—according to Lanois, a "description of what it was like to hang in Arkansas with Levon Helm in [Robertson's] old neighborhood."

Robertson played an electric-autoharp-like Suzuki Omnichord on the song. "He found a little chord sequence that was sweet and wonderful," recalled Lanois. "I recorded him and superimposed his storytelling, which I was secretly recording, on top. That was the birth of 'Somewhere Down This Crazy River.' It's kind of like a guy with a deep voice telling you about steamy nights in Arkansas."

Robertson recalled departed cultural icons—James Dean, Elvis Presley, and Marilyn Monroe—during "American Roulette" and paid homage to Richard Manuel (who had committed suicide a year before) on "Fallen Angel."

One of Robertson's earliest Native American–themed tunes, "Broken Arrow," with Gabriel on electric piano, later became a top-twenty pop hit for Rod Stewart, who covered it on his 1991 album *Vagabond Heart*. A year later, the Grateful Dead added it to their set list, with Phil Lesh singing lead. "I was proud to rip open my chest and bare my soul," said Robertson. "I'm not embarrassed to talk about these things anymore. Do you know what a skin walker is? It's a thing in Indian mythology. There are certain people born with this gift; they are able to actually get inside you and mess with your feelings and with your mind. I want a song to get inside me, to feel it, like the skin walker."

The album's smooth sound reflected the input of Lanois, Chapman stick player Tony Levin, and drummer Manu Katché. Rick Danko sang backup on "Sonny Got Caught in the Crossfire," while Garth Hudson played keyboards on "Fallen Angel" and "Sweet Fire of Love," which also featured U2—their lead singer Bono shared vocals with Robertson. A second song recorded with U2, "Testimony," was added as a bonus track when the album combined with its follow-up as the two-CD *Storyville* in 2005. The expanded disc also included Robertson's rendition of The Band's "Christmas Must Be Tonight," from the soundtrack of yuletide comedy *Scrooged*.

Partially recorded in New Orleans, *Storyville* celebrated the Louisiana city's musical heritage with ten new original tunes. New Orleans–based musicians, including Russell Batiste Jr.; the Neville Brothers, Aaron, Art, and Cyril; The Meters', George Porter Jr., Leo Nocentelli, and Zigaboo Modeliste; Big Chief Bo Dollis (The Wild Magnolias); Big Chief Monk Boudreaux (The Golden Eagles); and the Rebirth Brass Band, provided authenticity. Bruce Hornsby and Ginger Baker (Cream, Blind Faith) made guest appearances. Hudson played organ on three tracks; Danko sang on one. German director Wim Wilders would include "Breakin' the Rule" in the soundtrack of his mystery/science fiction film *Until the End of the World*, and several tunes would be heard in *Powwow Highway*, David Seals's 1989 satirical film about life on the Northern Cheyenne Indian Reservation. "To me, *Storyville* is a state of mind," said Robertson. "It [represents] the beginning of hot music—sensual music—in America. Whorehouse music, barrelhouse music, it all came out of this source. Storyville only lived for twenty years as a district, like you find in some European cities, where this music from the devil, ladies of the night, gambling, rambling, saloons, and cabarets are officially allocated to a certain neighborhood."

"My fascination with New Orleans started when I was fourteen years old in Toronto," Robertson told John Sinclair. "I was in a Huey 'Piano' Smith wannabe band, Little Caesar and the Consuls. Little Caesar wanted to be Huey Smith, and we played this music that made me think, wait a minute, there's something going on here—there is something about this whole thing that's different and unique. There's this mystery, there's this fun, there is this thing you can't quite put a finger on—it just separated it from the pack to me. That made me start to inquire about where it was coming from, and, when I found out this music came out of New Orleans, it began a lifelong interest in the city and its music for me."

Robertson further reconnected with his Native heritage after agreeing to prepare a soundtrack for TNT's six-hour examination of indigenous history, *The Native Americans*. Working with producer Jim Wilson of the Choctaw Nation in New Mexico, he used the opportunity to collaborate with some of Native America's greatest musicians and singers. "I had wanted to do something with Rita Coolidge for years," he said. "We had been talking about it for ages. I wanted to do something with Pura Fé, on and on, down the list of people that I wanted to bring into my group, which I called, 'The Red Road Ensemble.' I tried to use everybody in ways that were really special and dignified. On some of *Music for the Native Americans*, I used music that would fit into their world, but, with other pieces, I didn't care—I wanted sounds that were beautiful. It was somewhere between wanting to accommodate the documentary and going full circle in my life to where it began for me. It was really me being able to do what my imagination and my soul were telling me to do."

Before he embarked on a follow-up (*Contact from the Underworld of Redboy*), PBS asked Robertson to film a documentary, *Making a Noise: A Native American Musical Journey*, about his return visit to the Six Nations of the Grand River Reserve. "I wouldn't trade it for anything else that I've done," he said. "Floyd Westerman went with me. We were just experimenting together. We did not have a script or anything figured out ahead of time. It was a discovery process, and there's something so beautiful in that."

A focus on Robertson's exploration of his Native roots had been included on a segment of VH1's *Behind the Music*. "It showed me going to a peyote ceremony," he said, "although, obviously, you can't shoot footage during the ceremony, and some of the old peyote men weren't too keen about having cameras around. It was getting uncomfortable when one of these young peyote men said, 'We've got to be part of the future. It's part of our heritage.' He convinced the others that we were not doing a terrible thing. We had respect for boundaries."

Robertson has continued to find new outlets for his creativity. He has been working on a children's book, *Hiawatha and the Peacemaker*, based on a Six Nations legend. " It's a story that I heard at the age of around eight to nine," he said, "which is considered a young reader's age. I heard it on the Six Nations Indian Reserve (where my mom was born and raised), and the story was told to us by a very respected elder at the time. It's kind of extraordinary that we grow up thinking of Hiawatha as this character from Longfellow—from his poem—and he got Hiawatha mixed up with a different Indian. . . . Anyway, from that I'm doing sort of a whole other angle."

Together with his son Sebastian, Jim Guerinto, and Jared Levine, Robertson explored the lives and careers of twenty-seven musicians in *Legends, Icons, and Rebels: Music That Changed the World*. "Sebastian was working with kids at the time," he explained to *Paste* magazine, "and he was inspired by the fact that they weren't reacting like they were reacting to just great music, great songs. Like he said, 'Well, I'd put on the usual Humpty Dumpty songs or whatever, and every once in a while I'd slip in a Marvin Gaye and I'd change it around somewhere, Johnny Cash,' and he said it was extraordinary to witness what happened to all these kids in the room. Like a certain energy, a certain thing, and you could see their involvement in the feel of the music, as opposed to what we've been told that kids are supposed to listen to, and it was just an interesting discovery. This was years ago. 'You know, somebody should really do something about kids learning about really great recording artists, and so they've got some sort of foundation of taste and they know what the real deal is and you know what fluff is and what the real thing is.' I said, 'Well, that's an interesting thought.' Years later, we revisit this and we decide we're gonna do this, and it's taken many years to do this because I just wanted to get it so right. And we got it so right."

Robertson has been working on his autobiography. "I surprise myself at the details I remember," he said, "and I'm really enjoying revisiting these things, because I don't have any reason to think about this stuff. As I go along, I find that I have some stories to tell about this journey that I have been on."

Robertson has continued to explore his own music as well. With the help of Eric Clapton, Steve Winwood, bassist Pino Palladino, and drummer Ian Thomas, along with Robert Randolph, Tom Morello (Rage Against the Machine, Audioslave, The Nightwatchman), Trent Reznor (Nine Inch Nails), and Taylor Goldsmith (The Dawes), he released his first new album in twelve years, *How to Become Clairvoyant*, in April 2011. "I haven't tried to intellectualize it," Robertson told me, "but I'm doing the same thing that I did as a kid—walking between two worlds. Nobody says, 'You can't come in here and make that kind of music.' I feel privileged to be able to get away with it."

Robertson's songs on *How to Become Clairvoyant* represented his most personal writing. "When I was writing songs for The Band," he explained, "I didn't want to come in and say, 'Here's another fascinating song about me.' I was not comfortable with that at all. This is another thing from [my childhood days at] the Six Nations [Reserve]. I thought that, when I grew up, I wanted to be a storyteller like these elders. They told these stories and it gave me chills . . . the idea of being able to write a mythology based on real things, to invent fictional characters based on real people, of course, there is always personal stuff in there, anyway."

The opening track, "Straight Down the Line," recalled Robertson's earliest musical memories. "In the beginning of rock 'n' roll, it was referred to as the devil's music," he told Mike Ragogna. "I enjoyed the counterpoint of this over the years. In the back of my mind, I [wrote] this song about meeting Sonny Boy Williamson, [but] also about Mahalia Jackson and Frank Sinatra. In the black community, there was blues and gospel music, and the idea of putting those two things together (like Ray Charles did years ago) was very questionable. [Mahalia Jackson] made a statement saying, 'I do not play rock 'n' roll,' and Frank Sinatra said, 'This music will be around for six months and then it will be gone forever.' I think there is something about those bold statements that has stayed with me throughout the years, and I liked the idea of writing a song about that."

Robertson's "Axeman" paid homage to those who had inspired his guitar playing. "It was a way for Tom Morello and I to do something in tribute to all these guys," he explained to *Rolling Stone*. "I refer to Duane Allman, Stevie Ray Vaughn, and Jimi Hendrix, who I call Jimi James, in the song, because, when I met him, [that was the name he was using]. I also refer to RJ—Robert Johnson—Django Reinhardt, and Link Wray—so many of the guys who, if it weren't for them, we wouldn't be doing what we're doing. It was time to do a tip of the hat, I felt."

Another song, "When the Night Was Young," recalled the glory days of The Band. "The youth of the nation, and ultimately the youth of the world, really did have an incredible influence on what was going on," said Robertson. "There was a war going on, in the late '60s, [and] people at the Woodstock festival, and people around the country said, 'We don't agree with this; we're going to stand up and make some changes,' and they did. [The United States] had to pull out of that war because it was such a negative thing. . . . We were coming out of the period of the assassinations of the Kennedys and Martin Luther King Jr., and in some very powerful way, it brought people together. Music was the voice of the generation."

Robertson reflected on the breakup of The Band during "This Is Where I Get Off." "I've never much talked about it in public," he told Mike Ragogna, "and I've certainly never talked about it in song. . . . Sometimes you just start with the germ of an idea, and you really don't know where it's going to go until it unveils itself and lets you know what path you're following. When I started writing this song, I wasn't sure where it was going to go, but as it unfolded, it was a nice release to be able to talk about this, and to put it in a way of declaring that, when I did leave The Band, that was never the idea. As I put it in the song, 'walking out on the boys' was never the plan, because it wasn't. Everybody went off in different directions after *The Last Waltz* because there were projects that everybody was interested in doing, and everybody wanted to just freshen up and do something else. Then, the idea was we were going to come back together, do some writing, and try to make some great music. Everybody went off and did their own thing and nobody came back. . . . Nobody could retrace their footsteps, somehow, and everything evolved into different places. It wasn't about me standing up and saying, 'I'm quitting The Band.' That never happened."

EIGHT
Coda

More than a half century has passed since they came together as Ronnie Hawkins's Hawks. It has been more than four decades since they first played with Bob Dylan, and more than thirty-five years since the original quintet hosted *The Last Waltz*, but The Band's influence remains strong. Revered as pioneers of Americana, their unique blending of R&B, jump blues, gospel, folk, country, and rock continues to inspire a new generation of roots-oriented bands in the United States, including Old Crow Medicine Show, Alabama Shakes, Railroad Earth, and Spirit Family Reunion, and is embraced by musicians around the globe. "Americana doesn't really mean American," said British-born Richard Thompson, the recipient of a songwriter award from the Americana Music Association, to the *Boston Globe*; "it means roots music."

"I never really had a big strategy in mind," Robertson told BBC interviewer Clive Owen in April 2001. "I just followed the music, always, and when I had something to write about, something to express, that was the best time to make a record. [It] was all about writing songs that would have that timeless quality . . . no frills, no tricks, no nothing—the real shit—that was as much as any of us wanted out of the music.

Bibliography

Allen, Linda. *Washington Notebook: New Songs of the Northwest Sung by Northwest Musicians*. Victory. Audio CD.
Baxandall, Rosalyn, and Linda Gordon, eds. *Dear Sisters: Dispatches from the Women's Liberation Movement*. New York: Basic Books, 2001.
Boyd, Joe. *White Bicycles: Making Music in the 1960s*. London: Serpent's Tail, 2006.
Clapton, Eric. *The Autobiography*. New York: Broadway Books, 2007.
D'Ambrosio, Antonino. *A Heartbeat and a Guitar: Johnny Cash and the Making of Bitter Tears*. New York: Nation Books, 2009.
Dylan, Bob. *Chronicles, Volume 1*. New York: Simon & Schuster, 2004.
Editors of *Rolling Stone*. *The Rolling Stone Interviews*. Vol. 1. New York: Warner Paperback Library, 1971.
Harris, Craig. *The New Folk Music*. Crown Point, IN: White Cliffs Media, 1991.
Hawkins, Ronnie, with Peter Goddard. *Last of the Good Ol' Boys*. Toronto: Stoddart Publishing, 1989.
Helm, Levon, with Stephen Davis. *This Wheel's on Fire: Levon Helm and the Story of The Band*. New York: William Morrow and Company, 1993.
Heylin, Clifton. *Bob Dylan: The Recording Sessions 1960–1994*. New York: St. Martin's Press, 1995.
Hoskyns, Barney. *Across the Great Divide*. New York: Hal Leonard, 2006.
Kiersh, Edward. *Where Are You Now, Bo Diddley: The Artists Who Made Us Rock and Where They Are Now*. Garden City, NY: Doubleday, 1986.
Kooper, Al. *Backstage Passes & Backstabbing Bastards: Memoirs of a Rock 'n' Roll Survivor*. New York: Billboard Books, 1998.
Lesh, Phil. *Searching for the Sound: My Life with the Grateful Dead*. New York: Little, Brown, 2005.
Neer, Richard. *FM: The Rise and Fall of Rock Radio*. New York: Villard Books, 2001.
Santelli, Robert. *Aquarius Rising: The Rock Festival Years*. New York: Dell, 1980.
Smith, Joe. *Off the Record: An Oral History of Popular Music*. New York: Warner Books, 1989.
Weinberg, Max, with Robert Santelli. *The Big Beat: Conversations with Rock's Great Drummers*. Chicago: Contemporary Books, 1984.
Woliver, Robbie. *Bringing It All Back Home: Twenty-five Years of American Music at Folk City*. New York: Pantheon Books, 1986.

Index

"4 ½ Pantomime," 132
10cc, 130
"A Change Is Gonna Come," 137
"A Hard Rain's Gonna Fall," 20, 23
"A La Glory," 125
"A Mood I Was In," 140
A Musical History, 129
A Song Will Rise, 17
"A Train Robbery," 180
A Tree with Roots, 77
"Absolutely Sweet Marie," 36
"Acadian Driftwood," 144, 145
"Across the Great Divide," 95, 101, 136, 139
Adderly, Cannonball, 40
"Ain't Got a Home," 137, 138
Ain't in It for My Health, 87, 124, 181
"Ain't No More Cane (On the Brazos)," 60, 129, 162
"Ain't That a Lot of Love," 143
The Alabama Shakes, 89
Alaska, the Musical, 177
Alexander, Arthur, 181
Alexandra, Robertson, 97
Alk, Howard, 37, 67, 83, 136
"All around the World (Grits Is Groceries)," 59
"All I Wanna Do," 24
The Allman Brothers Band, 49, 89, 138, 139
Allman, Duane, 89, 190
Allman, Gregg, 183
"All Our Past Times," 146, 151, 172
The Almanac Singers, 5–7, 8, 12
The Amazing Rhythm Aces, 162
"Amazon (River of Dreams," 168
Ambient 4/On Land, 186
American Bandstand, 44, 51
American Son, 157
Amram, David, 120

Andersen, Eric, 71, 120, 170–171
Anderson, Marian, 18
The Animals, 50
Another Side of Bob Dylan, 19
Antonioni, Michelangelo, 95
"Are You Ready for the Country," 143
"Arkansas Hard Luck Blues," 41
Armstrong, Louis, 44, 61
Arnold, Jerome, 24, 26
Arnold, Kokomo, 154
"Atlantic City," 168
"At Last," 160
"Auld Lang Syne," 151
Avalon, Frankie, 3, 24, 55
Avis, Bill, 30

"Baby, Let Me Follow You Down," 33, 152
Bachman, Randy, 39
Bachman-Turner Overdrive, 39
Back to Mud Acres, 120
The Bacon Brothers, 174
Badfinger, 131
Baez, Joan, 5, 11, 17, 18–19, 23, 70, 71, 97
Bailey, Pearl, 124
Baker, Ginger, 90
Baker, Lavern, 53
"Ballad of a Thin Man," 21, 31, 33, 37
"The Ballad of Hollis Brown," 19
The Band: Breakup of original group, 153; Bob Dylan and, 1, 2, 28, 136, 140, 140–141, 141–142, 150–123, 167; *Easy Rider* and, 89; Festival Express and, 126, 129; Albert Grossman and, 11; Impact of Richard Manuel's suicide, 166; Influence of, 119; Glyn Johns and, 131; Last Waltz and, 148, 149–152, 155, 158; Recording and, 124, 126, 131, 137–136, 143, 144–145,

197

169; Reunion, 163, 163–164; John Simon and, 83–84; The Southland and, 94; Success and, 126; Summer Jam at Watkins Glen and, 138–140; Touring, 91, 92, 124, 147; Woodstock and, 122–123, 124
Bantu Choral Folk Songs, 12
Bartholomew, Dave, 132
Basement Tapes, 17, 60, 73, 76, 76–77, 85, 91, 100, 120
Basie, William "Count," 27, 134, 136
Batiste, Russell Jr., 188
The Beach Boys, 75, 94, 153. *See also* Brian Wilson
Bearsville, 71, 129, 130, 130–131
The Beatles, 22, 23, 37, 38, 43, 58, 75, 94, 123, 124, 147, 167, 176
The Beau Brummels, 93
"Beautiful Dreamer," 44
Beautiful Noise, 143, 147
"Beautiful Thing," 77, 146
"Be Bop a Lula," 75
Beck, 161
Beckley, Gerry, 153
Beckwith, Byron de la, 19. *See* The Call
Before the Flood, 141, 142
Belafonte, Harry, 40
Belew, Fred, 49
Bengali Bauls, 155
Berline, Byron, 144
Bernstein, Elmer, 161
Bernstein, Steven, 183
Berry, Chuck, 45, 51, 52, 53, 56, 75, 127, 137, 138, 139–140, 154, 161, 174, 175
Best of Everything, 160
The Best Revenge, 158
Betts, Dickey, 138
"Beyond the Breakers," 185
Big Country, 97
Big River, 177
Bikel, Theodore, 10, 15, 23
The Bill Doggett Band, 62
Bill Haley and the Comets, 75
"Biloxi," 130
Biograph, 1, 33, 35
The Birds Fly Home, 12
The Birds of Paradise, 12
Birdy, 187
Bishop, Elvin, 24

Bizio, Peter, 129
"Bizness Ain't Dead," 16
"Black Crow Blues," 19
The Black Crowes, 89, 97, 174, 175, 178
The Blackhawks, 40, 45
Blackwell, Otis, 54
Bland, Bobby "Blue," 27, 43, 45, 46, 59, 139, 151
The Blind Boys of Alabama, 181
"Blind Girl," 180
"Blind Willie McTell," 168, 185
Block, Rory, 120, 130, 178
Blonde on Blonde, 35, 36, 67
Blood on the Tracks, 77
Blood, Sweat, and Tears, 39, 83, 123, 127
Bloomfield, Mike, 22, 24, 26, 28, 83, 89
"Blowin' in the Wind," 14, 15, 16, 17, 18, 23
"Blue Moon of Kentucky," 157
Blue Rodeo, 186
Blue, David, 154
Blues Project, 119
"Blues So Bad," 154
"Blues Stay Away from Me," 42, 168
"Bo Diddley," 51
The Bobbettes, 62
Bono, 187
"Book Faded Brown," 169
Boone, Skip, 119
The Bootleg Series Vol. 1–3, 35
The Bootleg Series Vol. 10. Another Self Portrait (1969–1971), 120, 123
Bosch, Hieronymus, 21
Boudreaux, Big Chief Monk, 188
"Bound by Love," 169
Boyd, Joe, 25
Bramlett, Randall, 159, 162
Brand, Oscar, 23
Brando, Marlon, 137
Brickman, Marshall, 71
Bright Morning Stars, 121
Bringing it all Back Home, 13, 21, 34, 67
Britt, Elton, 176
Broadside, 7, 15
Broadside Ballads, volume one, 15, 16
Brock, Louise, 69
"Broken Arrow," 187
Brokenshaw, Frank T. "Brock," 69

Bromberg, David, 183, 184
Brook, Michael, 186
Brooks, Harvey, 29, 30
Broonzy, Big Bill, 10, 29, 90, 152
Brown, Bolton, 68
Brown, James, 42
Brown, Jim, 10
Bruce, Jack, 90
Bruno, Bruce, 27
Buchanan, Roy, 44, 54, 55, 56
Budd, Harold, 186
Bunuel, Luis, 35
Burgess, Albert Austin "Sonny," 45, 46, 48
Burnett, Chester Arthur "Howlin' Wolf," 44, 46, 53, 59
Burnett, T-Bone, 178
Burrito Deluxe, 185
Burstyn, Ellen, 150
Burton, James, 44, 54, 55
Busey, Gary, 159
Bush, Sam, 163, 174, 182
The Butterfield Blues Band, 11, 24, 26, 130, 133
Butterfield, Paul, 24, 43, 71, 83, 120, 130, 143, 148, 151, 154, 162, 167, 168, 170. *See also* The Butterfield Blues Band
Byrdcliffe, 65, 68, 69
The Byrds, 10, 23, 24, 29, 31, 76, 120, 164, 176

C. F. Martin and Sons, 86
Café Espresso, 70, 71
Cagle, Terry, 161, 163
Cahoots, 2, 60, 100, 131–132, 133
Cale, J. J., 169
"Caledonia Mission," 84, 85
The Call, 153–154, 185
Calloway, Cab, 45
"Calvary," 180
Camp Songs with Six to Eleven Year Olds, 12
Campbell, David, 161; Background of, 176–177; David Bromberg and, 184; FM radio on, 93, 146; Levon Helm and, 87, 174, 176, 183; Ollabelle and, 179
"Camptown Races," 44

"Can You Please Crawl out Your Window," 33, 35
The Canadian Squires, 27, 43
Capitol Records, 52, 74–75
"Caravan," 151
Carllile, Thumbs, 153
Carpenter, Mary-Chapin, 168
Carroll's Rehearsal Studio, 24
Carter, Benny, 134
The Carter Family, 76, 143, 180
Carter, Fred Jr., 54, 55, 154, 157
"Carry It On," 15
Case, Neko, 184
Cash, Johnny, 31, 37, 46, 76, 157, 168, 189
Cash, Roseanne, 177
Cashdollar, Cyndi, 164
The Cate Brothers, 157, 161, 166
Cate, Ernie. *See* The Cate Brothers
"The Caves of Jericho," 168; *Ceremonies of the Horsemen*, 141
Chad and Jeremy, 23
Chad Mitchell Trio, 10, 17
The Chambers Brothers, 26
Chandler, Len, 19
Chapman, Blondie, 153, 166
Chapman, Mike, 162
Charles, Bobby, 60, 134, 137, 151, 152, 154, 169
Charles, Ray, 27, 28, 40, 42, 58, 59, 134, 136, 160, 167, 190
The Charlie Daniels Band, 97
Charters, Sam, 26, 119
Cheap Trick, 130
"Chest Fever," 84, 85–86, 135, 139, 151
The Chicago Women's Liberation Rock Band, 98
Child Is Father to the Man, 83
"Chimes of Freedom," 24
"Christmas Must Be Tonight," 149, 187
Ciarlante, Randy, 164, 167, 168, 169, 170, 171
Civil Rights Movement, 14, 15, 17, 18, 19
The Clancy Brothers, 10
Clapton, Eric, 58, 82, 90, 122, 123, 127, 148, 151, 152, 153, 160, 166, 168, 169, 172
Clark, Gene, 164

Clarke, Michael, 164
Classic Albums — The Band, 98
Clemens, Clarence, 155
Clements, Vassar, 168
Cline, Patsy, 157
The Coal Miner's Daughter, 157–158
Coburn, James, 140
Cochrane, Eddie, 56
Cockburn, Bruce, 39, 186
Cocker, Joe, 89
Cohen, John, 72
Cohen, Leonard, 28, 39, 83, 184
Cohen, Robert "Bob," 15, 16
Collins, Howie, 20
Collins, Jay, 183
Collins, Judy, 178
The Color of Money, 42, 160
Coltrane, John, 60, 119
Colvin, Shawn, 163, 168, 177
"Come Rain or Come Shine," 160
"Come Together," 52
Considine, Shaun, 22
Cooke, Sam, 58, 137
Coolidge, Rita, 188
Cooper, Alice, 127
Copas, Cowboy, 42
Coppola, Francis Ford, 150
Corea, Chick, 134
"Corrina, Corrina," 20
The Corsairs, 12
Costello, Elvis, 23, 58, 133, 143, 174
Cotton, James, 46
The Cowboy Junkies, 39, 186
The Cowsills, 75
"Coyote," 151
"Crazy," 157
Cream, 90
Creedence Clearwater Revival, 44, 121
Cropper, Steve, 81, 154
Crosby, David, 146
Crosby, Harry Lillis "Bing," 151
Crosby, Stills, and Nash, 164, 165
The Crossing Guard, 160
Crow, Sheryl, 182
The Crowmatix, 169, 170, 185
Crowell, Rodney, 28
Crudup, Arthur "Big Boy," 20
Cummings, Burton, 39
Cunningham, Sis, 5

Cupid's Arrow, 154
Curtis, James "Peck," 49
Curtis, Tony, 90
Cushnie, Scott, 54
The Cyrkle, 83

Dane, Barbara, 15
Dangerfield, Rodney, 124
"Daniel and the Sacred Harp," 125
Daniels, Charlie, 97, 157
Danko, Eli Damian, 167
Danko, Rick: Andersen, Danko, and Fjeld and, 170–171; Background of, 57–58; Bass playing of, 58; Paul Butterfield and, 170; Death of, 172; Japan and, 171; Richard Manuel and, 159; Musical approach of, 72, 80; Outside projects of, 187–188; Solo career of, 171, 172; Vocals of, 58, 81. *See also* The Band, The Hawks
Danko, Terry, 58
Darling, Erik, 9, 12
Das, Purna, 155, 185
The Dave Clark 5, 23
Davenport, Darius, 119
Davis, "Little" Sammy, 175
Davis, Jesse Ed, 154
Davis, Miles, 119, 134
Davis, Ossie, 15
Davis, Reverend Gary, 24, 152
The Dawes, 190
"Dead Man's Curve," 75
Dean, James, 187
Dear Mr. President, 7
"Dear Mrs. Roosevelt," 77
"Death of Harry Simms," 7
Dee, Ruby, 15
Deep Sea Chanteys and Whaling Ballads, 7
The Delmore Brothers, 42, 168
Demara, Ferdinand Waldo Jr., 90
Dement, Iris, 163
DeNiro, Robert, 119, 150, 160
Denver, John, 10, 89
DePalma, Brian, 119, 150
"Desolation Row," 21, 30, 33
DeShannon, Jackie, 89
Dewey, John, 68
Di Prima, Diane, 151

Diamond Jubilation, 178
Diamond, Neil, 143, 147, 149, 151
Diddley, Bo, 53, 151
"Did She Mention My Name," 84
"Different Drum," 71
Dimitroff, Sita, 119
"Dirge," 140
Dirt Farmer, 179, 180–181, 182
The Dixie Hummingbirds, 178, 184
Dixon, Delores, 15. *See also* New World Singers
Dixon, Willie, 24, 27, 54, 160, 168
Doherty, Kevin, 169
Dollis, Big Chief Bo, 188
Dollmaker, 158
Domino, Antoine "Fats," 53, 132–133, 137, 159
Donohue, Tom "Big Daddy," 93
Donovan, 139, 184
Don't Cry Now, 70
"Don't Do It," 124, 134, 139, 152
Don't Look Back, 37
"Don't Think Twice, It's Alright," 14, 17
"Don't Wait," 169
"Don't Ya Tell Henry," 132, 135
The Doors, 127
Dr. John (Malcolm John Rebennack, Jr.): *Carney* and, 159; Guest appearances of, 134, 137, 143, 155, 166, 184; Influence of The Band on, 93; The Last Waltz and, 151, 152; Libby Titus and, 70; Midnight Ramble and, 174; RCO All-Stars and, 154
Dorsey, Lee, 133
Douglas, Jerry, 163
"Down in the Flood," 76, 120, 135, 142
"Down South in New Orleans," 60
"Drag Strip City," 75
"Drown in my Own Tears," 42
Duboff, Steve, 75
Duncan, Isadora, 68
Dunn, Donald "Duck," 73, 154, 157
Dupree, Champion Jack, 168, 169, 174, 184
Dupree, Robbie, 163
Dylan, Bob: The Band and, 1, 2, 5, 36, 77, 91, 122, 135–136, 168; The *Basement Tapes* and, 73, 74, 76–77; Electric music and, 2–3; Folk music and, 3; Forest Hills and, 30–31; Albert Grossman and, 11, 14; Happy Traum and, 16; The Hawks, 28, 29, 32, 35; Influence of, 15, 17, 80, 170; The Isle of Wight Festival and, 123; Levon Helm and, 181, 183; The Last Waltz and, 152; Sarah Lownds and, 65; The March on Washington and, 18, 19; Motorcycle accident of, 66–67; Newport Folk Festival and, 23–26; The New World Singers and, 15; Politics and, 17, 19, 20; Tiny Tim and, 83; Woodstock and, 69, 70, 71
Dylan, Jakob, 65, 183
Dylan, Jesse, 65, 122

Earle, Steve, 174, 180
Easy Rider, 89, 95
Eat the Document, 37, 67
Eaton, Jimmy Van, 49
Eberhardt, Cliff, 163
Ed Sullivan Show, 19, 23, 124
Edward Sharpe and the Magnetic Zeroes, 129
Electric Dirt, 88, 178, 181–182
The Electric Flag, 26, 83
Elliott, Ramblin' Jack, 3, 5, 44
"Endless Highway," 139, 140
Eno, Brian, 186
Eoff, Ron, 163
Ertegun, Ahmet, 16
"Eternal Love," 59
"Evangeline," 145, 151, 161
Evans, Gil, 130, 134, 160
Evans, Jimmy "Lefty," 54
Evars, Medgar, 19, 95
"Even if it's a Pig—Part Two," 181
"Everlasting Love," 161
The Everly Brothers, 13, 56

F. S. Walcott's Rabbit's Foot Minstrels, 174
Fagen, Donald, 70
Faier, William "Billy," 69–70
Faithful, Marianne, 167, 184
"Fallen Angel," 187
Farina, Richard and Mimi, 70

Farrell, Joe, 134
Fast Folk Musical Magazine, 163
Fé, Pura, 188
"Feelin' Good," 180
Feliciano, Jose, 44
"Ferdinand the Imposter," 77, 90
Ferlinghetti, Lawrence, 151
Festival Express, 126–129
"Fever," 42
Fiore, Bob, 129
Fjeld, Jonas, 170, 171
Fleck, Bela, 168, 177
Foghat, 130
Folk music, 3–11, 12, 13, 15, 25, 29, 36, 38, 69
Folksongs of Four Continents, 12
"Follow Me, I'm the Pied Piper," 75
Fonda, Jane, 158
Fonda, Peter, 89
Forbert, Steve, 177
"Forbidden Fruit," 144
Forces of Nature, 49
Foreigner, 130
Forest Hills Tennis Stadium, 26, 29
"Forever Young," 17, 152, 169
Forte, Fabian, 3, 36, 56
Foster, Jodie, 159
"Fortune Teller," 132
"Forty Days," 51
"Four Strong Winds," 151
Foster, Stephen, 44
The Four Quarters, 62
Four Tops, 42, 135, 139
Frankie Lymon and the Teenagers, 51
Franklin, Aretha, 89
"Freak's Lament," 159
Freddy and the Dreamers, 23
Freedom Singers, 15, 23
Freeman, Bobby, 93
Freewheelin', 17, 20
Friedman, Kinky, 177, 178, 181
"French Girls," 169
Frizzell, William Orville "Lefty," 44, 53, 57
"From a Buick 6," 21, 31
Fuller, Blind Boy, 152
Funicello, Annette, 56
"Furry Sings the Blues," 151
"Further on up the Road," 151

Gabriel, Peter, 187
Garcia, Jerry, 97, 129, 176, 181. *See also* The Grateful Dead
The Garden of Earthly Delights, 21, 159
"The Garden Party," 138
Garland, Jim, 178
Garnier, Tony, 177
Garth Hudson Presents: A Canadian Celebration of The Band, 186
Gaskon, Leonard, 20
"Gates of Eden," 21, 22, 30, 33
Gaye, Marvin, 134, 189
Gayton, Clark, 183
Geffen Records, 161
Geffen, David. *See* Geffen Records
"The Genetic Method," 86, 128
Gene Vincent and the Bluecaps, 75
"Georgia on My Mind," 59, 149, 150
Georgia Peach, 185
Gerde's Folk City, 13, 15
Gerry and the Pacemakers, 75
Gersh, Gary, 161
"Get Off the Track," 125
"Get Out of My Life, Woman," 133
"Get Up Jake," 134, 136, 138
The Ghost of Tom Joad, 180
Gibson, Bob, 10, 11, 23
Gilbert, Ronnie. *See* The Weavers
Gill, Vince, 28, 181
Gillum, William McKinley "Jazz," 152
Ginsberg, Allen, 19, 76, 120
The Gipsy Kings, 184
Give It Up, 70
Glazer, Tom, 5
Gleason, Ralph, 34, 96, 99, 100, 102, 136
Glosson, Lonnie Elonzo, 41
Glover, Henry, 42–43, 143, 154, 167, 168
"Go Go Liza Jane," 27
Going Home, 55
Going My Way, 151
Goldberg, Barry, 24, 26, 83
The Golden Eagles, 188
"Goodnight, Irene," 8
Gorgoni, Al, 22
"Got Me a Woman," 180
Graham, Bill, 1, 92, 122, 140, 143, 148, 152
"The Grand Coulee Dam," 77
Grand Funk Railroad, 131

The Grapes of Wrath, 101
The Grateful Dead, 89, 122, 126, 128, 136, 138, 139, 142, 163, 172, 185, 187
Great Big Sea, 186
The Great Imposter, 90
The Great White Wonder, 76
The Greenbrier Boys, 71. *See also* John Herald
Greene, Jackie, 99
Gregg, Robert "Bobby," 21, 22, 34, 36
Griffin, Paul L., 21, 22
Griffith, Nanci, 163
Grogan, Emmett, 152
Grossman, Albert Bernard: Background of, 10–11; The Band and, 67, 72, 74, 92; Bearsville and, 130; Bob Dylan and, 14, 29, 31, 65, 66, 123; Newport and, 24; Other clients and, 65, 84, 131; Peter, Paul, and Mary and, 11–12, 13–14; Woodstock and, 23, 67, 71, 126, 129
Grossman, Sally Anne, 65
"Groundhog," 137
"Growing Trade," 88, 181
Grunt, Blind Boy, 76
Guard, Dave. *See* The Kingston Trio
Guerinto, Jim, 189
The Guess Who, 39
Guip, Justin, 183
Guralnick, Jake, 178
Guralnick, Peter, 178
Guthrie, Arlo, 10
Guthrie, Woodrow Wilson "Woody," 2, 3, 5, 7, 8, 10, 12, 14, 15, 16, 28, 41
Guy, Buddy, 126, 127

Half Pint, 45
Hall and Oates, 131
Hall, Jim, 119
Hall, Willie, 49
Hamilton, Frank, 9, 70
Hammond, John, 20, 120
Hammond, John Jr., 21, 27, 49, 168
Hampton, Lionel, 134
The Handsome Strangers, 178, 183
Hank Ballard and the Midnighters, 42
Hardy, Jack, 163
Harms, Dallas, 39

Harris, Emmylou, 145, 151, 157, 174, 184, 187
Harrison, George, 38, 82, 90
"Havana Moon," 154
Havens, Richie, 28, 71, 97, 123
Hawes, Baldwin "Butch," 5
Hawes, Bess Lomax, 5
Hawes, Pete (Joe Bowers), 5
Hawkins, Delmar Allen "Dale," 43, 44
Hawkins, Ronnie: Background of, 40–41, 43–45; The Band and, 81, 134, 148, 151; Changing personnel and, 54, 55; Rick Danko and, 57, 58; The Hawks and, 2, 27, 39–40, 51; Levon Helm and, 48; Garth Hudson and, 59, 62; Richard Manuel and, 59; Robbie Robertson and, 53–54, 54–55, 55, 56; Sun Records and, 46, 49
Hawkins, Skipper, 43
The Hawks, 2, 27–28, 28, 29, 34, 39–41, 48, 51, 53, 54–57, 57, 62, 76, 81
Hayes, Buddy, 44
Hays, Lee Elhardt, 5, 7–8. *See also* The Almanac Singers, The Weavers
"Hazel," 140, 152
Head Over Heels, 146
"Heaven's Pearls," 181
"He Don't Love You (And He'll Break Your Heart)," 27
Hellerman, Fred. *See* The Weavers
"Hello, It's Me," 130
Helm, Amy: Background of, 173–174, 175, 183; *Dirt Farmer* and, 173, 179–180; The Handsome Strangers and, 183–184; Levon Helm and, 57, 70, 173, 182; Ollabelle and, 178–179
Helm, Jasper Diamond "JD," 48
Helm, Mark Lavon "Levon": Background of, 47, 48, 49; Larry Campbell and, 176–178, 178–179; Rick Danko and, 172; Bob Dylan and, 28, 29, 30–31, 31, 32, 77, 140, 141, 168, 183; Cancer and, 173–174, 179, 182; Henry Glover and, 43, 143; John Hammond, Jr. and, 28; Garth Hudson and, 60, 85; Influences on drumming of, 49; Legacy of, 182, 183; Movies and, 157–158; Muddy Waters and, 143; Outside projects

of, 142, 146, 153, 154, 157, 167; The RCO All-Stars and, 152, 154; Recording and, 130, 131, 143; Reflecting on The Band's collapse, 125, 138, 148, 153; Richard Manuel and, 59, 85, 162, 165, 166; Robbie Robertson and, 57, 87–88, 125, 182; Solo career of, 161–162, 180, 181–182; Libby Titus and, 70; Sonny Boy Williamson and, 50. *See also* The Hawks, The Band
Helm, Linda, 48
Helm, Sandy, 166, 181, 182
"Help!," 22
"Helpless," 143, 151
Hendrix, Jimi, 71, 121, 122, 125, 129, 190
Henry, Clarence "Frogman," 137
Herald, John, 70–71, 83, 120
Herb Alpert and the Tijuana Brass, 132
"Hey Boba Lou," 54
Hiatt, John, 125, 169, 181, 182, 183
Hiawatha and the Peacemaker, 189
"High Cotton," 169
Highway 61 Revisited, 21, 22, 28, 34, 35, 67
Hill, Joe, 4–5
Hirt, Al, 132
Hirth from Earth, 147, 185
"Hobo Jungle," 144, 145
Holland–Dozier–Holland, 134
The Hollies, 23, 75
Holly, Buddy, 2, 53, 54, 56, 139, 170
Hollywood Bowl, 26, 31
Holt, Will, 14
"Holy Cow," 133, 137
Holy Soul Jelly Roll, 120
"Honeycomb," 51
"Honky Tonk," 62
Hooker, Earl, 175
Hooker, James, 162
Hooker, John Lee, 44
Hopkins, Sam "Lightnin'," 24
Hopper, Dennis, 89
Hornsby, Bruce, 188
"Hot Sticker," 75
Hot Tuna, 174, 178
House, Son, 27
How to Become Clairvoyant, 190–191

Howard, Harlan, 157
Howlin' Wolf (Chester Arthur Burnett), 44, 46, 53, 59
Hudson, Garth: Background of, 59–62; Rick Danko and, 171; John Hammond, Jr. and, 28; Richard Manuel and, 165; Outside projects of, 70, 137, 143, 146, 153, 160, 167, 178, 184, 185; Maud Hudson and, 185; Solo career of, 185. *See also* The Hawks, The Band
Hudson, Maud, 184–185
Humperdinck, Engelbert, 23
Hunter, Robert, 181
Hurt, Mississippi John, 119
The Hutchinson Family, 125
"I Ain't Got No Home," 77
"I Am A Union Woman," 7
"I Can See a New Day," 16
"I Don't Believe You (She Acts like We Never Have Met)," 19, 152
"(I Don't Want to Hang Up) My Rock and Roll Shoes," 121
"If I Had a Hammer (The Hammer Song)," 14, 18
"If I Should Fail," 169
"If You Gotta Go, Go Now," 24
"I'm Stickin' with you," 51
"In a Station," 59, 85
The Indigo Girls, 184
Industrial Workers of World (IWW), 3–4
"I Pity the Poor Immigrant," 123
Isaacs, Byron, 178, 180, 183
"I Shall Be Released," 58, 76, 85, 86, 91, 120, 121, 135, 139, 152, 166
The Isle of Wight Festival, 123, 131
"I Still Miss Someone," 37
"It Ain't Me Babe," 19, 23, 123
"It Makes No Difference," 144, 150, 184, 185
"It Takes a Lot to Laugh, It Takes a Train to Cry," 21, 22, 25, 181
"It's Alright, Ma (I'm Only Bleeding)," 21
"It's All Over Now, Baby Blue," 25, 30, 33
"It's Only Make Believe," 47
Ives, Burl, 5, 8

"I Wanna Be Your Lover," 33, 35
"I Want You," 35, 143
"I Will Not Go under the Ground (Let Me Die in My Footsteps)," 16
"I'll Keep It with Mine," 36

Jackson, Al, 49
Jackson, Aunt Molly, 7
Jackson, Benjamin "Bull Moose," 42
Jackson, Mahalia, 18, 190
James, Clifton, 49
James, Elmore, 56, 76
Jameson, James, 58
"Java Blues," 153
"Jawbone," 59, 97, 98
The Jefferson Airplane, 122, 146
Jeffreys, Garland, 178
"Jemima Surrender," 98
Jenkins, Gordon, 8
Jennings, Waylon, 89
Jericho, 42, 168
Jerry Garcia Band, 97
Jessie, Young, 51
"Jet Pilot," 35
Jim Kweskin Jug Band, 26
Jim Weider's ProJECT PERCoLATOR, 186
The Jodimars, 75
Johanson, Jai Johanny, 138
"John Brown," 16
John Wesley Harding, 77, 155
John, Elton, 80, 89
John, William "Little Willie," 42–43
"Johnny B. Goode," 139
Johns, Glyn, 131, 157
Johnson, Howard, 134, 154, 183
Johnson, Johnnie, 169, 175
Johnson, Robert, 27, 49, 122, 190
Jones, Booker T., 154
Jones, Brian, 37, 125. *See also* The Rolling Stones
Jones, Elvin, 134
Jones, Grandpa, 42
Jones, Mickey, 36
Jones, Norah, 174, 184
Jones, Rickie Lee, 160
Jones, Tommy Lee, 158
Jones, Willard "Pop," 48
"Jon the Generator," 71

Joplin, Janis, 59, 84, 123, 125, 126, 129, 167
Jordan, Louis, 174
Jordan, Steve, 174
Jost, Paul, 169
Jubilation, 169–170, 181
The Jungle Bush Beaters, 49
"Jupiter Hollow," 145
"Just a Glass of Water," 35
"Just another Whistle Stop," 59
"Just Like Tom Thumb's Blues," 21, 31, 33, 35

Kalb, Danny, 119
Kalmusky, Ken, 165
Kaplansky, Lucy, 178
Katché, Manu, 187
"Katie's Been Gone," 90
Kaufman, Murray "Murray the K," 30
Kaukonen, Jorma. *See* Hot Tuna, Jefferson Airplane
Kaz, Eric, 70, 119
K-Doe, Ernie, 132
Keith, Bill, 71, 120, 177
Keller, Helen, 5
Keltner, Jim, 155
Kemper, David, 177
Kennedy, John Fitzgerald, 18, 23, 31, 95
Kennedy, Robert, 125
Kenner, Chris, 132
Kennerley, Paul, 157, 180
Kerouac, Jack, 19
"Key to the Highway," 90
King Curtis (Ousley), 89
"Kingfish," 181
"King Harvest (Has Surely Come)," 58, 84, 101, 101–102, 136, 150
King, Martin Luther Junior, 18, 125
The King Biscuit Boys, 49
King Biscuit Time, 49
King, Carole, 75, 140
The King of Comedy, 160
King, Earl, 154
King, Riley "BB," 28, 44, 46, 160, 178
The Kingston Trio, 10, 16, 74
The Kinks, 23
Kleinow, "Sneaky" Pete, 176
Knight, Marie, 178
Knight, Robert, 161

Koerner, Spider John, 3
Konikoff, Sandy, 36
Kooper, Al, 22, 24, 25, 26, 29–31
Kornfeld, Arthur Lawrence "Artie," 75, 121–122
Kosek, Kenny, 178
Kottke, Leo, 100
Kraus, Dr. Dennis, 179
Krause, Bernie, 9
Krauss, Alison, 132, 178
Kristofferson, Kris, 140, 174
Kudlets, Harold "The Colonel," 39

Ladder 49, 161
Lampell, Millard. *See* The Almanac Singers
Landy, Elliot, 94
lang, k.d., 177
Lang, Michael, 75, 121
Langhorne, Bruce, 20, 21
Lanois, Daniel, 186–187
Larkin, Patti, 163
"Last of the Blacksmiths," 133
"The Last Tennessee Waltz," 130
"Last Train to Memphis," 169
The Last Waltz, 43, 57, 60, 89, 97, 145, 148–149, 149, 153, 155, 158, 163, 167, 172, 182, 185, 191, 193
Late Again, 17
"Laugh Laugh," 93
Lauper, Cyndi, 177
Lavin, Christine, 163
"Lawdy Miss Clawdy," 46
Lawrence, Erik, 183
"Lay Lady Lay," 123
Lay, Sam, 24, 26. *See also* The Butterfield Blues Band
"Leave Me Alone," 27, 43
Led Zeppelin, 129
Ledbetter, Huddie "Leadbelly," 8, 129
Lee, Albert, 99
Lee, Spike, 20
Lee, William "Bill," 20
The Legend of Jesse James, 157, 180
Leiber, Jerry and Stoller, Mike, 28
"Lemon Tree," 27
Lennon, John, 52, 127, 134, 138
Lenoir, J. B., 180
"Leopard Skin Pill-box Hat," 36

Lerner, Murray, 136
Lesh, Phil, 179, 187
Levin, Tony, 187
Levine, Jared, 189
Levy, Moise "Morris," 43, 51, 51–52, 54
Lewis, Jerry, 160
Lewis, Jerry Lee, 29, 46, 48, 56, 127, 138, 174
"Lieberstraum," 140
"Life Is a Carnival," 88, 132, 134, 136, 139, 148, 150, 174
Lightfoot, Gordon, 11, 28, 84
"Like a Rolling Stone," 21, 22–23, 25, 31, 33, 37, 123, 135
Linden, Colin, 168
Lindley, David, 154
Lipscomb, Mance, 24
"Little Birds," 180
"Little Body Rinktum Ti-mee-oh," 48
Little Caesar and the Consuls, 53, 188
Little Feat, 89
Live at Breeze Hill, 171
Live at the Academy of Music 1971, 2, 136
Live at the Palladium, NYC, 154
Live at the Wolf, 185
Live from the Lone Star, 178
"Living the Blues," 76
Lloyd, Charles, 83
"Lo and Behold," 76
Lockwood, Robert Jr., 49
Lofgren, Nils, 155
Lomax, Alan, 4, 5, 7, 8, 16, 19
Lomax, John, 8, 19
Lombardo, Guy, 28, 39
"The Lonesome Death of Hattie Carroll," 20
"Lonesome Suzie," 59, 85, 90
Lone Star Café, 70, 162, 177
"Long Black Veil," 41, 129, 184
"Long Distance Operator," 90
"Look Out Cleveland," 99
"Looking for a Love," 143
Lopez, Trini, 14, 36
Los Lobos, 184
Love at the Greek, 147
"Love Has No Pride," 70
"Love Minus Zero/No Limit," 21, 24, 30, 141
"Love the One You're With," 161

"Loving You Is Sweeter than Ever," 135, 139, 143
Loveless, Patty, 181
Lovelle, Herb, 20
The Limelighters, 10
The Lovin' Spoonful, 21, 94, 176. *See also* John Sebastian
Lownds, Hans, 65
Lownds, Sara, 65, 122
Lowrey, 60, 86
Lucas, George, 150
Lunceford, Jimmy, 123
Lynn, Loretta, 157

MacDonald, Rod, 88, 163
Macho, Joseph Jr., 21, 22
"Maggie's Farm," 21, 25, 31, 33
"Magic Bus," 161
Mahal, Taj, 134
Makem, Tommy, 10
Making a Noise, 189
Malo, Raul, 181
Malone, Tom, 154
"Mama Let Me Lay It on You," 152
Manfred Mann, 23, 75, 76
Mann, Herbie, 16
Mann, Thomas, 68
"Mannish Boy," 151
"Mansion on the Hill," 46
Manuel, Arlie, 165
Manuel, Paula, 166
Manuel, Richard: Background of, 58, 59; Legacy of, 166; Outside projects of, 137, 164; Piano playing of, 63; The Rockin" Revols and, 59, 165; Singing of, 58–59, 80, 81, 85, 98; Solo career of, 165; Songwriting of, 59, 134; Suicide of, 165–166. *See also* The Hawks, The Band
"Many Thousand Gone," 16
The March on Washington for Jobs and Freedom, 18–19
Margolin, Bob, 143
Marini, Lou, 154
Martha and the Muffins, 186
Martin, George, 59
Martin, Mary, 18, 28, 33
Martinez, Hirth, 147, 185
"Mary Lou," 51

"Masters of War," 23, 69
Matisyahu, 161
Maverick, 68
Mayer, John, 183
Mayfield, Curtis, 81, 89
McCall, Jane Byrd, 68
McCartney, Paul, 37, 133
McClintock, Harry "Haywire Mac," 3
McGhee, Brownie, 5, 10, 174
McGuinn, Roger, 10, 168. *See also* The Byrds
McLuhan, Marshall, 83
Mean Streets, 150, 158
Meat Loaf, 131
"Medicine Sunday," 35
The Memphis Jug Band, 15
Menkes, Sigmund, 69
Merideth, James, 17
The Meters, 188
Midnight Ramble, 173, 174–175, 175, 183
"Midnight Train," 35
Miles, Buddy, 26, 83
"Milk Cow Boogie," 154
Miller, Buddy, 177, 182
Miller, Steve, 51
"Million Dollar Bash," 76
Mingus, Charles, 71, 134, 136
Minnelli, Liza, 150
"Minstrel Boy," 123
Mississippi Burning, 129
"Miss Otis Regrets," 70
Mitchell, Brian, 180, 183
Mitchell, Joni, 39, 140, 143, 151
"Mixed Up Changes," 20
"Mixed-up Confusion," 20
Moby Grape, 146
"Mockingbird," 140
Modern Jazz Quartet, 119
Modern Romans, 153
Monroe, Bill, 48, 100, 157
Monroe, Marilyn, 187
Moondog Matinee, 133, 137, 138, 140, 151
The Moody Blues, 94
Moore, Sam, 23
Morales, Hector, 122
Moreira, Airto, 134
Morello, Tom, 190
Morrison, John G., 4

Morrison, Van, 28, 72, 132, 148, 151, 160, 167, 184
Morrissey, Bill, 163
Moss, Wayne, 36
"Most Like You Go Your Way and I'll Go Mine," 36
"Mother-in-Law," 132
"Motorpsycho Nightmare," 19
"The Mountain," 180
"Mountain Jam," 139
"Move along Train," 181
Mr. Dynamo, 54
"Mr. Lee," 62
"Mr. Tambourine Man," 21, 23, 24, 25, 29, 30, 33, 37, 123
Mud Acres, 120
Muldaur, Geoff, 26, 71, 184
Muldaur, Maria, 71, 120
Mullican, Moon, 42
Mumford and Sons, 89, 129
Muscle Shoals All-Stars, 162
Music from Big Pink, 2, 41, 43, 76, 79, 82, 84, 85, 86, 90
Musick, Stan. *See* The Call
Musselwhite, Charlie, 28
"My Babe," 54
"My Baby's in Love with Another Guy," 160
"My Back Pages," 19
My Morning Jacket, 174, 183
My Son the Folksinger, 10
"Mystery Train," 137, 151

Nance, Jack, 47, 49
Nash, Graham. *See* Crosby, Stills, and Nash
Nashville Skyline, 77
"The Nazz are Blue," 130
Near, Holly, 10
Nebraska, 180
"Need Your Love So Bad," 42
Neer, Richard, 93, 146
Nelson, Rick, 44, 59
Nelson, Willie, 157, 161, 177, 181
Nesmith, Mike, 71
The Neville Brothers, 187, 188
Nevins, Tara, 178
The New Lost City Ramblers, 72
"New Mexico," 153

New Morning, 77, 141
New Orleans, 27, 34, 44, 60, 93, 132, 133, 134, 137, 151, 181, 188
New Riders of the Purple Sage, 89, 126, 129
New York Dolls, 130
New York Rock and Soul Revue, 70
Newman, Randy, 94, 181
Newport Folk Festival, 11, 12, 23–26, 31, 35, 70, 182
The New World Singers, 15, 16, 16–17
"The Night They Drove Old Dixie Down," 94, 96, 97, 100, 136, 139, 140, 178
"The Night You Took Me to Barbados in My Dreams," 70
Nile, Willie, 177
Nine Inch Nails, 190
Nirvana, 161
Nitty Gritty Dirt Band, 174
"No More Auction Block for Me," 15
No Reason to Cry, 146
North, Alex, 159
Northern Lights-Southern Cross, 144, 146
"Not Fade Away," 139
"Number One," 35

"Obviously Five Believers," 36
O'Connor, Sinead, 184
Oakley, Berry, 138
Ocasek, Ric, 160
Ochs, Phil, 5, 15, 170
Odetta, 3, 10, 11, 129
Of Mice and Men, 101
"Oh, Freedom," 19
Oh Mercy, 187
Old Crow Medicine Show, 89, 129, 193
Oldies but Goodies, 138
Ollabelle, 178–179, 181
"On a Night Like This," 140
"Once Upon a Time," 153
On the Beach, 142
"One of Us Must Know (Sooner or Later)," 36
"Only a Hobo," 16, 120
"Only a Pawn in Their Game," 19, 23, 69
Only Slightly Mad, 184
Ono, Yoko, 123, 127

"Ophelia," 60, 88, 144, 145, 150
"Orange Juice Blues (Blues for Breakfast)," 90
Orbison, Roy, 45, 46, 51
Orchestral Wives, 160
Osborne, Joan, 42, 89
Otis, Johnny, 54
Out on the Street, 168
Owens, Buck, 74, 124
Owens, Frank, 22
"Oxford Town," 17, 20

Pacheco, Tom, 169
Packer, Larry, 148, 164
"Pagan Knight," 159
"Pain in My Heart," 132
Palladino, Pino, 190
Palmer, Robert, 42, 96, 151, 160
Parton, Dolly, 184
"Party Doll," 51
Pat Garrett and Billy the Kid, 140
Paturel, Bernard and Mary Lou, 70
Paul, Les, 72
Paulman, George, 48
Paulman, Jimmy Ray "Luke," 46, 48, 87
Paxton, Tom, 15, 123
Paycheck, Johnny, 163
The Pearl, 186
Pearl Jam, 169
Peckinpah, Sam, 140
The Pencils, 162
Penderecki, Krzysztof, 137
Penfound, Jerry, 63
Pennebaker, Donn Alan "D.A.," 37
Penniman, Little Richard, 2, 3, 53, 56, 127, 129, 138–139, 167, 170, 174, 181
The People's Revolutionary Band, 128
People's Songs, 7–8
Perkins, Carl, 40, 45, 46
Perkins, Joseph William "Pinetop," 143, 151
Pet Sounds, 94
Pete the Bear (Peter Derimigis), 54
Peter and Gordon, 23
Peter, Paul, and Mary, 10–14, 17, 18, 23–28, 69, 71, 76
Peterson, Oscar, 39, 40
Petty, Tom, 160, 168
"Phantom Engineer Cloud," 22

Phillips, Samuel Cornelius "Sam," 46
Phish, 99
Planet Waves, 2, 140–141, 152, 169
Platinum High School, 47
"Play Something Sweet," 157
"Please Mrs. Henry," 76
Poco, 146
The Pointer Sisters, 132
Pomus, Doc, 54, 134
"Poor Old Dirt Farmer," 180
Porter, Cole, 70
Powell, Jess, 62
Powwow Highway, 188
Presley, Elvis, 20, 22, 40, 44, 46, 56, 137, 154, 157, 174, 187
Preston, William Everett "Billy," 155, 167
The Pretenders, 160
Prine, John, 183
"Promise Yourself," 59
The Psychedelic Furs, 131
"Puff, the Magic Dragon," 14, 17
Purim, Flora, 134

Quatro, Suzi, 44
"Queen Jane Approximately," 21
"Quinn, the Eskimo," 145, 150
"Quit Your Lowdown Ways," 130

Ra, Sun (Herman Blount), 20
Raffi, 186
Raging Bull, 158, 160, 162
"Rag Mama Rag," 84, 95, 96, 139
"Rags and Bones," 144, 145
"Rain Down Tears," 154
"The Rain, the Park, and Other Things," 75
"Raining in My Heart," 139
"Rainy Day Women #12 and 35," 123
"Raised on Robbery," 140
Railroad Earth, 193
Rainey, Ma, 174
Raising Sand, 132
Raitt, Bonnie, 70, 119, 130
Randolph, Asa Philip, 18
Randolph, Robert, 183, 190
Raney, Wayne, 41
Rankin, Kenny, 21
Ratdog, 89

The RCO All-Stars, 152
Reagon, Bernice Johnson, 23
Rebirth Brass Band, 188
Reconcile, George, 177
Red Headed Stranger, 161
"Red Rubber Ball," 83
The Red Road Ensemble, 188
Redding, Otis, 132
Reece, Florence, 7
Reed, Aaron Corthen "AC," 45
Reed, Jimmy, 27, 59, 175
"Reflection/Adagio," 161
Reinhardt, Django, 190
"Remedy," 168
Renaldo and Clara, 152
"Revolution Blues," 142
Reynolds, Nick, 10
Reznor, Trent, 190
Rhythm Ranch, 177
Richards, Keith, 184
Richardson, J. P., "The Big Bopper," 56
"Ride Your Pony," 133
The Right Stuff, 158
Riley, Billy, 40, 46
"Ring Your Bell," 144, 145
Rinzler, Ralph, 71
Rivers, Johnny, 36
Robbie and the Robots, 53
Robertson, Dominique, 65, 82
Robertson, Robbie: Background of, 52–53; Roy Buchanan and, 54, 56; Rick Danko and, 58, 172; Neil Diamond and, 147; Bob Dylan and, 1, 11–12, 12–15, 16, 37, 38, 136, 140, 142; California and, 140; *Carney* and, 159–160; The Chelsea Hotel and, 67; Eric Clapton and, 90–91; Film and, 161; Garth Hudson and, 60; Albert Grossman and, 67; Guitar playing of, 81–82; Inspiration of, 101; Intellectual pursuits of, 35, 56; John Hammond, Jr. and, 10; Levon Helm and, 57, 87–88, 172, 182; Little Willie John and, 42; Richard Manuel and, 58, 137, 165, 166; Martin Scorsese and, 149, 150, 158–159, 160; The Mississippi Delta and, 55; Outside projects of, 70, 137, 140, 147, 161; Jesse Winchester and, 130; *The Works* and, 137. *See also* The Hawks, The Band
Robertson, Sebastian, 189
Robinson, Chris, 175
Robinson, Earl, 5
Rock of Ages, 2, 76, 99, 133, 135, 136, 148
"Rockin' Chair," 60, 94, 99, 129, 135
Rockin' Revols, 59, 126, 165
Roderick, Judy, 119
Rodgers, Jimmie, 44, 51, 176
The Rolling Stones, 19, 23, 28, 38, 44, 121, 123, 125, 130, 132, 134, 142, 149, 167
Ronstadt, Linda, 70, 71
Rooney, Jim, 71, 120, 163
Rotolo, Suze, 17, 19, 69
Rounder Records, 120
The Royal Teens, 22
Rubin, Alan, 154
"Ruler of My Heart," 132
"The Rumour," 135
Rundgren, Todd, 11, 130–131
Rush, Tom, 184
Ruskin, Bayard, 18
Ruskin, John, 67
Russell, Catherine, 178
Rydell, Bobby, 56

"The Saga of Pepote Rouge," 149
Sahl, Mort, 12
Sahm, Doug, 177
Sainte-Marie, Buffy, 39, 84
"The Same Thing," 168
Santana, 129
Saturday Night Live, 149, 154
Scorsese, Martin, 24, 42, 89, 149–150, 151, 155, 158–159, 160–161
Scott, Clifford, 62
Scrooged, 187
The Sea to the North, 185
Sebastian, John, 21, 70, 71, 94, 120, 130, 174, 184. *See also* The Lovin' Spoonful
Sedgwick, Edie, 65
"See You Later, Alligator," 134
Seeger, Charles, 5
Seeger, Pete, 10, 12, 14, 15, 16, 23, 26, 77, 100. *See also* The Almanac Singers, The Weavers

The Seeger Sessions, 180
Self Portrait, 76, 120
"(Seems Like) A Freeze-Out," 35
Sergeant Pepper's Lonely Hearts Club Band, 94
"Seven Days," 146
Sex Kittens Go to College, 47
Sexton, Charlie, 177
"Shadows and Light," 151
"Shake It," 153
Shane, Bob. *See* The Kingston Trio
Shangri-La, 77, 143, 144, 149, 151, 152, 154
"The Shape I'm In," 58, 139, 150
Shear, Jules, 168
"She Belongs to Me," 21, 30
Sherman, Allen, 10
Shindell, Richard, 178
"Shine Your Light," 161
Shocked, Michelle, 89
Sholle, John, 120
"Short Fat Fanny'," 80, 161
"Short Shorts," 22
Shutter Island, 161
Siebel, Paul, 120
Simon and Garfunkel, 21
Simon, Carly, 70
Simon, John, 82, 88, 99, 168
Simon, Paul, 21, 83, 137, 178
Sinatra, Frank, 88, 190
Sing Out, 7, 72
"Sing, Sing, Sing," 154
"Single Girl, Married Girl," 180
Sir Douglas Quintet, 177
"Sitting on a Barbed Wire Fence," 22
Sledge, Milton, 162
"Sleeping," 59, 125
Slim, Memphis, 24
"Slippin' and Slidin'," 129
"Sloop John B," 94
The Smith, 89
Smith, Bessie, 27, 76, 100, 174
Smith, Huey "Piano," 188
Smith, Patti, 130, 131
Smith, Russell, 162
Smooth Talk, 158
Snow, Hank, 39, 53
Snow, Phoebe, 70
Sod-Buster Ballads, 7

Soles, Steve, 119
"Someone Like You," 54
Something/Anything, 130
"Somewhere Down This Crazy River," 187
The Song Swappers, 12
Songs for John Doe, 6
Songs of Leonard Cohen, 83
Sonic Youth, 161
Sonnier, Jo-El, 153
Sonny and Cher, 23, 75
"Sonny Got Caught in the Crossfire," 187
The Sons of the Pioneers, 43, 176
Sound Outs, 121
"Sounds of Silence," 21
South, Joe, 36
"Southern Accents," 160
Southern, Terry, 89
Spector, Phil, 52, 138
Spielberg, Steven, 150
Spinosa, Maria. *See* The Crowmatix
Spirit, 130
Spirit Family Reunion, 193
Spooky Tooth, 89
Springsteen, Bruce, 7, 22, 27, 40, 89, 166, 168, 180
St. Peters, Crispian, 75
Stage Fright, 2, 59, 124–125, 125, 126, 131, 134
"Stage Fright," 2, 57, 59, 124–125, 125–126, 126, 131
Stages, 171
"Stand Up," 169
"Standing on a Mountain Top," 157
Stanley, Carter, 181. *See also* The Stanley Brothers
Stanley, Ralph, 176. *See also* The Stanley Brothers
The Stanley Brothers, 90, 100
Staples, Mavis, 89, 183, 184. *See also* The Staples Singers
The Staples Singers, 89, 151, 181
Starr, Ringo, 28, 148, 152, 155, 167, 181. *See also* The Beatles
Stax Records, 73, 154
Steinbeck, John, 101
Steppenwolf, 127
Stevens, Wallace, 68

Stewart, Dave, 160
Stewart, Rod, 187
"Stewball," 71
Stills, Stephen, 152, 161. *See also* Crosby, Stills, and Nash
Stone, Sly (Sylvester Stewart), 93, 121, 122
Stoner, Rob, 177
"The Stones I Throw," 27
Stookey, Noel Paul, 12. *See also* Peter, Paul, and Mary
Storyville, 187–188
Stratton, Dayton, 164
"Stuff You Gotta Watch," 168, 181
"Subterranean Homesick Blues," 21
"Such a Night," 151
Sumlin, Hubert, 53
"Summer in the City," 176
Sun Records, 39, 46, 49, 51
The Sun Records Quartet, 39
"Superstition," 100
The Supremes, 23, 89, 138
"Susie Q," 44
"Sweet Fire of Love," 187
Sweet Honey in the Rock, 23
Swervedriver, 161
"The Swim," 93
Szelest, Stan, 164, 167

"T'ain't Nobody's Business," 160
"Take Me to the River," 157
"Talkin' Devil," 16
"Talkin' John Birch Society Blues," 19, 23
"Talkin' World War III Blues," 23
Talking Heads, 157, 160
Talking Union, 7, 12
Talley, James, 163
Tape from California, 5
Taplin, Jonathan, 130, 133
Tarantula, 19, 67
Tart, Chris, 161
Taupin, Bernie, 80, 89
Taxi Driver, 150, 158
Taylor, Cecil, 20
Taylor, Dudlow, 49
Taylor, James, 119, 140
Taylor, Livingston, 184
"Tears of Rage," 59, 60, 76, 84, 85, 90

"Teenage Prayer," 76
"Temporary Like Achilles," 35, 36
The Temptations, 89
"Tennessee Jed," 181
Ten Years After, 122
Ten Years and Forty Days, 175
Terry, Sonny, 5, 10
"Testimony," 187
Thaler, Dr. Edward, 66
"Third Man Theme," 151
"Thirty Days," 51
The Three Blisters, 61
They Might Be Giants, 130
Thigpen, Ed, 40
"This Is Where I Get Off," 191
"This Land Is Your Land," 14
"This Wheel's on Fire," 76, 85, 139, 150
Thomas, David Clayton, 39
Thomas, Ian, 190
Thomas, Irma, 132
Thomas, Rufus, 174
Thompson, Richard, 193
Thornton, Billy Bob, 174
Thumper & the Trombones, 53
Thursday Afternoon, 186
Till, John, 59, 126, 165
Time Out Of Mind, 187
Times Like These, 146, 172
"The Times They Are a'Changin'," 17, 31
"Time to Kill," 126, 135
Tiny Tim (Herbert Khaury), 83
Titus, Libby, 57, 70, 173
"To Kingdom Come," 81
"To Ramona," 24, 30, 123
Tom Petty and the Heartbreakers, 160
Tony Mart's, 28
"Too Much of Nothing," 17, 76
Toussaint, Allen, 132–133, 134, 137, 148, 157, 169, 174, 175
Trampled by Turtles, 89
Traum, Artie, 11, 119, 164, 168. *See also* Happy and Artie Traum, Woodstock Mountain Revue
Traum, Happy and Artie, 11, 76
Traum, Harry Peter "Happy," 14, 15, 20, 71, 72, 119, 120, 121, 177, 182. *See also* The New World Singers, Happy and Artie Traum, Woodstock

Mountain Revue
Travers, Mary Allin, 12. *See also* Peter, Paul, and Mary
Travis, Randy, 181
Trischka, Tony, 177
True Endeavor Jug Band, 119
Tubb, Ernest, 45
The Tubes, 130, 131
"Tura-Lura-Lural," 151
Turner, Gil. *See* New World Singers
The Turtles, 23, 24
"Twilight," 142
Twitty, Conway (Harold Jenkins), 3, 39, 47, 49
Tyson, Ian and Sylvia, 126, 128, 130
"Tzena, Tzena, Tzena," 8

U2, 161, 187
"Uh-uh-uh," 27
"The Unfaithful Servant," 60, 98, 99, 101, 136
The Unforgettable Fire, 187
"Union Maid," 7
United Mine Workers, 7
Until the End of the World, 188
Upchurch, Phil, 58
"Up On Cripple Creek," 100–101, 135, 139, 150

Vagabond Heart, 187
Valens, Ritchie, 56
Van Ronk, Dave, 13
Van Zandt, Stevie, 93
Vaughn, Stevie Ray, 190
Vee, Bobby, 2
Vega, Suzanne, 163
The Velvet Underground, 127
Venus and Mars, 133
Viridiana, 86
"Visions of Johanna," 36
Vollmer, Sredni, 165, 171
Von Schmidt, Eric, 33, 76

Walker, Ken, 127, 128–129
"Walking to New Orleans," 134
Walsh, James H., 3
Walsh, Joe, 155, 183
Warhol, Andy, 35, 65
Warwick, Dionne, 89

"Washer Woman," 154
Washington, Jackie, 186
Wasn't That a Time, 10
"Watermelon Picking Time in Georgia," 157
Waters, Muddy (McKinley Morganfield), 26, 28, 43, 44, 56, 59, 71, 119, 130, 143, 148, 149, 151, 161, 167, 168, 174, 175, 181
Waters, Roger, 183, 184
Watkins Glen, Summer Jam at, 138–140
"We Can Talk," 59, 101
"We Shall Overcome," 19, 23
The Weavers, 8–10
"Wedding Song," 140
Wednesday, 3AM, 21
Weider, Jim, 163, 164, 165, 168, 168–169, 171, 182, 183, 186
"The Weight," 85, 86–88
Wein, George, 11, 23, 24, 25
Weinberg, Max, 40, 166
Weir, Bob, 89, 127. *See also* The Grateful Dead
Weissberg, Eric, 71
Wellstood, Dick, 20
Westerman, Floyd, 174
Wheeler, Cheryl, 178
"When I Go Away," 178, 181
"When I Paint My Masterpiece," 60, 132, 135, 168
"When the Ship Comes In," 17
"When You Awake," 59, 97
"Where Do We Go from Here," 133
"Where I Should Always Be," 169
"Which Side Are You On," 7
Whispering Pines, Live at the Getaway, January 1985, 59
"White Cadillac," 169
White, Hervey, 68
White, Josh, 5, 10, 12
Whitehead, Ralph Radcliffe, 68
The Who, 23, 38, 49, 123, 132, 134, 161
"Who Killed Davey Moore," 23
The Whole Enchilada, 185
"Why Do Fools Fall in Love," 51
"Wide River to Cross," 180
Wilco, 184
The Wild Magnolias, 188
"Will the Circle be Unbroken," 143

Williams, Big Joe, 174
Williams, Dar, 178
Williams, Hiram King "Hank," 44, 46, 53, 57, 76, 157, 176
Williams, Lucinda, 181, 183
Williams, Teresa, 178, 183
Williamson, John Lee Curtis "Sonny Boy, 49
Williamson, Sonny Boy (Alex "Rice" Miller, 49
Willis, Edgar, 58
The Will Rogers Follies, 173
Wilson, Brian, 75, 94. *See also* The Beach Boys
Wilson, Jim, 188
Wilson, Tom, 20–21, 22
Winchester, Jesse, 130
Winfrey, Oprah, 55
Winter, Johnny, 122, 127
Winwood, Steve, 190
"With God on Our Side," 19, 23, 24
Wobblies, 3
Woman Blue, 119
Wonder, Stevie, 70, 100, 134, 135
"Wonderful Remark," 160
Wood, Ron, 19, 152, 168
Woodstock (town): History of, 68–71
Woodstock Mountain Revue, 120, 163, 164
Woodstock Music and Art Festival, 5, 75, 121–123, 125, 126, 127, 136, 139, 146
Woodstock Winter, 169
"Working in a Coal Mine," 133
Wray, Link, 53, 190
Wrecking Ball, 187
"The W. S. Walcott Medicine Show," 136, 139, 148, 150, 174

Wyman, Bill, 28. *See also* The Rolling Stones

XTC, 130

Yankovic, Frankie, 83
Yankovic, Weird Al, 83
"Yankee Lady," 130
Yarborough, Glenn, 10
The Yardbirds, 23, 50, 130
Yarrow, Peter, 11–12, 25, 69, 83, 137. *See also* Peter, Paul, and Mary
"Yazoo Street Scandal," 90
Yellin, Bob,. *See* The Greenbrier Boys
Yellow Moon, 187
Yes, We Can, 133
"Yes We Can Can," 132
Yoakam, Dwight, 181
"You Ain't Goin' Nowhere," 76
"You Angel You," 140
You Are What You Eat, 83
"You Can't Catch Me," 52
"You Can't Lose What You Never Had," 181
"You Got Me," 154
"You Say You Love Me," 77
"You See Me," 169
"You'd Better Move On," 181
The Youngbloods, 143
Young, Eugene Edward "Snooky," 134
Young, Jesse Colin, 143. *See also* The Youngbloods
Young, Neil, 39, 142, 143, 148, 151, 152, 168, 186

Zabriskie Point, 95
Zappa, Frank, 71

About the Author

Passion for music provides fuel for Craig Harris. Exploring an eclectic range of music (and photographing musicians) since 1971, the New York–born and Massachusetts-based writer, musician, and educator's articles, reviews, and photographs have appeared in newspapers (*Boston Globe, Boston Phoenix,* and *Village Voice*), in magazines (*Sing Out, Global Rhythm,* and *Dirty Linen*), and on websites (AllMusic.com). The author of *The New Folk Music* (White Cliffs Media, Crown Point, IN) and *The Heartbeat, Warble, and Electric Powwow: Native America's Musical Tapestry* (pending), he was a major contributor to *Music Hound Folk Music: Essential Album Guide* and *Music Hound World Music: Essential Album Guide* (Music Sales Corporation, New York). Playing drums and percussion since his preteens, Harris has performed in concert or recorded with Rod MacDonald, Jonathan Edwards, Greg Brown, CJ Chenier & His Red Hot Louisiana Zydeco Band, the Fast Folk Music Revue, Jim Kweskin Jug Band, the Gaea Star Band, Stillbridge, and the late Merl Saunders and Rick Danko, and he produced two albums for Western Massachusetts–based Miles Orgasmic. Possessing a master's degree in education and teaching certification in music, he taught in public and charter schools for a quarter of a century before launching his award-winning multicultural, intergenerational, and participatory Drum Away the Blues program in 2007.

www.ingramcontent.com/pod-product-compliance
Lightning Source LLC
Chambersburg PA
CBHW051058230426
43667CB00013B/2347